HOW
TEACHERS
TAUGHT

Research on Teaching Monograph Series

HOW TEACHERS TAUGHT

CONSTANCY AND CHANGE IN AMERICAN CLASSROOMS 1890-1980

Larry Cuban

STANFORD UNIVERSITY

Longman

New York & London

How Teachers Taught

Longman Inc., 1560 Broadway, New York, N.Y. 10036
Associated companies, branches, and representatives
throughout the world.

Developmental Editor: Lane Akers
Editorial and Design Supervisor: Russell Till
Production and Manufacturing Supervisor: Ferne Y. Kawahara

Library of Congress Cataloging in Publication Data

Cuban, Larry.
     How teachers taught.

     Bibliography: p.
     Includes index.
     1. Education—United States—History—19th century.
2. Education—United States—History—20th century.
3. Teaching. I. Title.
LA216.C82 1984   370'.973   83–17559
ISBN 0–582–28481–3

MANUFACTURED IN THE UNITED STATES OF AMERICA
9 8 7 6 5 4 3 2 1   92 91 90 89 88 87 86 85 84

Contents

Aerial Classroom, Geography Lesson, Los Angeles Public Schools, 1927

Foreword

Those who conduct research on teaching rarely consider historical investigations germane to their work. There is a sense in which history is treated as arcane, esoteric, and of little import to the concerns of practice and policy. In reading this book, I am convinced that precisely the opposite is true. Carefully conducted historical inquiry may well provide us with the most powerful guides available. Any study of teaching that purports to provide guidance for future practice or policy makes two kinds of claims. First, we must believe that the particular classrooms studied were representative of classrooms at large at the time the investigation was conducted. Second, we must further believe that the classrooms of interest to us, at a time and place typically different from those investigated, bear sufficient resemblance to those studied to provide helpful insights.

Certainly it can be argued that the past prefigures the future, but the present never exactly mimics the past. Do we gain better advice from investigations plucked out of the temporal and cultural–ideological context in which they occurred; or are we better informed through studies that extend self-consciously through time, attempting explicitly to explain the phenomena described by connecting them meaningfully to other events occurring concurrently as well as to those that have preceded? In an unpublished essay, Lee Cronbach refers to educational research and evaluation as "quantitatively assisted history."

When we think of historical inquiry, we often imagine a scholar reading the letters, journals, newspaper accounts, and official documents of a given period and then aggregating those diverse forms of personal or collective impressions into the individual impression of the historian. As we read this monograph by Larry Cuban, we can begin to see how the line that divides history from sociology or psychology, hence educational history from the mainstream of empirical educational research, is a thin one. Cuban makes use of classroom observation records collected over many decades for diverse purposes—the evaluation activities of the Eight Year Study; system-wide monitoring of curriculum and organizational changes in the public school systems of New York, Washington, Denver, and North Dakota, among many others; and hundreds of photographs of classrooms which he uses inventively to infer how teaching was conducted during those periods. Never is any one source of data—photographs, personal diaries, classroom observations, district reports and evaluations, published articles, or even his own observations—taken as evidence by itself. Cuban is a careful historian who insists on carefully juxtaposing data sources, searching for both corroborative consistency as well as provocative contradiction between data sources, among different school sites during the same era, and among similar school settings during different decades.

Much of the richness communicated through this book is a consequence of the unique background brought to the enterprise by its author. Larry Cuban began as a classroom teacher, spending fourteen years teaching secondary social studies in the school districts of Cleveland, Ohio, and Washington, D.C. He trained returned Peace Corps volunteers to teach in inner-city schools and subsequently directed staff development for a major program in the District of Columbia public schools. His interest in history as a subject area finally led him to Stanford University, where he studied educational history under David Tyack and wrote a masterful dissertation on the careers of three big-city superintendents. His *School Chiefs under Fire* was based on that dissertation.

But Cuban was not content to study historically the administration of large school districts; he was committed to making that history as well. Upon completing his doctorate in educational history he was appointed Superintendent of the Arlington County, Virginia, Public Schools, a position he held for seven years until he returned to Stanford in 1981 as a member the School of Education faculty.

There are those who will read this volume as a pessimistic assessment of the failures of school reform. Despite the energy and rhetoric that has supported the reform of educational institutions in the direction of ''progressive'' ideals, especially student-centered instruction in activity-based classrooms in which subject area instruction is correlated and integrated, the general picture Cuban draws is of a rather stable, teacher-centered pedagogy sustaining itself from New York to Denver, from North Dakota to Michigan, from 1900 to 1980. But the picture drawn by Cuban is far more subtle than that. He finds that the portrait is not monolithic. Some reforms take better than others. Some settings (e.g., the elementary school) are more fertile ground for planned change. Even in the failures of reform he derives lessons for future planning and innovation. He asks not only why the reforms were not sustained, but what was right and adaptive about the traditional methods whose resilience he documents so vividly. From the very stability of certain instructional forms, he asserts, we may learn important principles regarding the fundamental character of school-based education—principles that can guide our future attempts to improve the quality of public education.

We thus confront the dual perspectives of historian and schoolman, the dispassionate ''long view'' of the disciplined scholar and the impassioned and practical concern of the front-line decision maker. It is a rare blend, which may occasionally offend the sensibilities of the historiographer who prefers his scholarship bland and distant. Yet this is scholarship of the highest, most meticulous order. Evidence for each assertion is carefully marshalled and contradictory findings meticulously examined. Replications are sought in adjacent decades and/or concurrent events in similar districts. Quantitative and qualitative indicators are used without fear of combining the incompatible. While undoubtedly a work of history, Cuban has written a masterful example of flexible inquiry that can be read with profit by all members of the research on teaching community. The highest praise I can give a piece of educational research is that it contributed substantially to my own education. *How Teachers Taught* did so for me, and I trust it likewise for many others in the worlds of scholarship, policy, and practice.

LEE S. SHULMAN
Stanford, California

Acknowledgments

I began this study as a school superintendent and completed it as a professor. The blend of practice with teaching and research at the university reaffirms my deeply held belief that worthwhile knowledge draws from both worlds. Indeed, the separation of practice from theory, of practitioners from researchers, is more often than not a divorce that is more symbolic than real. My quarter-century of experience in public schools, shuttling back and forth between teaching and administering, persuaded me that the daily realities of classrooms and schools produced knowledge of much worth but that required conceptual frameworks to improve my understanding of what those things I faced daily meant. The interplay between knowledge derived from experience in schools and that which researchers studied helped me greatly in grasping the meaning of both organizational and individual behavior in public schools.

This study of classroom teaching over the last century is part of my journey in trying to understand the complexity of the process of change in schools. Because I taught for many years and served as a school superintendent for seven years, I needed to discover answers to some longstanding questions I had about the process of teaching both in schools where I taught and those where I served as an administrator. The questions I ask and the answers I found construct the boundaries of this study.

Any investigation that takes eighteen months to complete requires the help of many kind individuals willing to share their time and advice. Historical research often means time spent in libraries. In New York City, Pauline Pincus who served in the school system's Professional Library was especially helpful in tracking down sources I could not find elsewhere. Robert Morris of Teachers College took time to introduce me to their newly acquired archives from the New York City Public Schools. Lillian Weber gave me a morning to tell of her efforts in New York, her views of the informal education movement in the late 1960s and early 1970s, and some persistent issues in schooling. Her insights helped me to revise a number of assumptions.

Gordon York, Assistant Superintendent of the Grand Forks, North Dakota Public Schools and Glenn Melvey, Fargo Assistant Superintendent of Instruction, arranged visits for me to each of the schools I had requested. I appreciated the patience of the principals and teachers who put up with my note-taking and questions.

In Denver, Ellengail Buehtel who directs the district's professional library helped me locate a number of sources that I had given up on ever finding. John Rankin in the Public Information Department was especially gracious in arranging for me to use student yearbooks, clipping files, and photographs stored in the basement of the administration building.

Researching the Washington, D.C. schools in two time periods was made easier by the sources located in the District of Columbia Public Library's Washingtonia Room. In the school system, Erika Robinson and Maggie Howard of the Division of Research were especially helpful in locating sources and patient with my use of their space. Bill Webb in the Media Center let me see photographs of classrooms taken since the mid-1960s.

Gordon York, Assistant Superintendent of the Grand Forks, North Dakota Public Schools and Glenn Melvey, Fargo Assistant Superintendent of Instruction, arranged visits for me to each of the schools I had requested. I appreciate patience of the principals and teachers who put up with my note-taking and questions.

Reviewers of the manuscript followed my instructions to give it a tough, close reading. I appreciated the prompt and full responses from Elisabeth Hansot, Carl Kaestle, Joseph Kett, Marvin Lazerson, Kim Marshall, and David Tyack. They are absolved of responsibility for any errors in fact or judgment that persist in the final study.

One reviewer deserves special mention. The editorial board for this series asked Lee Shulman, a colleague who joined the Stanford University faculty in 1982, to review the manuscript. His gentle and wise touch helped me eliminate some confusions I had created, and he urged me to pursue my arguments about teacher practices to their logical conclusion. His insights were helpful.

I also want to acknowledge the help of Charles Missar, Librarian for the National Institute of Education. He was especially gracious and patient with an ex-superintendent unlimbering rusty research muscles. I appreciated his help a great deal. And NIE itself deserves a brief acknowledgment for the original study which they funded and from which this book derived. I feel awkward thanking an organization for betting that a school superintendent could carry off a complex historical investigation. Usually, I thank individuals but a large number of people were involved in making the decision to fund this research. I thank them for having confidence in this practitioner-researcher.

Finally, as in every single writing venture I have undertaken, my wife Barbara has helped at some stage with either the mechanics, proofreading, or providing support. Thanks.

I have written a great deal over the last twenty years about education. I cannot say what it has amounted to but, as for this study, I can say it was the most satisfying. It scratched an itch that had been bothering me for a number of years.

LARRY CUBAN

Introduction

I have worked as a public school teacher, administrator, and researcher in four school systems for a quarter-century. Over the years basic questions on schooling arose that seemed unanswerable or had, for me, no persuasive answer either in my experience or in the research literature. Let me share a few of these questions that have troubled me.

I have been in many classrooms in the last decade. When I watched teachers in secondary schools a flash of recognition jumped out of my memory and swept over me. What I saw was almost exactly what I remembered of the junior and senior high school classrooms that I sat in as a student and as a teacher in the mid 1950s. This acute sense of recall about how teachers were teaching occurred in many different schools. How, I asked myself, could teaching over a forty-year period *seem*, and I mean to underline the word, almost unchanged?

Longtime union leader Albert Shanker made a similar observation that only gave further weight to my question.

> Ten thousand new teachers each year enter the New York City school system as a result of retirement, death, job turnover, and attrition. These new teachers come from all over the country. They represent all religions, races, political persuasions, and educational institutions. But the amazing thing is that, after three weeks in the classroom you can't tell them from the teachers they replaced.[1]

His observation underscored the puzzling question of apparent uniformity in instruction over time.

During the last decade, serving as a decision-maker in two local school districts, I have had to deal with another question that puzzled me: in institutions so apparently vulnerable to change as schools why do so few instructional reforms get past the classroom door? These questions, I believe, are linked. The apparent uniformity in instruction irrespective of time and place is related to the apparent invulnerability of classrooms to change.

In a paper commissioned by the National Institute of Education (NIE), I sought answers to these questions through a study of curriculum change and stability since 1870.[2] In examining how various forces shaped the curriculum and their consequences for classrooms over the last century, I used the metaphor of a hurricane to distinguish between curriculum theory, courses of study, materials, and classroom instruction. Hurricane winds sweep across the sea tossing up twenty foot waves; a fathom below the surface turbulent waters swirl while on the ocean floor there is unruffled calm.

As tricky as metaphors can be, I compared that hurricane to any newly trumpeted curriculum theory. Professional journals, for example, echo pro and con arguments on a new theory. Letters to editors and sharp rebuttals add to the flurry. Books are written and reputations are made. Conferences host both skeptics and advocates. Professors of education teach the new wisdom to their students. Yet most publishers continue producing texts untouched by that theory, and most teachers use methods unmarked by controversy, slogans, journal articles, or convention programs. I used this metaphor for its utility in illustrating distinctions between theory, content, materials, and, most important, impact upon teaching behavior.

In this NIE paper I found that curriculum theories did influence professional ideologies and vocabularies, courses of study, and some textbook content. But I did not find much evidence of significant change in teaching practices. However, I did not systematically or comprehensively examine primary sources or research any school districts. I used, for the most part, secondary sources and a few primary documents that were available. Based upon this initial review I found evidence of a seemingly stubborn continuity in the character of instruction despite intense reform efforts to move classroom practices toward instruction that was more student-centered.

Deepening the paradox further, the limited evidence suggested that teaching practices seemed uncommonly stable at all levels of schooling touching students of diverse abilities in different settings over many decades despite extensive teacher education. In dealing with this paradox researchers have tied more knots than they loosened. Some writers assert that student-centered teaching practices were embraced by teachers, while others argue that such classroom changes are seldom institutionalized. Common to all writers is severely limited evidence about what teachers have done in classrooms.[3]

Scanty evidence about the stable or changing character of instruction drove me toward asking a fundamental question: how did teachers teach? The fragments of knowledge about what teachers did in their classrooms needed to be brought together to give a cumulative clarity. This study begins that task.[4]

In trying to answer the question of how teachers taught, I will use the framework of the previous reform efforts directed at altering classroom pedagogy. By investigating teaching practices before, during, and after reform impulses in the twentieth century aimed at changing what teachers routinely do, a clearer sense of what has persisted and what has changed in classrooms should emerge. But what to look for in classrooms marked by a bewildering variety of student and teacher behaviors? While there is a rich variety of instructional practice and no single study can do justice to the intricate complexity of classroom teaching, a useful tool for revealing a portion of that complicated topography is available. The concept of describing instruction as a continuum stretching from teacher-centered to student-centered contains a limited but useful set of indicators describing important dimensions of what teachers did in their classrooms. Not aimed at capturing the richness of the classroom, this continuum nonetheless provides a handy wedge in prying open the closed doors of classrooms that existed decades ago and mapping, in a preliminary fashion, their pedagogical terrain.

Before proceeding further, let me state plainly what I mean by teacher- and student-centered instruction. Teacher-centered instruction means that a teacher controls what is taught, when, and under what conditions within his or her classroom. Observable measures of teacher-centered instruction are:

- Teacher talk exceeds student talk during instruction.
- Instruction occurs frequently with the whole class; small group or individual instruction occurs less frequently.
- Use of class time is determined by the teacher.
- The classroom is usually arranged into rows of desks or chairs facing a blackboard with a teacher's desk nearby.

Student-centered instruction means that students exercise a substantial degree of direction and responsibility for what is taught, how it is learned, and for any movement within the classroom. Observable measures of student-centered instruction are:

- Student talk on learning tasks is at least equal to, if not greater than, teacher talk.
- Most instruction occurs either individually, in small (2 to 6 students) or moderately sized (7 to 12) groups rather than the whole class.
- Students help choose and organize the content to be learned.
- Teacher permits students to determine, partially or wholly, rules of behavior and penalties in classroom and how they are enforced.
- Varied instructional materials are available in the classroom so that students can use them independently or in small groups, e.g., interest centers, teaching stations, and activity centers.

- Use of these materials is either scheduled by the teacher or determined by students for at least half of the academic time available.
- Classroom is usually arranged in a manner that permits students to work together or separately in small groups or in individual work space; no dominant pattern exists and much movement of desks, tables, and chairs occurs in realigning furniture and space.

These concepts of teacher- and student-centered instruction should be viewed as tools to help in determining what happened in classrooms. As conceptual tools they are limited because they are arbitrary; they often lack precision. At different times, for example, student-centered instruction is used as a synonym for progressive practices or the open classroom. Further, they simplify complex classroom events. Nevertheless, even with these shortcomings, these concepts can help sort out, however crudely, various teaching patterns, especially when these patterns are arrayed on a continuum. Of even greater importance is to weigh these shortcomings against the simple fact that there are so few studies that have captured what teachers have done in classrooms over time.

In using these constructs, I do not assume that actual changes in practice moved solely from teacher- to student-centered; traffic flowed both ways regardless of reformers' intentions. Individual teachers stopped at various places along the way. Nor do I assume that changes in teaching behavior were an all-or-nothing embrace of an entire approach. Quite often, as this study will show, teachers incorporated into their repertoires particular practices they found useful. An elementary school teacher in 1929, for example, whose only classroom change in years was to divide her class into two groups for reading, teaching one in the front of the room while the rest worked at their desks on an assignment, had added a new practice to her arsenal of teaching methods. Or take a high school history teacher in 1933 who began using examples from contemporary political life to enliven his students' study of the French Revolution.

While pedagogical progressives of the time might have winced at my wording and labeled such changes as trivial, these teachers had adopted progressive practices, albeit selectively. On a continuum there needs to be space for progressive teacher-centered instruction as there would be space for the various types of student-centered instruction more familiar to progressive reformers.

The various adaptations of progressive pedagogy that teachers incorporated into their practices are just as puzzling, if not interesting, as what was ignored. The range of teaching practice contained in this study tries to describe a variety of teaching behaviors.[5]

Despite individual teaching differences, observers can, I believe, still categorize instructional patterns by careful attention to at least five visible areas of classroom decision making over which teachers have direct influence. These classroom indicators can suggest dominant forms of instruction, especially when they combine to create patterns.

1. Arrangement of classroom space
2. Ratio of teacher to student talk
3. Whether most instruction occurs individually, in small groups, or with the entire class
4. The presence of learning or interest centers that are used by students as part of the normal school day
5. The degree of movement students are permitted without asking the teacher[6]

In seeking to describe classroom practices I had to narrow my scope. No judgments will be made about the effectiveness of teacher- or student-centered instruction, nor will comparisons be made among teaching practices. Finally, this study will not deal with the emotional climate of the classroom or the relationship between adults and children—as important as these issues are. The central research issue for me is to determine how stable certain teaching behaviors were decade after decade in the face of mighty efforts to move toward student-centered instruction—not the relative value of teacher-centered instruction in achieving student outcomes. However, there is little point in determining which teaching behaviors produce improved student performance until researchers find out which teaching acts persist over time, which have changed, and why.

Given these limits, an obvious question arises: if this research will not reveal what is "good" or "poor" teaching or how some teachers are better than others at creating positive classroom climates, then what will be the practical use of the research? This is a fair question because it raises the issue of the intersection between research and practice. Without getting into the merits of applied or basic research or the value of incremental knowledge, I anticipate broader uses of this study.

Because so little is known by researchers, policymakers, school administrators, teachers, and citizen-advocates about what has remained stable and what has altered in teaching over the last century, investigating the seeming persistence of certain instructional practices can illuminate both the potential and the limits to classroom change. Exploring the terrain of the classroom since the turn of the century should reveal what is durable and what is transient, what is open to improvement and what is invulnerable to reform. By simply knowing more about the instructional quark that is the classroom, citizens and professionals can come to have reasonable expectations about what teachers can and cannot do, what schools can be held accountable for and what is beyond their reach. Such modest outcomes offer practical directions for the periodic surges of reform that sweep over public schools.

Since the late 1950s, reforms in curriculum (e.g. new math), governance (e.g. community control), instruction (e.g. team teaching) have tried to alter teacher behavior in the classroom. There should be a page in the *Guinness Book of World Records* on failed classroom reforms, for few ever seem to have been incorporated into teachers' repertoires. Perhaps in studying directly how teachers have taught, reliable clues will emerge that suggest paths that both teachers and reformers might pursue more realistically, if not usefully.

Moreover, establishing that which is enduring and that which is changeable in the classroom aids the professional educators responsible for turning out the next generation of teachers. While formal teacher education is one of several ways of improving classroom instruction, state legislators across the country have opted for stiffening certification requirements and mandating entry-level tests for new teachers. While these may be a politically satisfying response to popular unease with public schools, anyone knowledgeable about the complexity of classroom instruction knows that such solutions are marginal in their impact on teacher effectiveness. What is less marginal and more useful is to determine what knowledge and skills teachers have used in performing classroom tasks year in and out, decade after decade. To uncover what is changeable and what is stable in teaching offers university teacher-educators ingredients for a well-grounded approach to what candidates for the profession should know and be able to perform once they enter the classroom. Similarly, to know what is persistent and predictable in teaching offers school administrators paths to pursue in working with experienced teachers.

There is a tangible usefulness for teachers in this examination of classroom practice. For teachers to be reliably informed that colleagues a century ago coped with similar situations, found solutions that worked in their classrooms, and adapted to working conditions that, while not identical, were undeniably alike, may give practitioners pride in how their predecessors coped with adversity and a clear sense of identity with a profession that is afflicted with self-doubts and diminished public esteem. Furthermore, for teachers to know that some classroom practices have persisted for over a century while others are of more recent origin may suggest to them a basis for accurately estimating what classroom changes are feasible, given existing conditions. Finally, understanding that what has persisted and what has changed in American schools was less often due to what individual teachers did in their classrooms but stemmed from factors beyond their immediate influence may suggest to teachers proper targets for change in the classroom, school, and community. Most instructional reforms in the last century were generated outside the school and were shoved downward into the classroom. Were teachers to be more informed about the history of classroom instruction perhaps they would voice their preferences based upon a firm knowledge of what can and cannot be done in classrooms as they are presently organized.

There is also another less direct, more subtle use that I see for this study of classroom instruction. Powerful metaphors dominate the thinking of practitioners, policymakers, and scholars on schooling. J. M. Stephens writes that the common metaphor for schools is the factory. This image, like that of a machine, reinforces rational decision making, suggesting that every facet of schooling is a candidate for planned change. Switch the metaphor to farming, he says, and schooling looks very different. In agriculture you start with an ancient, stable process and build your efforts around the sun, climate, seeds, plants, and what insects are likely to do. By understanding the durability and limits to the process, he argues, you can improve production. But you cannot, he continues, ignore these "older organic forces you have little control over." You have to work through them. This is a fundamentally different way of viewing teaching and has tangible consequences for what can and cannot be done with and for classroom teachers.[7]

I believe that many school officials, policymakers, and researchers carry these or similar images in their heads. Such pictures shape their decisions. Historical maps of teaching practices over the last century carry, at the least, potential for determining the accuracy of these metaphors and, in turn, suggest directions for the persistent reforms undertaken by citizens and professionals alike. I take up these points again in the final section.

Two specific questions guide this study:

- Did teacher-centered instruction persevere in public schools during and after reform movements that had as one of their targets installing student-centered instruction?
- If the answer is yes, to what extent did it persist and why? If the answer is no, to what extent did instruction change and why?

In order to answer these questions I have drawn historical maps of teacher classroom practices in three cities and many rural districts during the 1920s and 1930s; in two cities and one state for the decade between 1965 and 1975; and one middle-sized school district in a metropolitan area between 1975 and 1981. The two periods when reformers tried vigorously to install student-centered teaching practices were the progressive years in the early decades of this century and the more recent, briefer period when informal learning and open classrooms captured the enthusiasm of both professionals and citizens.

To determine how teachers taught, I have used a variety of sources:

- Photographs of teachers and students in class
- Textbooks and tests teachers used
- Student recollections of their experiences in classrooms
- Teacher reports of how they taught
- Reports from persons who visited classrooms, e.g. journalists, parents, and administrators.

- Student writings in school newspapers and yearbooks
- Research studies of teacher behavior in classrooms
- Descriptions of classroom architecture, size of rooms, desk design and placement, building plans, etc.

Historians have to cope with the twin problems of selectivity of evidence (i.e. what survives and is available may be a typical of the category) and the biases of sources (e.g. a photographer in 1900 posed students to illustrate the "New Education"). To counter these perennial problems I have sought multiple and varied sources over two periods of time in a number of different settings—elementary and high school, urban and rural. Questions of selectivity will still arise but the use of several sources at various times in many settings should partially offset the inherent problems that accompany similar studies.

From these sources I have gathered descriptions of over 1,200 classrooms for the years 1890 to 1980. These descriptions will be embedded within a larger set of data from each district including studies of teachers, and other sources that indirectly reveal teaching practices in almost 6,000 other classrooms. In addition, I included national data on how teachers taught in order to give a context for the local practices that I describe.

The patterns of teaching practice described in this study, the historical maps I mentioned earlier, represent only a tiny fraction of what teachers did in classrooms. Anyone familiar with a classroom knows the kaleidoscopic whirl that it is—although its pace, intensity, and complexity are often obscured by student compliance and by teacher-established routines. To the infrequent observer, the classroom, after 30 minutes, may seem humdrum, even tedious. How, then, can I capture only one slice of this whirl after it has disappeared?

The historian of classroom teaching is in the same bind as the paleontologist who carefully and softly brushes away the dust from a jaw fragment of an apparent human ancestor. The bone is an infinitesimally small fragment of the skeleton; the skeleton an even tinier fraction of the population that the scientist wants to describe. The "bones" I have had to deal with are photographs and written accounts of various participants. Capturing what happened in a classroom after it occurred is similar, but not identical to the paleontologist's search for relevant evidence.[8]

Historian David Fischer suggests another metaphor. History is like trying to complete an unconventional puzzle. Take a Jackson Pollock painting, cut it into a puzzle with thousands of parts. Throw out the corner pieces, most of the edges, and half of the rest. The task of putting it all together approximates what historians do.[9]

Putting it all together also means an effort to make sense of what is reconstructed. In a study of continuity and change in American classrooms over the last century, how I can explain the various practices that may have persisted in spite of determined reforms to alter them or the new techniques that teachers incorporated into their repertoires?

EXPLANATIONS FOR CONSTANCY AND CHANGE

There are a number of explanations for classroom stability in the face of reforms and changes that were embraced. I raise them now to alert readers to both the range and character of arguments that I will consider as the descriptions of classroom practice unfold in the next five chapters.[10] Consider the following possible explanations for classroom practices that have endured.

Schools are a form of social control and sorting. The ways schools are organized, the curriculum, and teaching practices mirror the norms of the socioeconomic system. Those instructional practices that seek obedience, uniformity, and productivity through, for example, tests, grades, home-work, and paying attention to the teacher prepare children for effective participation in a bureaucratic and corporate culture. Consistent with this argument is that certain teaching practices become functional to achieve those ends: teaching the whole class encourages children to vie for the teacher's attention and encourages competitiveness; teacher questions reward those students who respond with the correct answer; rows of chairs facing a teacher's desk produce a uniform appearance, reinforcing the teacher's authority to control the behavior of the class. Thus, the argument goes, the practices encouraged by student-centered instruction ill-fit the character of the society children would enter and classrooms became inhospitable arenas for small group instruction, expression, student deci-sion making, etc. Teacher-centered instruction, however, endured because it produces student behaviors expected by the larger society.

The organizational structure of the school and classroom drove teachers into adopting instructional practices that changed little over time. The archi-tecture of the classroom, compulsory attendance, age graded classes, dividing the day into periods, the Carnegie Unit, and other structural imperatives emerged from irresistible impulses inherent in public school-ing: getting a group of students to acquire knowledge while maintaining an orderly class. Within a classroom 30 or more students are required to listen and follow the directions of a teacher who must make over a thousand decisions daily about what to teach, how to teach, maintaining a buzzing but orderly calm, and how to secure student interest in the tasks at hand.

Tied to structures over which they had little influence teachers conserved their time and energy to cope with conflicting demands. They created resilient and adaptable approaches to deal with many students in a small space for long periods of time. Rows of desks permitted easy surveillance. Teaching the entire class as a single group was simply an efficient use of valuable teacher time so as to cover mandated subject matter while monitoring any untoward noise or movement in the room. Lecturing, numerous teacher questions, and seatwork are simple ways of conveying knowledge and managing a group efficiently. Teachers invented a practical pedagogy to cope with a complex classroom.

Student-centered techniques that stress informal student seating, small group work, individual creativity, and learning centers around the room generate a noisier, messier classroom. Far more energy is required from the teacher in managing varied tasks, constructing numerous materials for students, and tolerating their freedom to move and talk when they wish. Such a classroom would be out of step with existing classroom and school structures, the argument goes, and most difficult to install.

The culture of teaching itself tilts toward stability and a reluctance to change. This culture is shaped by the kinds of people recruited into the classroom, how newcomers learn to survive, and the prevailing values in the school supporting existing approaches. People who become teachers, according to this explanation, themselves watched teachers for almost two decades before entering their own classrooms. They tend to use those practices that they observed in teachers that taught them. Whole class discussions, supervised study, homework assignments drawn from one text, seatwork, tests, and an occasional film were familiar methods to new teachers in their own schooling. Such techniques seemed to work in the classes of the teachers they admired. Rather than make fundamental changes in practice such as small group instruction, planning lessons with students, and letting the class choose what to do, refining traditional approaches and introducing occasional variations would be consistent with the tenets of the conservative culture characteristic of teaching.

Two other explanations may account for more change than stability in teaching practices.

Ideas about how children develop, the role of the school, classroom authority, and the place of subject matter in instruction determine teaching practices. Those classrooms where teachers believed that a child's interest in the outdoors needed to be cultivated by tying instruction to science, writing, reading, and math constructed very different classrooms from colleagues who believed that work and play were separate activities with the latter to occur only after the former had been completed. This explanation stresses that ideas shape behavior; teachers committed to a child-centered progressivism, informal education, or a teacher-dominated setting shaped their classrooms and activities consistent with those ideas.

What determines instructional practice is whether or not reforms were effectively implemented in classrooms. According to this argument, when efforts to modify what teachers did were systematically executed, classrooms changed. Where efforts were ill-conceived, haphazardly adapted, and partially implemented, classrooms remained insulated from the directives and dreams of reformers. Planned change in classrooms occurred with some frequency when the ideas where carefully designed and put into practice.

Of the five explanations, the first three account for the durability of teacher-centered instruction and the last two explain where classroom change may have occurred. Consider these various arguments in reading the next five chapters.

The book is divided into three sections. Part I covering 1900–1940 consists of three chapters. Chapter 1 opens with a description of teaching at the turn of the century including the progressive reforms of these years. This description is followed by a chapter of case studies on New York City, Denver, Colorado, and Washington, D.C. during the 1920s and 1930s. Chapter 3 surveys teaching practices nationally during these two decades, including rural schools. Part II contains two chapters. Chapter 4 treats informal education between 1965–1975. In it, case studies of Washington, D.C., New York City, and North Dakota are summarized. Chapter 5 offers an intensive look at classroom teaching in one school district employing over one thousand teachers since 1975. Part III, the final chapter, is an essay on continuity and change in teaching during this century.

Earlier I compared my task to that of fossil seekers. Let me shift disciplines to that of the thirteenth century cartographer trying to map a new world on the basis of what information seafarers brought back, what had been written in books, and informed guesses. The maps he produced contained numerous mistakes yet sea captains who used them explored the seas and returned with new information that reshaped subsequent maps. This study is in the tradition of that thirteenth century mapmaker.

NOTES

1. "Interview with Albert Shanker," *Principal*, Vol. 53, No. 3, March/April, 1974, p. 48.
2. Larry Cuban, "Determinants of Curriculum Change and Stability, 1870–1970," in Jon Schaffarzick and Gary Sykes (eds.) *Value Conflicts and Curriculum Issues* (Berkeley, Calif.: McCutchan Publishers, 1979).
3. The writers who argue for stability often cite John Goodlad's study. These researchers drew conclusions based upon observations in the late 1960s of 158 classrooms in 67 schools across the nation. See *Looking Behind the Classroom Door* (Worthington, Ohio: Charles A. Jones, 1974). Writers who assert that

progressive theories have penetrated the classroom include Lawrence Cremin, *Transformation of the School* (New York: Vintage, 1961) and Charles Silberman, *Crisis in the Classroom* (New York: Random House, 1971). Other investigators have asserted that the instructional practices proposed by reformers did not get past the classroom door. See David Tyack, *The One Best System* (Cambridge: Harvard University Press, 1974) and Theodore Sizer, *Places for Learning, Places for Joy* (Cambridge Mass.: Harvard University Press, 1973). One writer who did investigate what happened in schools during the 1930s was Arthur Zilversmit, "The Failure of Progressive Education, 1920–1940," in Lawrence Stone, (ed.) *Schooling and Society* (Baltimore: John Hopkins Press, 1976), pp. 252–61. What historians have written about student-centered classrooms penetrating classrooms is taken up in more detail in chapter 1.

4. For the nineteenth century Barbara Finkelstein has done a signal service by researching teacher autobiographies, student recollections, textbooks, teaching manuals, and the like for primary school instruction. Other than the journal articles she has published based upon her doctoral research, this line of investigation has interested few researchers. See Barbara Finkelstein, "Governing the Young: Teacher Behavior in American Primary Schools, 1820–1880," (Unpublished Ed. D. Dissertation, Teachers College Columbia University, 1970).

I cannot fully explain why so few researchers have tried to recapture what happened in classrooms other than the difficulty or the tediousness of the task (which, I suspect, is a partial explanation). The typical researcher, as Dan Lortie has pointed out, "has concentrated on learning rather than teaching and has generally employed models and techniques at some distance removed from the realities of the classroom." Dan Lortie, *Schoolteacher* (Chicago: University of Chicago Press, 1975), p. 70.

Consider that the major policy study of the mid-1960s concentrated upon facilities available to students and used standardized test results as the basis for determining whether schools were effective. Far removed from classrooms, the Coleman Report, nonetheless, had profound consequences for both the public view of schooling, practitioners' aspirations for their students, and initially channeling research away from classrooms.

Where research has dwelt on teaching, it has been more fascinated with proving one method better than another (to no avail) or promoting one observational instrument over another. While those traditions of research are undergoing important changes now, few investigators have examined exactly what teachers have done in classrooms. David Berliner, in a thoughtful comprehensive review of problems researchers need to be aware of in investigating elementary classrooms, stressed that "until we know more about what teacher behavior fluctuates and how and ... why it fluctuates over time relating teaching behavior to student outcomes must remain primitive." David Berliner, "Studying Instruction in the Elementary Classroom," in Robert Dreeben and Alan Thomas (eds.) *The Analysis of Educational Productivity* (Cambridge Mass.: Ballinger Publishing Co., 1980), p. 202. There is also a growing body of ethnographic literature on what happens in classrooms that has appeared over the last decade. I will cite some of these sources when I deal with the post-1965 years.

5. I can illustrate this important point by a personal note. In the late 1950s when I began teaching social studies, an observer could have easily categorized me as wholly teacher-centered. Each week in class my students sat in rows of movable chairs with tablet arms; we carried on, more often than not, teacher-led discussions interspersed with mini-lectures from me, student reports, an occasional debate or class game to break the routine. Over 90 percent of the instructional time with students was spent with the whole group.

By the early 1960s I had begun to incorporate into my teaching practices such techniques as using student-led discussions, dividing the class into groups for varied tasks, preparing instructional materials to replace the textbook, and other approaches that could be summed up loosely as being part of the "new social studies."

By the early 1970s one class of the five I taught daily would spend the entire 50 minute period going from one teaching station to another. I used these stations at least once a week, sometimes more, depending on how much material I had developed for the teaching stations. Most of the week, however, was spent in teacher-led discussions, supervised study periods, group meetings for particular projects, student reports, mini-lectures, and other approaches. Students sat in a horseshoe arrangement of desks and chairs with the open end of the shoe facing my desk and the blackboard. What was studied, the methods used, how time and classroom space was allocated, I decided.

Again, if required to make a judgment about how I taught, my dominant pattern of instruction remained teacher-centered, yet I had incorporated into my instruction certain practices not there a decade earlier.

I offer this personal reference to illustrate the point of how at least one teacher changed some practices, yet did not necessarily substantially alter a basic teaching pattern.

6. The rationale for using these indicators is taken up in more detail in the Appendix.

7. J. M. Stephens, *The Process of Schooling* (New York: Holt, Rinehart and Winston, 1967), p. 11. David Tyack pointed out to me that progressives Ellwood Cubberley and Franklin Bobbitt used both metaphors.

8. Donald C. Johanson and Maitland A. Edey, *Lucy: The Beginnings of Human-kind* (New York: Simon and Schuster, 1981), p. 120.

9. David H. Fischer, *Historians' Fallacies* (New York: Harper and Row, 1970), p. 134.

10. Elaborations of these explanations occur in the final chapter and are cited there.

Part I

Progressivism and Classroom Practice, 1890–1940

1

Teaching at the Turn of the Century: Tradition and Challenge

At P.S. 8 in New York City, William Chatfield taught the sixth grade. While he taught many subjects, he enjoyed the teaching of history enough to submit an article to *New York Teachers' Monographs*, a journal that printed contributions from city teachers. A glimpse of how Chatfield taught his sixth graders history in 1900 emerges from his description. He wrote that the course of study for the second semester of the sixth grade covered the French and Indian War through the end of the War of 1812. Chatfield described how he included the main points of this half-century of American history and how he taught the subject matter.

> The general method has been to first furnish the pupils with an outline of the work to be covered and to assign lessons from the text in conformity with this, and then to lead them by conversations to discover the reasons and think out the results.
>
> A part of the time each week is given to oral instruction and at the end of the week a written exercise is required of each pupil. In this he attempts to show what he has gathered from the oral work, his reading and the text book.
>
> Maps and pictures are freely used to illustrate the work, the former being drawn upon the blackboard and copied by the pupil. Upon these maps are indicated the movements of the opposing forces; and brief statements are made of events which have made certain places and localities noted. The pictures are gathered from many sources and are distributed in the class.

Chatfield pointed out how he connected the climate and geography to "causes aiding or preventing certain results," and what people did for a living. Finally, to "leave a lasting impression, the principal events are memorized in chronological order."[1]

I know little else about William Chatfield or, for that matter, his thousands of colleagues across the city. Few historians know what happened in those classrooms. Much is known about school district governance, squabbles over schools, who taught and what was taught, yet very little is known of what teachers did in classrooms. The few historians who have studied practice prior to progressive reformers' involvement with public schools have reconstructed a partial picture of classroom activities from teacher biographies, student recollections, popular textbooks on methods, visitors' impressions, and the context within which teachers worked, i.e. class size, room arrangement, school organization, courses of study, or school board rules.[2]

Public schools near the turn of the century were diverse. For example, in 1890 there were 224,526 school buildings housing almost 13 million students in elementary (including grades seven and eight)* schools, and 222,000 in high schools. Together these students constituted 69 percent of the age 5–17 population. Over 77 percent of the children attended schoolhouses in rural areas, then defined as districts outside of towns and cities of 4,000 or more people.[3]

By the 1890s over a half-century had already passed since the common school movement had spread across the growing nation. Public schools, particularly in cities, had established organizations and practices that would be familiar to observers a century later. Schools were graded. School was in session nine months out of each year. Teachers were expected to have had some formal training beyond a grammar or high school education. Each teacher had a classroom to herself (by 1890, 65 percent of all primary and grammar school teachers were female; 60 percent of high school staffs were female). Rows of desks bolted to the floor faced a teacher's desk and blackboard. (Movable desks were introduced in the early 1900s but did not become commonplace until the mid-1930s.)[4] Courses of study set the boundaries and expectations for what had to be taught and when. Report cards and homework had already become standard features of the urban classroom in the 1890s. In brief, a terrain familiar to teachers and students today had been constructed a century earlier in urban classrooms.

But rural schools differed. By 1890, rural school boards spent $13.23 per pupil while city boards spent $28.87. In particular, one-room schoolhouses received less of everything. They were housed in older, makeshift facilities with insufficient books, supplies, and equipment. In ungraded schools, teachers with little formal education themselves coped with five

---

* Distinctions between primary (grades 1–4) and grammar (grades 5–8) schools were common at this time. I will use the word elementary to include both types of schools and those with grades 1–8.

year olds and young adults simultaneously. Students attended school fewer weeks a year than their urban cousins. These schools, soon to become the object of a vigorous campaign for improvement through consolidation, were the sites where most Americans were taught the basics. By 1910 rural schools still enrolled 67 percent of all children; per pupil expenditure had increased to $26.13, but remained well below the $45.74 that city systems spent.[5]

What did teachers do in these urban and rural classrooms? Did teaching differ by setting? According to Barbara Finkelstein, who examined almost one thousand descriptions of elementary school classrooms between 1820 and 1880, teachers talked a great deal. Students either recited passages from textbooks, worked at their desks on assignments, or listened to the teacher and classmates during the time set aside for instruction. Teachers assigned work and expected uniformity from students both in behavior and classwork. Teachers told students "when they should sit, when they should stand, when they should hang their coats, when they should turn their heads...." Students often entered and exited the room, rose and sat, wrote and spoke—as one. "North and south, east and west, in rural schools as well as urban schools," she concluded,

> ... teachers assigned lessons, asked questions and created standards of achievement designed to compel students to assimilate knowledge and practice skills in a particular fashion. It was a fashion dictated by the textbooks usually—and often with dogmatic determination.[6]

Finkelstein found three patterns of teaching in these elementary schools. The "Intellectual Overseer" assigned work, punished errors and had students memorize. The "Drillmaster" led students in unison through lessons requiring them to repeat content aloud. A third pattern, "Interpreter of Culture," she found only occasionally. Here the teacher would clarify ideas and explain content to children. She found less than a half dozen descriptions of this instructional pattern.[7]

Documenting these patterns, she provides richly detailed accounts of monitorial schools established in cities by Joseph Lancaster and his followers in the 1820s, where group recitations and standardized behavior were routine and rural one-room schools, where individual students sat before the teacher on the recitation bench and raced through their memorized text selections in the few minutes they had with the teacher.

Consistently, Finkelstein stresses that the regularities in teaching behavior she found crossed geographical and organizational boundaries. The settings, she concluded, had little to do with what teachers did in their classrooms. Nor could she find much change over time. "One gets the impression," she writes, "that there was little linear change in the conduct of classrooms in the period from 1820 to 1880." Carl Kaestle, however, noted that there was less corporal punishment, more uniformity in texts, some grouping by ability, and more grading of levels in these decades.[8]

Washington, D.C. Elementary Classroom, Black School, 1900 (*Frances B. Johnson Collection, Library of Congress*).

Washington, D.C. Elementary Classroom, White School, 1900 (*Frances B. Johnson Collection, Library of Congress*).

Washington, D.C., Elementary Classroom, White School, 1900 (*Frances B. Johnson Collection, Library of Congress*).

Other primary sources not included in her study support the existence of the Overseer and Drillmaster patterns. As with Finkelstein's study, identification and frequency of occurrence in these types cannot be determined. Articles written by New York City grammar school teachers in 1900, for example, describe how they taught composition, science, geography, and arithmetic. These accounts reveal reliance upon whole group instruction, drill, and recitation; uniformity in practice turns up repeatedly in the teachers' descriptions. There were, however, a sizable number of teachers who told how they used various materials in addition to the text, modified lessons to fit children's interests, and developed special topics for students to pursue, providing evidence for the Interpretor of Culture type though this is two decades after the period Finkelstein studied.[9]

Photographs of elementary school classrooms were posed since camera technology of the period required subjects to remain immobile twenty or more seconds while film was exposed. Typically, they show rows of children with hands folded atop their desks staring into the camera with a teacher standing nearby. Activities appear occasionally. One Washington, D.C., photograph shows 27 children sitting at their desks, cheeks puffed up, ready for the teacher's command to blow on the pinwheel that they are holding in both hands. In the vast majority of these photos the teacher is the center of attention; sometimes a student under the watchful gaze of the teacher, demonstrates a point at the blackboard, recites a passage, or reads to the class. Exceptions could be seen, however, in a series of posed photos taken in 1899 in Washington, D.C., classrooms to portray the "New Education." In almost 300 prints of elementary teachers, nearly 30 show groups of students working with relief maps in geography, rabbits and squirrels for a lesson on rodents, watching a teacher carve into a cow's heart to show the parts of an organ, taking a trip to the zoo, and similar activities. The remaining 90 percent of the prints show students sitting in rows at their desks doing tasks uniformly at the teacher's direction.[10]

Corroborating photographs and teacher descriptions further are the pen portraits of elementary classrooms drawn by Joseph Rice, the pediatrician-journalist who observed 1,200 teachers in 36 cities during a 6 month period in 1892. Rice's articles in a popular magazine painted teaching in urban schools as grim, dreary, and mechanical, the latter a favorite epithet of his. Instruction was married to drill and sing-song recitations, lacking sensitivity to children as individuals, Rice said.[11]

As a self-proclaimed reformer, he described in clear, if not minute detail, the deadening drill, memorization, and "busywork" students mindlessly pursued at the teacher's order. In Boston, Rice witnessed a teacher beginning the lesson with a question:

> "With how many senses do we study geography?"
> "With three senses: sight, hearing, and touch," answered the pupils.
> The children were now told to turn to the map of North America in their geographies, and to begin with the capes on the eastern coast. When the map had been found each pupil placed his forefinger upon "Cape Farewell," and when the teacher said "Start," the pupils said in concert, "Cape Farewell," and then ran their fingers down the map, calling out the names of each cape as it was touched.... After the pupils had named all the capes on the eastern coast of North America, beginning at the north and ending at the south, they were told to close their books. When the books had been closed, they ran their fingers down the cover and named from memory the capes in their order from north to south.
> "How many senses are you using now?" the teacher asked.
> "Two senses—touch and hearing," answered the children.[12]

In New York, Rice spoke with a principal about unquestioned obedience to the teacher's direction for order. Asking her whether the children in one classroom were allowed to turn their heads, the principal told Rice: "Why should they look behind them when the teacher is in front of them."[13]

In 6 months of school visits Rice found untrained teachers, unimaginative methods, and textbook-bound instruction in most classrooms except for a few cities that he extolled. I will return to these exceptions later in this chapter.

Other sources that support the existence of the teaching types that Finkelstein found are surveys of school conditions conducted by the educational experts of the day. Take, for example, the 1913 Portland, Oregon survey directed by Stanford University professor Ellwood P. Cubberley. The survey team visited 50 elementary classes in 9 schools. Except for teachers in the primary grades, the observers were highly critical of the instruction they viewed. Some excerpts:

- *Geography*: "All the work observed ... was abstract and bookish in the extreme.... The assignment for study and the questions, almost without exception, called for unreasoning memorization of the statements of the book."

- *Arithmetic and grammar:* "... the teaching of these subjects seemed on the whole, to be the best teaching observed. It is true that much of the technical grammar had little meaning for most of the children...."

- *History*: "There was not the slightest evidence of active interest in the subject; the one purpose seemed to be to acquire, by sheer force of memory, the statements of the assigned text...."[14]

Newton (Mass.) Superintendent Frank Spaulding drafted the report on elementary instruction. "Passive, routine, clerical," he wrote, "are the terms that most fittingly describe the attitude of principals and grammar grade teachers toward their work." Except for one lesson "in all my visits to grammar-grade rooms, I heard not a single question asked by a pupil, not a single remark or comment made to indicate that the pupil had any really vital interest in the subject matter."[15]

While the survey report blamed a "mechanical system" of courses of study and quarterly examinations for suffocating imaginative teaching, there is a persistent problem in interpreting these survey conclusions. Often it is impossible to gauge precisely whether conclusions apply to all, the overwhelming majority, or most of the classrooms. Even more difficult is to disentangle the observers' desires for improvement from what they see.

Additional data buttressing Finkelstein's reconstruction of teaching practice come from evidence found in various articles and books by educators of the period about teaching methods. Take, for example, Vivian Thayer's *The Passing of the Recitation*. A professor involved in efforts to make curriculum child-centered, his book traces the history of the recitation—a reform introduced initially to improve instruction—to its use in 1928 when the book was published.

Thayer pointed out how the child-centered ideas of Pestalozzi, as translated by his followers at places like the Oswego (N.Y.) Training School in the 1860s were disseminated throughout the country. Yet within decades adherents of "object teaching" were being accused of "mechanizing instruction." Similarly, enthusiastic American followers of Johann Frederich Herbart took his description of how the child's mind worked and by the 1890s, according to Thayer, had converted these ideas into a "method of instruction which requires that children, in the acquisition of new knowledge, move in lockstep fashion through five steps in learning." Detailed lesson plans included precise actions to be taken by the teacher, devices for holding the class's attention and carefully crafted assignments. These planning techniques resulted from implementing Herbart's theories into classroom practice, Thayer observed; in classrooms such techniques centered even more attention, if not influence, upon the teacher.[16]

After summarizing the ideas of major nineteenth century pedagogical thinkers and their impact upon practice, particularly the recitation, Thayer concluded that by the 1920s,

> ... the developments since Lancaster have led to little more than pouring of new wine into old bottles. We teach different subjects and we have altered the content of old subjects. We have originated more economical devices for learning and we have profited from careful studies in the technique of acquiring skill and information. We classify and grade our pupils more skillfully. But withal we have not fundamentally reconstructed the recitation system which Lancaster devised a little more than a century ago.[17]

Different evidence drawn from the conditions within which teachers worked and their training is oblique and offers less direct support for the classroom practices that Finkelstein outlined. I enter these points now into the discussion in order to highlight linkages between what teachers do, the conditions under which they teach, and their training. I will return to these connections between context and practice later.

Urban classrooms had between 40 to 48 desks per room. These classrooms were constructed to house 40 to 60 students. Estimates of class size at the turn of the century are rough but suggest that few desks were long empty, especially in the rapidly growing cities of the northeast and midwest. To staff these crowded classrooms, teachers had to be found who would survive and stay. Yet teaching was an insecure job. Trustees decided each year whether or not the teacher would be rehired. Political and family ties played a large role in appointments. Moreover, the jobs demanded a great deal from applicants who often lacked advanced education. Teachers, expected to cover up to ten subjects daily, often had limited training beyond their own grammar or high school education.

With a largely untrained corps of teachers expected to teach a variety of subjects and skills it comes as no surprise that textbooks flourished. By the 1880s textbooks had already become the teacher's primary tool and the student's main source of knowledge. Also published courses of study determined for teachers what had to be taught and when. These syllabi were often studded with page listings from textbooks for each subject.[19]

Exactly how powerful these working conditions were in shaping how teachers organized their classrooms for instruction is difficult to estimate. That class size, prescribed texts and curriculum, and lack of training had some influence, however, is obvious in teachers pointing to these conditions as factors affecting their performance.

Were high school classrooms at the beginning of the twentieth century similar to those in elementary schools? To set a framework for answering the question some demographic information might help.

HIGH SCHOOL CLASSROOMS

In 1890 just over 220,000 students attended 2,526 high schools in the country for an average of 86 days a year, although attendance varied by section of the country. A decade later, enrollment had increased sharply to 519,251 students in just over 6,000 high schools. New schools were appearing at the average rate of one per day. Uncommon as it was for a 17-year-old to attend a high school, it was even more unusual for that teenager to graduate. Of the 200,000 who went to high school in 1890, representing 1 percent of the total population, only 11 percent graduated. And of those who went to school and received diplomas, females consistently outnumbered males.[21]

High school teachers had more training and education than their grammar school colleagues. In New England, for example, where high schools began, 56 percent of the teachers were college graduates and 21 percent had done some work beyond high school. In Buffalo (N.Y.) of the 182 high school teachers in 1914, 72 percent had graduated either from college or a formal teacher training school.[22]

Additional schooling beyond high school was often necessary since teachers were called upon to teach many subjects. Since half of the high schools enrolled less than a hundred students, often one or two teachers taught the entire curriculum. Twenty-three of fifty-nine Connecticut high schools had one or two instructors to teach the complete course of study. Henry King of Albany, Missouri, to cite one case, was responsible for teaching botany, zoology, Latin, history English, etymology, and arithmetic. In city high schools, enrollments were larger and faculties were organized into departments by the early twentieth century.[23]

The curriculum was geared to prepare students for college in the late nineteenth century. In 1893, 44 percent of high school students took Latin; 56 percent took algebra. In 1900, most students enrolled in English, U.S. and English history, algebra, geometry, Latin, earth science, and physiology. College entrance exams shaped the course of study and activities as much as the rhythm of the school year.[24]

And teaching? If few historians studied elementary classrooms at this time, none has yet examined secondary ones. Clues do appear in pictures of classrooms with row after row of bolted-down desks; rooms in newly

Washington, D.C. Western High School, White, Chemistry Lesson, 1900 (*Frances B. Johnson Collection, Library of Congress*).

built schools set aside for "recitation"; and master schedules with the major portion of time allotted to this formal activity. Beyond these contextual clues, little is known about what happened in these classrooms. Since the major focus of this study is in the period after 1920 I can only offer a few fragments of evidence that may suggest a partial picture of practice. The subject deserves a full study.

Consider Steele High School in Dayton, Ohio, in 1896. The city's only high school or "people's college" was the subject of a detailed report by Malcolm Booth at the end of his first year as principal. Submitted to Superintendent W. J. White, Booth's report sketches out the teaching conditions at Steele and what teachers reported they did in classrooms.

Steele High School enrolled 846 students (60 percent female) in 1895–1896, an academic year lasting 36 weeks, a month shorter than the previous year. The 1896 graduating class had 92 students (71 percent female). For the first time the high school was open from 8:30 A.M. to 1:00 P.M. instead of two daily sessions. The school day was divided into 6 periods of 41 minutes each, running back-to-back except for a 15-minute recess between 11:18 and 11:33.[25]

The curriculum contained four courses of study (Classical, Scientific,

English, and Commercial) covering 4 years. The content of each course was outlined in the principal's report including the textbooks used, assignments, and what was expected of the students. To teach over 25 required courses to over 800 students there were 26 teachers (38 percent female). They taught 6 periods daily (with about 30 students in each class). These six classes seldom meant teaching the same lesson six times. While Mr. Kincaid in the Classical Department, for example, taught only two subjects, Latin and Greek, he probably had five different lessons to teach daily: Senior Latin, Junior Latin, Second Year Greek, First Year Latin, and Junior Greek. Each class had different texts and requirements. Also each class—Junior Greek, for example—included in the "Outline of Courses of Study" the notation "(5)" which meant that Mr. Kincaid was expected to hold five "recitations per week."[26]

To teach botany, physiology, geometry, Latin, Greek, and advanced German demanded schooling beyond the grammar grades. Fifty-four percent of Steele's faculty had graduated from college; fifteen percent had attended either normal school or college; the remainder had finished high school.[27]

Turning to the classroom, some hints of what occurred during the 41-minute period surfaced in course descriptions that teachers submitted to the principal. English teacher Charles Loos, an 1869 graduate of Bethany (W.Va.) college, 8 year veteran at Steele, and one of the three highest paid staff ($1,500 per year) described the methods English teachers used to teach mythology to third and fourth year students:

> The myths are to be studied at home and recited topically, none being omitted or left to careless reading.... The myths must be reproduced as exercises in narration, comparison, and description.... This study is to be accompanied by constant exercise in composition, both written and oral, with special emphasis upon good sentence structure and pronunciation.[28]

In teaching the novel, Loos and other English teachers planned the following:

> In recitation the class must be prepared to give an outline of the part studied and show its connection with what has preceded; to discuss the characters as they appear, show how they affect other characters and the plot in general....
> The recitation should cover oral and written reports, rapid questioning, informal discussion and the reading aloud of certain illustrative passages.[29]

Physics and botany teacher August Foerste, Harvard Ph.D. (1890), and appointed to Steele in 1893, wrote Booth that science instruction had improved with the Board of Education's recent purchase of equipment.

> With this apparatus it was possible for the teacher to perform, in the presence of the class, most of the experiments mentioned in the book. The

pupils were required to make notes during the experiment, and then to describe it at length in their note book.[30]

Foerste urged the purchase of more equipment so that students could do work individually and create projects such as "an electric bell and burglar alarm, a telegraph sounder and relay, and a telephone" so that students do "practical application of physical laws." These ideas, he said, "are not wild." It is not essential for the "pupil to be a skilled mechanic in order to make them a success *educationally*" (original emphasis). This teacher's concern for practical application of knowledge and projects worked on by individual students was unique in the reports submitted to the principal.[31]

Although Marie Durst, at Steele for 8 years, included in her report on French and German a concern for daily usage of language, she said that "most of the classes in modern languages are too large. The teacher has no opportunity for giving any individual attention." As to method, instruction is given in the language to be taught and "the pupils are led to express themselves in that language as soon as they have acquired a sufficient vocabulary." For grammar and translation, Durst used dictation frequently since "they train the ear to the strange sounds and require the strictest attention." Also, she added, students learn correct pronunciation and fluent speech by "memorizing and reciting selections of high literary merit."[32]

Such reports reveal teacher intentions and, in various portions, describe practice. No verification of what happened in their classes is available. A decade later, in another city, however, a professor did sit in classes and reported what she saw and heard. Romiett Stevens visited an unspecified number of schools in and around New York City between 1907 and 1911 to study the use of questions in classrooms. Using a stopwatch and a stenographer she observed 100 English, history, math, foreign language, and science teachers that principals had identified as superior. She recorded the number of questions that they asked. In a related study, she followed ten classes through each period of the day to get a sense of the aggregate impact of teacher questioning.[33]

Stevens found that teachers asked an average of two to three questions per minute; the average number of questions that students faced daily totaled 395. The lowest number of questions she found in her observations of 100 classrooms was 25; the highest, 200. "The teacher," she commented, "who has acquired the habit of conducting recitations at the rate of from 100 to 200 questions and answers per classroom period of 45 minutes has truly assumed the pace that kills." Of the 100 teachers she visited, 28 asked questions at that pace.[34]

With teacher questioning dominant, Stevens calculated exactly how much time during a lesson was devoted to teacher and student talk. Using 20 stenographic reports, she found that teachers were talking 64 percent of the time. Of the 36 percent of talk that belonged to students, much of it was brief, usually one word responses or short sentences. There were exceptions. Stevens found 2 of the 100 classrooms she observed unusual. Of the 34 questions asked in one science class, 25 came from students. In a history lesson, the teacher let the students use the textbook while the class answered questions. General practice, according to Stevens, was to close the text and put it away once the teacher began asking questions.[35]

Stevens' writing reveals a distaste for rapid-fire teacher questioning where the "pupils follow as a body, or drop by the wayside." To ask between two to three questions a minute, "we commit ourselves as 'drivers' of youth instead of 'leaders,'" she wrote. With teachers assigning lessons for the next day, students taking the book home to memorize the lesson, and the next day teachers telling students to close their books and recite answers from the pages read, Stevens concluded that teachers were "drillmasters instead of educators."[36]

Three years after Stevens' study was published, a survey of Buffalo (N.Y.) schools was completed by the New York State Commissioner of Education's staff at the request of the city superintendent. A portion of that report deals with high schools.

In 1914, Buffalo had 4 high schools with 182 teachers. "Inspectors," as the members of the survey team were called, visited classrooms of all teachers and reported their conclusions in narrative form. Some excerpts suggest patterns although specific figures are missing in the report. Of the 25 English teachers who were each visited 3 times for at least 15 minutes on each occasion, the inspectors reported on the teaching of grammar:

> Instruction in grammar is usually much too detailed and formal. It is composed largely of such work as copying, composing, and correcting short illustrative sentences, selecting single types of constructions from sentences frequently too easy for the pupil, completing elliptical sentences, memorizing terms and definitions, diagramming and parsing in routine fashion.[37]

For the 23 modern language teachers (Spanish, French, and German), the inspectors observed that "the usual method was to have one pupil read a paragraph, then to put a few simple questions to him about the part read, then to ask for forms and explanations of syntax." The survey team concluded that assignments were often ambiguous and recitations were poorly delivered, except for four teachers whom they praised. "Usually the teacher sat uncomfortably behind her desk and let the pupils answer the questions."[38]

State Department officials observed 32 math teachers. Recitation, again, was the primary teaching method. Most math teachers, the report stated, "called on most of the pupils for some part of the recitation." Inspectors criticized math instruction in the four high schools for giving insufficient attention to preparing students for the new work of the next day.[39]

Science teaching impressed the inspectors. Student time in the classes of the 15 teachers was divided between laboratory and recitations. In labs, students worked on completing exercises using equipment and facilities that the observers felt were adequate. "There was little evidence," their report said, "of slavish following of directions. . . ." For recitations, the "questioning was well calculated to test both the memory of a statement and ability to apply the definitions and principles." In two classes, student reports consumed the lesson. "This appeared to be the habitual practice," they reported. In other classes student responsibility was less defined "with the result that the recitation became a lecture punctuated by occasional questions." In a number of classes the work was carried on with "splendid enthusiasm."[40]

History instruction was also viewed favorably by the team of observers. Except for the minority (number unspecified) whose teaching is "formal and mechanical" because they limit themselves to the text, required readings and notebook work, the majority of "skillful" teachers use maps, field trips, discussions, debates, and other subjects in the curriculum to make history "vivid and interesting."[41]

Such evidence drawn from surveys, reports, visitors' impressions, and photographs is piecemeal. It is suggestive, not comprehensive. A complete study of high school instruction would, I believe, fill in the gaps and include the finer lines that go into a full portrait of teaching. Yet even with this broad outline teaching patterns emerge from the unorderly jigsaw pieces presented here.

When elementary and high school instruction are taken together, similarities appear. Generally, classes were taught as a group. Teacher talk dominated verbal expression during class time. Student movement during instruction occurred only with the teacher's permission. Classroom activities clustered around teacher questions and explanations, student recitation, and the class working on textbook assignments. Except for laboratory work done in science classrooms, uniformity in behavior was sought and reflected in classroom after classroom with rows of bolted-down desks facing the blackboard and the teacher's desk.

There were also differences between the two levels of instruction at the turn of the century as today. Subject matter was stressed far more in the higher than in lower grades. Teaching was splintered in high schools, that is, students traveled from class to class to meet with different teachers for about an hour at a time. Not so at the elementary school where the teacher generally would spend the day with the same students. Classes in high schools were smaller than in elementary schools and high school teachers had more schooling than their colleagues in the lower grades.

Taking the similarities and differences together, teacher-centered instruction, as defined by the categories listed above, clearly dominated the instances of instruction that appear in the evidence I offered here. This should come as no surprise considering the times.

Embedded within teacher-centered instruction were a set of assumptions about schools, children, and learning consistent with the profound changes occurring at the turn of the century in the larger culture. Notions of bureaucratic efficiency, organizational uniformity, standardization, and a growing passion for anything viewed as scientific were prized in the rapidly expanding industrial and corporate sector of the economy. School officials and teachers came to share many of these beliefs as well. Harnessed to an infant science of educational psychology that believed children learned best through repetition and memorization, these social beliefs, reinforced by the scientific knowledge of the day about learning, anchored teacher-centered instruction deeply in the minds of teachers and administrators at the turn of the century.[42]

STUDENT-CENTERED INSTRUCTION

What were the concepts of student-centered instruction practiced in the public schools at the turn of the century? Two forms existed. A common-sense, atheoretical, practical version appeared in rural one-room schools due, in large part, to the conditions existing in those settings. The lack of materials, isolation, group feeling engendered by an intuitively flexible teacher produced classrooms that permitted cooperative work, individual attention, use of content drawn from the community, and tolerance of student movement. The other more prominent and theoretical form were the innovative efforts tried in small, mostly private, schools.

The origins of this latter form can be traced back to Rousseau's *Emile* as elaborated further by educational reformers Froebel and Pestalozzi. In America the conversion of these reformers' ideas into schools that viewed the child, not the teacher or subject, as the proper focus for instruction, can be found in the work of Edward Sheldon, Francis Parker, John Dewey, and their earnest disciples who spread interpretations of each man's work throughout the country. No one definition of student-centered instruction or the "New Education" nor progressivism bound these men together other than the conviction that schools could do a far better job of linking a child's life inside the classroom to the world outside the schoolhouse door.

The point of reviewing, however briefly, the work of Sheldon, Parker, and Dewey is to establish that varied concepts of student-centered instruction were practiced in schools operated by these men and their followers throughout the late nineteenth and early twentieth centuries.

Edward Sheldon, teacher of orphans in "ragged" schools, secretary and organizer of a public school system, fervently embraced Pestalozzi's ideas, as translated by the English Home and Colonial Infant Society. "Object teaching," as Pestalozzian principles in the hands of Sheldon and others came to be labeled, concentrated upon the experience of children, their perceptions, and language in order to develop in an orderly manner their powers of reasoning. A child's experience was supposed to replace books; how a child developed was to replace courses of study; and the teacher's careful direction of instruction was to replace recitation.[43]

Object teaching, according to two writers, penetrated magazines, books, conferences on teaching, reports and courses of study at the elementary level, especially in arithmetic, oral instruction, geography, and natural science. In classrooms, however, object teaching became, in Thayer's phrase, "dismal formalism." Reprints of actual lessons reveal teachers asking questions about objects, adding little knowledge to the students, and controlling the entire pace, structure, and outcomes of the lesson. Examples of lessons used at the Oswego State Normal and Training School contained specific points that teachers were expected to make with classes, clear instructions of how to lead students to correct observations. If anything, these instructions resemble scripts.[44]

While object teaching was still in evidence by 1900, it was often indistinguishable from the dreary, tedious recitations that Rice and other school critics condemned. Nonetheless, the ideas about children's development and expression underlying object teaching had had an impact. Perhaps that may explain the letter Sheldon received in 1886 from the principal of the Cook County Normal School, Francis Wayland Parker. "You," Parker wrote, "touched every child in America." Strong praise, indeed, from the person John Dewey called the "Father of Progressivism." Parker had taught in country schools. During the Civil War he served in the Union Army, was seriously wounded in the throat, and rose to rank of Colonel.[45]

Returning to teaching he soon became principal of a Normal School in Ohio. His wife died shortly thereafter. Using a trust fund that a relative had left him, he went to Europe to study both philosophy and pedagogy. Coming back to America he could not find a position until School Board President Charles Francis Adams invited him to Quincy (Mass.).

In the years he served Quincy, a school system with 40 teachers and 1,600 students in 7 schools including a high school, Parker rapidly changed the curriculum, methods of instruction, and materials. Within a few years Quincy became a mecca for educators interested in the "New Education," as one admirer of Parker called it. Parker disclaimed any innovation saying:

> I repeat that I am simply trying to apply well established principles, principles derived directly from the laws of the mind. The methods springing from them are found in the development of every child. They are used everywhere except in school. I have introduced no new method or detail. No experiments have been tried, and there is no peculiar "Quincy System."

Perhaps. But John Dewey in a speech on Parker's work in Quincy asked: "Did you ever hear of a man, who starting as superintendent of schools had reached a point in his career twenty-five years later where the anniversary of that beginning was an event to be marked by the educators of the nation?"[46]

Parker went on to serve as principal of the Cook County Normal School which eventually became part of the University of Chicago. He served as principal and director for almost two decades before he died in 1902. In the "Practice School" Parker and his staff, many of whom were graduates of the Oswego Normal School, developed further ideas and instructional and curricular techniques that implemented the Colonel's often quoted sentence: "The child is the center of all education."[47]

In the 1880s the eight-grade school had a kindergarten, library, printing plant to provide classroom materials and to publish teacher-written units, physical education equipment, manual training, and 20 acres of nearby land that became a center for nature study. Parker believed in intergrating ("correlation" was the word used then) the various subject areas. Children seeing connections between science, art, math, geography and being able to express these connections became one of the primary aims and achievements of the school. Beyond linking subjects, teaching basic skills through integrated content, and heavy reliance upon expression through art, music, and drama, the school also taught cooking, sewing, pottery-making, weaving, gardening, and bookbinding.[48]

When a veteran school superintendent visited classrooms in the Normal School in 1892 he went away impressed by how easily and without any overt coercion students did what practitioners called "busywork" in public schools. Superintendent J. W. Greenwood of Kansas City saw no fear of the teacher in children. No copying occurred. The work was done rapidly, without any apparent order. Each student "goes at it in a hurry and rushes 'his job' along. It is the kindergarten idea carried up through the grades." In the upper grades, Greenwood observed practices that were similar to laboratory work, "each keeping a record of his own experiments." The grim uniform recitation with which the Kansas City school chief was familiar was absent from Parker's school. He, like thousands of visitors including the peripatetic pediatrician Joseph Rice, went away quite taken with the Colonel's achievements.[49]

When Parker died in 1902 memorial services were held at the University of Chicago. John Dewey spoke.

> Twenty-five years ago, in Quincy, Massachusetts the work he undertook was the object of derision. . . . To many he seemed a faddist, a fanatic. It was only twenty-five years ago; and yet the things for which he then stood are taken today almost as a matter of course, without debate, in all the best schools of the country.[50]

Dewey knew Parker well. When Dewey moved his family to Chicago in 1894, he enrolled his son, Fred, in the first grade of the Practice School. The next year, Fred's sister Evelyn attended the school. When Dewey and his wife began an experimental school, they took their children out of

Parker's school and entered them into their new Laboratory School at the University of Chicago.

Far more has been written about Dewey than Sheldon and Parker. Rather than trying to recapture the essence of his Dewey's career as an influential theorist and practitioner, a task others have done, I will mention briefly the years 1896–1903 when he served as Director of the experimental school. In the Laboratory School he worked directly with children, teachers, and parents implementing his ideas of learning and child development into classroom practice.

In reading through teacher recollections, courses of study, teacher reports, and students' remembrances it is easy to conclude that the Laboratory School with its curriculum centered upon Man's occupation rather than separate subjects, upon reading and writing learned through activities rather than through isolated tasks, and group activities guided rather than directed by teachers, were simply features of just another progressive school. That would be a mistake since in the 1890s there were few schools in the country, public or private, that risked shaping an entirely new curriculum around children's interest in adult work, family and community ties, group cooperation, and democratic practices—not for its own sake but toward larger goals. As a private school of 140 children (1900) and 23 teachers including Ella Flagg Young as Supervisor of Instruction, and later Chicago Superintendent of Schools, the Laboratory School was openly experimental, advancing ideas and trying innovations that would become familiar, if not clichés, a generation later.

Consider the first few months of school for Group III, the six-year-olds. Daily the class would gather and review the previous day's work and plan for the day, "each child being encouraged to contribute." The plans for the day's work were decided upon and delegated by the pupils. At the end of the period, another group meeting summarized the results of the work and suggested new plans. Projects determined and built by the children included a miniature farm house, barn and cultivated land made out of large blocks, twigs and soil. Plans were discussed and drawn up using rulers to make the model to scale. This group also cleaned up a five by ten foot space in the school yard to plant winter wheat. As they proceeded through the school year, the class discussed plowing, what seeds to plant, how to plant, harvesting and using the grain to make flour, and then making bread. "When they talked about grains in the classroom," a teacher wrote, "they cooked cereals in the kitchen." Measuring and other uses of numbers were easily incorporated into building the farm model and producing the winter wheat.[51]

During these first few months of school "an interest in reading also developed."

> All the things they had found in their outdoor excursions were placed on a table. Sentences were written on the board, such as: "Find a cocoon," and the

child who could read it was allowed to run and get the cocoon. After playing this game a few times, the same sentences were shown printed in large type, so that they would get the printed form simultaneously with the script. They seemed very eager to read and decided themselves to make a weekly record of their work.[52]

For older students, the same focus upon active involvement, occupations, group discussion and decision making with the teacher acting as a helper prevailed. The typical program for nine- to twelve-year-olds was:

Subject	Hours a day	Hours a week
history and geography	1	5
techniques (reading, writing, numbers)	½	2½
science or	1½	2 or 2½
cooking or		1½
textile or shop		2
art		1½
music	1 or ½	1½
gymnasium		2½
modern languages	½	2½
	4½	21½

Opportunities to make decisions, use manual skills learned in classrooms, and to work cooperatively presented themselves, for example, in a schoolwide project of building a clubhouse where students in the Camera and Dewey (for debating and discussion) clubs could meet. Mayhew wrote that this "enpterprise was the most thoroughly considered one ever undertaken by the school." Because it provided a home for clubs away from the main building "it drew together many groups and ages and performed a distinctly ethical and social service."[53]

Writing in 1930, former student Josephine Crane recalled what she learned at the Laboratory School.

> First as to the Sciences, no matter how young we were—too young to understand very much—we were given a chance to use our eyes, to observe facts of nature more closely....
>
> Secondly, the activities—carpentry, cooking, weaving, sewing, art—all trained our hands and fingers to be useful.... People have often asked me where I learned to use my hands, and how it is I so easily learn to do new things with my hands. I tell them it is because I was trained to use my mind and hands and eyes together. I was trained to observe and given a chance to use what I observed in what I did.
>
> Third, the building of the clubhouse—the real and practical work—helped us to see what architecture really is. We got far more out of that than out of books.
>
> Fourth, I learned responsibility. When I was quite young, I was asked to teach art for two months to a younger class.... When I went into the room for

the first time I had to realize that I must do something! I learned how to teach that way and this is responsibility finally realized.[54]

For teachers as well as students it was an exciting place to be. Grace Fulmer, a teacher at the Laboratory School who left to direct a similar school in Los Angeles, recalled her two years (1900–1902) working under John Dewey.

> It was Mr. Dewey's idea that each child should be free to develop his own powers to some ultimate purpose through the guidance of one whose experience was richer. Such also was his own relation to the teachers in his school. I know there were things in my own work of which he did not approve and yet I always felt free to work in my own....

The Dewey School, as it was often called by teachers and friends, lost its namesake in 1904 when he accepted an appointment at Teachers College, Columbia University.[55]

Beyond the direct efforts of these men, there were public schools that partially or thoroughly implemented the "New Education" or "scientific pedagogy" as Rice and other enthusiasts labeled it. Writers who cite Rice for his description of mindless instruction often ignore his warm portraits of schools where the curriculum was correlated and where teachers introduced science work, encouraged children's expression in writing and art, and practiced manual training in the elementary school.[56]

From St. Paul, Minneapolis, Indianapolis, and La Porte (Indiana), Rice quoted liberally from student work and described teacher activities that unified the curriculum. In La Porte, for example, he found instances of the "perfect lesson." It is "one that not only interests the child, but one that uses his energies to the best advantage."

> From the start the pupils are encouraged to be helpful to each other. Already in the first school year the children begin to work together in groups and to assist each other in making and recording observations of plants and animals, of the wind and the weather.... In the classrooms are found small square tables around which the pupils sit, particularly when doing busy work, performing tasks in which all the members of the group take part....
>
> At the group tables things are made with which the rooms are decorated at the bi-monthly festivals which have become a custom at La Porte. Much of the number work is done at the group tables....

Rice conceded that such school districts were a minority in 1892. He found 4 school systems of the 36 he visited implementing the principles he advocated. Far more teachers stood and students sat in conventional recitation-bound classrooms, according to Rice.[57]

Just over two decades later John Dewey and his daughter Evelyn visited schools embracing progressive practices. In *Schools of Tomorrow*, the Deweys documented the spread of schools with "tendencies toward greater freedom and an identification of the child's school life with his environment and outlook, and even more important, the recognition of the role education must play in a democracy." While most of the schools they describe are private, the Deweys devote much space to the Gary (Indiana) schools under Superintendent William Wirt,* one public school in Chicago and two Indianapolis public schools, one of which served Black students. Concentrating on themes where teachers encourage student expression, group work, and a close fit between the content studied and the immediate environment, the Deweys described a movement they believed was spreading across the nation. "More and more," John Dewey wrote, "schools are growing up all over the country that are trying to work out definite educational ideas.[59]

Thus various versions of teacher-centered and student-centered instruction existed at the turn of the century. The extent of each, their variations, and what impulses generated them cannot easily be determined although it would be reasonable to conclude that by 1915 when the Deweys' book appeared the dominant practice in most public schools continued to cluster around teacher-centered patterns in furniture arrangement, grouping, instructional talk, student movement, and class activities. Variations of student-centered patterns appeared most often in small (less than 300 students), private (although public schools implementing these approaches did exist), elementary schools—few, if any, high schools were described.

While teacher-centeredness prevailed in most classrooms, different conceptions of the school's role and teaching were slowly being converted into practice. Challenges to the conventional wisdom of the day on what subject matter was best for students and how teachers should deal with children began to appear in Quincy, La Porte, Chicago, New York City, and Washington, D.C. These challenges to the beliefs and practices of teacher-centered instruction grew in the decades that followed and produced classrooms where teachers tried to be faithful to the traditional and new sets of beliefs, creating mixes of practices that mirrored larger conflicts between the values of individual growth and group goals, scientific efficiency and creative expression, education and socialization.

The decades after 1900 saw an increase in efforts to introduce student-centered teaching practices in public schools. By 1940, the

---

* The Gary Schools during Wirt's tenure became a showplace of pre–World War I progressivism. Merging the impulse toward economy with the child-centered school impulse, Wirt created student communities out of schools through scheduling students into different spaces and activities within a building. Called platoon schools, Wirt's innovations, promoted by journalists and reformers, swept across the nation in the decade following its introduction in Gary. Because of the political controversy triggered by its abortive implementation in New York City in 1917, the Gary School Board and Superintendent asked a foundation to conduct an impartial survey of its schools. Directed by Abraham Flexner, the survey team inspected each of the innovations including classroom instruction and produced an eight volume report. Finding much merit in the Gary Plan, Flexner did conclude, however, that classroom instruction in the academic subjects, primary grades through high school, was mechanical and, if anything, conventional.[58]

vocabulary of pedagogical progressives had rapidly turned into the conventional educational of the times as expressed by both teachers and administrators. The next chapter explores how conventional that wisdom had become in urban and rural classrooms in the 1920s and 1930s.

NOTES

1. Sidney Marsden Fuerst (ed.), "Methods in New York Schools," *New York Teachers Monographs*, Vol. II (New York: June, 1900), pp. 106–7.
2. Lawrence Cremin, *Transformation of the School* (New York: Vintage, 1961); Tyack, *One Best System*; Finkelstein, "Teacher Behavior in American Primary Schools."
3. *Report of the Commissioner of Education*, 1890–1891, (Washington, D.C.: Government Printing Office, 1894), Vol. 1, p. 43 and Vol. 2, p. 792; 1900–1901 (Washington, D.C.: Government Printing Office, 1902), Vol. I, p. xi; 1911, (Washington, D.C.: Government Printing Office, 1912), Vol. II, pp. xxvi, xxviii.
4. Department of the Interior, *Biennial Survey of Education*, 1920–1922, (Washington, D.C.: Government Printing Office, 1924), Vol. I, pp. v, 2, 4; Henry Eastman Bennett, "Fifty Years of School Seating, *American School Board Journal*, March, 1940, Vol. 100, pp. 41–3, 125.
5. *Report of the Commissioner of Education*, 1911, (Washington, D.C.: Government Printing Office, 1912), Vol. II, p. xxix.
6. Finkelstein, "Teacher Behavior, 1820–1880," pp. 22, 86.
7. Barbara Finkelstein, "The Moral Dimensions of Pedagogy," *American Studies*, (Fall, 1974), pp. 81–2, 84.
8. Finkelstein, "Teacher Behavior, 1820–1880," pp. 174–5, 179; Carl Kaestle, *Pillars of the Republic* (forthcoming).
9. Fuerst, pp. 8, 132.
10. The Frances Benjamin Johnson collection of photographs is lodged in the Library of Congress; other photos are reproduced in Tyack, *One Best System* and O. L. Davis, Jr. "Schools of the Past: A Treasury of Photographs" (Bloomington, Ind.: Phi Delta Kappa Educational Foundation, 1976).
11. Joseph M. Rice, *The Public School System of the United States* (New York: Arno Press, 1969).
12. ibid., pp. 139–40.
13. ibid., p. 32.
14. ibid., pp. 116, 118.
15. ibid., p. 119.
16. V. T. Thayer, *The Passing of the Recitation* (Boston: D.C. Heath and Co., 1928), pp. 7, 9–12.
17. Ibid., p. 12.
18. John Folger and Charles Nam, *Education of the American Population* (Washington, D.C.: Government Printing Office, 1967), pp. 84–5; Rice, 58–9, 76, 159–60.
19. *Report of the Educational Commission of the City of Chicago* (1898) cited in William C. Bagley, "The Textbook and Methods of Teaching," National

Society for the Study of Education, *The Textbook in American Education*, Part II, (Bloomington, Ill.: Public School Publishing Co., 1931), p. 8; see also various volumes of *New York Teachers Monographs* (1900–1904) in which teachers describe how they use syllabi.

20. In Nancy Hoffman, *Woman's "True" Profession* (New York: McGraw-Hill, 1981), see selection from Margaret Haley's speech to the National Education Association in 1904; selection from an anonymous teacher in *Atlantic* Monthly (July, 1896); and selection from Myra Kelly, *Little Citizens*.
21. Ed Krug, *The Shaping of the American High School*, Vol. I, (New York: Harper and Row, 1964), pp. 5, 14, 169; Theodore Sizer, *Secondary Schools at the Turn of the Century* (New Haven: Yale University Press, 1964), pp. 5, 39, 53; Tyack, p. 576.
22. Sizer, pp. 44, 46; Education Department of the State of New York, *Examination of the Public School System of the City of Buffalo* (Albany, N.Y.: University of the State of New York, 1916), p. 55.
23. Sizer, pp. 45, 53; see also Buffalo Survey.
24. Sizer, p. 66; David Tyack, "The History of Secondary Schools in Delivering Social Services," Stanford University, June, 1978, p. 3.
25. Dayton, Ohio Annual Report of the Board of Education, 1895–1896 (Dayton Board of Education, 1896), pp. 13, 49, insert after p. 250.
26. ibid., p. 250.
27. ibid., pp. 13, insert after p. 250, 274.
28. ibid., pp. 58–9.
29. ibid., pp. 59–60.
30. ibid., p. 64.
31. ibid., p. 65.
32. ibid., pp. 76–7.
33. Romiett Stevens, *The Question as a Measure of Efficiency in Instruction* (New York: Teachers College, Columbia University, 1912), Contributions to Education, No. 48.
34. ibid., pp. 11, 15–17.
35. ibid., p. 11.
36. ibid., p. 25.
37. Buffalo Survey, p. 127.
38. ibid., pp. 132–3.
39. ibid., p. 134.
40. ibid., pp. 140–2.
41. ibid., p. 138.
42. Raymond Callahan, *Education and the Cult of Efficiency* (Chicago: University of Chicago Press, 1962), chapters 1–5; Tyack, pp. 39–59.
43. Thayer, p. 7.
44. Thayer, pp. 7–8; see Ned H. Dearborn, *The Oswego Movement in American Education* (New York: Teachers College, Columbia University, 1925), pp. 159–69 for thirteen lessons taken from Sheldon's *Elementary Instruction*.
45. Dearborn, p. 97; Cremin, p. 129.
46. Lelia E. Patridge, *The Quincy Methods* (New York: E. L. Kellogg and Co., 1889), p. 657; Jack Campbell, *The Children's Crusader: Colonel Francis W. Parker* (New York: Teachers College Press, 1967), p. 78; Cremin, p. 130, citing an 1879 report by Parker; Ida Heffron, *Francis W. Parker* (Los Angeles: Ivan

Deach, Sr, 1934), p. 25.

47. Charles Marler, "Colonel Francis W. Parker: Prophet of the 'New Education'" (Stanford University unpublished dissertation, 1965), p. 108; Campbell, p. 119.

48. Marler, p. 179; Campbell, pp. 130–2.

49. Marler, citing a report from J. M. Greenwood, "A Visit to Colonel Parker's School in December, 1892."

50. John Dewey, "In Memoriam, Colonel Wayland Parker," June, 1902 in *Elementary School Teacher and Course of Study*, Vol. II, pp. 704–8.

51. Katherine Mayhew and Anna C. Edwards, *The Dewey School: The Laboratory School of the University of Chicago* (New York: D. Appleton–Century Co., 1936), pp. 80–4.

52. ibid., pp. 84–5.

53. ibid., pp. 228–32.

54. ibid., p. 405.

55. ibid., p. 395.

56. Rice, p. 184.

57. ibid., pp. 207, 229.

58. *See*: Abraham Flexner and Frank Bachman, *The Gary Schools* (New York: General Education Board, 1918), pp. 77, 79, 80–3, 160; for long–term effects of Wirt's efforts, see W. Lynn McKinney and Ian Westbury, "Stability and Change: The Public Schools of Gary, Indiana, 1940–1970," in William Reid and Decker Walker, (eds.) *Case Studies in Curriculum Change* (London: Routledge and Kegan Paul, 1976).

59. Evelyn Dewey and John Dewey, *Schools of Tomorrow* (New York: E. P. Dutton and Co., 1915), preface; also see Scott Nearing, *The New Education* (Chicago: Row, Peterson, and Co., 1915) and *Rainbow Promises of Progress in Education* (Institute for Public Service, 1917).

2

Behind the Classroom Door
in Three Cities, 1920–1940

It was a large sunny room with ample windows letting in light to the rear and left. The window sill held potted plants, some of which had begun to flower. Just above the sill pasted to the window glass were drawings made by the children. Doors and the ledges above the blackboards held placards: "factors," "numerator," "denominator." Above the front blackboard in careful, neat script was written: SELF-CONTROL. On one door was posted the Declaration of Independence; on another one was the membership of the American Junior Red Cross, 1924.

This was Mrs. Spencer's fourth grade class. Forty-two children sat in rows, facing the teacher's desk and SELF-CONTROL, awaiting the teacher's direction. Fifteen bright children from 4A and 27 dull ones from 4B, according to Mrs. Spencer, made up her class. An arithmetic lesson was underway.

"Little helpers to the board," Mrs. Spencer directed. "George, Edith, Fred, Gertrude, each take two children who need helping." A dozen children arrayed themselves in groups of three around the room. "Begin at page 101 in your book and start with the first example. You others, in your seats, begin at page 115, example 4. Yes, you may talk to one another about your work." A quiet hum arose.

The teacher moved around the room helping individual students. After awhile she looked at her watch and announced: "The coaching period is over. To your seats." As the children scurried back to their seats and settled back, Mrs. Spencer went to the board and wrote

$$37\frac{1}{2}$$
$$-25\frac{1}{2}$$

"Who can give me the least common denominator? Fanny? I called on you because you weren't paying attention. Well, then, Sam, you tell us. Ten, that's right. Now, then, Sam, what do we—oh, I hope you know it—what do we do next?" A long pause. A girl answers. "Oh, dear," says Mrs. Spencer, "there's a girl named Sam." A long pause. Finally the teacher accepted an answer from another student.

"The arithmetic period is over," she announced. "Keep your papers in your books. Your homework is example 2 on page 114: 117,799 divided by 3,648." Stephen, the nine-year-old sitting directly in front of the teacher's desk for reasons that the entire class knows, fidgeted in his seat. Mrs. Spencer asked him what is wrong.

"She keeps sticking her feet into my back," he says.

"Oh, dear, how dreadful! Such little tiny feet going right through a big thick bench right into your big strong back. I suppose you are too seriously hurt to go to Mr. Hazen's room and fetch me the map of Asia. You're not? Well, and you David, go and get the map of Europe from Miss Flynn." As if launched by a sling shot both boys were at the door. "Remember to say 'Please,' Mrs. Spencer said and turned to the class," Always be—

"Polite," they responded.

"Yes, always be polite, it's worthwhile, you'll find." Looking around the room, she said: "Stretch up-deep breath-out-that's better."

"Take out your geographies and turn to the map of Asia. Page 185."

"Henry, what is Asia?"

"Asia—Asia—," Henry grasped for an answer.

"Class?"

"Asia is a continent," they chorused.

"Well, what is the meaning of 'continent', Elsie,?"

"A continent is the largest division of land."

"Right, when I talk about a continent, what do I mean? I mean land."

Stephen came back with the map of Asia in hand and placed it expertly atop the ledge above the blackboard. "Thank you, Stephen, it looks fine."

Question followed question with occasional children going to the map to use a pointer. Recess came and went.

"Time for writing," Mrs. Spencer said. "Monitors pass the papers. Everyone up and straight and tall and do your very best. Write your names. Don't forget to end with the upstroke. Two or three forgot about the upward stroke last time. It's just as bad as coming to school with your clothes unbuttoned or your necktie off. Write these words." On the board, she wrote: mountain, camp, August, glove, song, thumb, itself. "Do your very best. We have only a week or two more before promotion day." Three girls sighed and covered their faces.

Pens scratched. Feet shuffled. Paper crumpled. Mrs. Spencer reviewed the words, asking certain students to spell the words without looking at their papers.

"Time for reading. And we are going to exchange readers with Miss

Flynn's class. We shan't use our own readers today, but instead let's act out one of the stories. Let's do the Mad Tea Party. Who remembers it best?" The teacher chose four children. They knew the lines by heart and acted out the parts as only enthusiastic nine-year-olds could. "Fine. You were all good," Mrs. Spencer said.

"Now we'll have a drill game on the word 'bring,'" Mrs. Spencer told the class. The game brought the morning to a close.[1]

The school in which Mrs. Spencer taught in 1924 had received city-wide notice and praise as a progressive school. Her principal believed her to be an exemplar of progressive teaching in his building. Although Agnes DeLima, the journalist who observed this class, was a passionate advocate of child-centered schools similar to ones operated by Elizabeth Irwin, Felix Adler, and others, she described this fourth grade teacher sympathetically. Yet she felt that Mrs. Spencer and other teachers like her conducted sincere but colorless imitations of the private experimental schools. She believed that progressive classes in experimental schools would die if placed within public schools. Large class size, administrative indifference or hostility, and a generally negative attitude toward child-centered classrooms would kill such efforts. Who, then, were the progressives? Mrs. Spencer? Her building principal? Staff in the experimental schools? The problem, of course, is in the word itself. The ideas nested in "progressivism" were diverse and ambiguous, appealing strongly to dissimilar reformers in the decades bracketing World War I.

Historians Lawrence Cremin, Michael Katz, and David Tyack distinguished between various educational streams within the larger political movement. Among the educational reformers, for example, Tyack described the administrative progressives (e.g. Teachers College's George Strayer, Stanford University's Ellwood Cubberley, Frank Spaulding, veteran superintendent) who used the latest concepts in scientific management to streamline the school district's organizational and instructional machinery. He distinguished these progressives from social reformers (e.g. George Counts, John Childs, Willard Beatty) who advocated using the schools as an instrument for national regeneration, and the pedagogical progressives (e.g. Francis Parker, Flora Cooke, William Wirt, William H. Kilpatrick) who saw the child central to the school experience. Although substantial differences existed between, and among, the pedagogical reformers, they all drew deeply from the well of John Dewey's ideas.[2]

I will concentrate on the changes in the classroom in the interwar period and the efforts of the pedagogical reformers. I shall not deal with administrative progressives, reconstructionists, and other reformers except to the extent that they tried to modify existing classroom instruction.

No uniformity marked these pedagogical reformers except for a common antipathy to "fixed grades in the schools, fixed rules for the children, and fixed furniture in the classroom." Between these child-centered school advocates deep and sharp differences surfaced in curriculum, instruction, degrees of choice open to children, the role and extent of art and play in the classroom, and a host of other issues.[3]

Given their strong, negative views of the public schools and despite the diversity of doctrines implicit in the practices they advocated, there remained a core consensus on what constituted a school focused upon children. For the most part pedagogical reformers wanted instruction and curriculum tailored to children's interests; they wanted instruction to occur as often as possible individually or in small groups; they wanted programs that permitted children more freedom and creativity than existed in schools; they wanted school experiences connected to activities outside the classroom; and they wanted children to help shape the direction of their learning. The tangible signs of these impulses that bound philosophers, curriculum theorists, psychologists, and practitioners together were class-rooms with movable furniture, provisioned with abundant instructional materials, active with children involved in projects, and traffic between the classroom and the larger community. These commonalities leave un-touched cleavages over the project method, how much freedom a child should have in school, the teacher's role in setting goals, the amount of time spent on basic skills, and the like. The commonalities, nonetheless, do suggest where in the classroom to look for changes in practice.

Between the hundreds of thousands of students these professors taught, the readers of their books, the thousands of newspaper and magazine articles written about the schools they or their followers directed, the hundreds of courses of study and textbooks that incorporated these ideas, and the scores of school systems that bought movable desks and chairs, their ideas seemed to touch schools across the nation. *Time* pronounced it to be so in 1938. "No classroom," the anonymous writer declared, "escaped its influence."[5]

CLASSROOMS IN THE CITY

To what degree, if at all, teachers embraced these ideas and practiced them in their classrooms can be seen in the following case studies of New York City, Denver, and Washington, D.C. In the 1920s and 1930s, city school systems were acknowledged as the frontier of innovation. If new ideas about schooling were to be implemented, city schools were the obvious places to observe what happened.

All three districts had superintendents who built national reputations as strong leaders committed to improving schools. New York and Denver, at different times in the two decades, were recognized as leaders in initiating new programs that put progressive practices into classrooms. In the largest public school system in the world, the superintendent launched the Activity Program, the single largest experiment (about 75,000 students participated) ever to test progressive ideas in classrooms. Denver, a school district with over 45,000 students, became a national pacesetter by starting a unique program of changing curriculum through involving hundreds of teachers who wrote progressive concepts into courses of study. Denver also furthered its reputation as a laboratory testing student-centered concepts with its participation in the Progressive Education Association's national experiment to improve the high school curriculum. Called the Eight Year Study (1933–1941), all of Denver's junior and senior high schools joined the program.

Although Washington, D.C. had a superintendent noted in professional circles as an administrative progressive whose tenure spanned the entire period, the schools were inconspicuous on the national scene as instructional innovators. What makes the District of Columbia worth examining is how a racially segregated school system adopted a number of progressive approaches resembling closely what New York City and Denver had undertaken and what occurred in classrooms as a result.

By looking at classroom teaching in these three districts during a two-decade period of peak interest in and acceptance of progressive ideas, a sense of how much teaching had remained stable since the turn of the century and what had changed in classroom in districts renowned for their administrative and instructional reforms may emerge.

New York City Schools

The numbers stagger the imagination; they intimidate. Imagining 683 schools, 36,000 teachers, and 1,000,000 children (1930) in one school district boggles the mind of anyone west of the Hudson River. Glossy annual reports of the system tried to capture the massiveness of the school operation with comparisons: the increase in children attending school between 1920 and 1921 equaled the number of students going to school in Nashville, Tennessee. If you lined up all the children in the district, arms apart, they would stretch from New York to Toledo, Ohio. Or if the superintendent visited classrooms for ten minutes each, eight hours a day, five days a week, he would have done nothing else but observe each teacher once in three years.[7]

Size alone made New York's schools unique. Yet the school district's size should not obscure the rich history of tensions and resolutions in ethnic, religious, political, and class issues mirrored, on a smaller scale, in cities across the nation in the first half of the twentieth century. These varied issues in the school system's history have been described by a number of historians. I will not cover the same ground. My attention is on what teachers did in classrooms, a topic to which these researchers devoted little space.[8]

Some narrative, however, is necessary to set the stage for what Sol Cohen called the "ultimate triumph" in 1934 when the Public Education

Association (PEA), a reformist cadre dedicated to transforming schools into child welfare institutions, saw "its conception of progressivism in school principles and procedures capture New York City school officialdom."[9]

The Setting Between 1898 and 1940, the largest public school system in the country had four superintendents to cope with social changes that schools could only adjust to, not alter: massive growth in school enrollment; sharply increased ethnic diversity; and, after 1930, cutbacks in salaries, positions, and programs resulting from the Depression and World War II.

Enrollment growth and diversity taxed the ingenuity, skills, and stamina of William Maxwell, who served as the first superintendent of the consolidated 5-borough district for 20 years. As a pragmatic school reformer who organized a bureaucracy while retaining interest in the "New Education," he had to cope with such basic needs as providing a seat for every student so that the schools could reach out, through the child, to improve the community. His tenacity, vigor, and persistence left a string of accomplishments recognized by his contemporaries: greater uniformity in curriculum and instruction than had ever before existed; more schools to house students, expanded social services, after-school and summer programs, broader curriculum, and key administrative initiatives (e.g. Board of Examiners) that would indelibly mark organizational routines for years to come. Combining the administrative progressives' passion for uniformity with concern for classroom practice, Maxwell cast a long shadow that few of his successors could escape, even if they were so inclined—and none seemed to be.[10]

The three superintendents who followed Maxwell came up through the ranks as teacher, principal, district superintendent and associate superintendent. In the latter position, each became a member of the Board of Superintendents, a body that advised the Superintendent on personnel and program recommendations to the Board of Education. Each person that assumed the top post had sat in every key chair in the system as he rose through the ranks.

William Ettinger served as superintendent for six years (1918–1924). A teacher and principal for over a quarter-century before being elevated to a district superintendency, he worked for another decade in that position before joining fellow associate superintendents. Shortly after, at the age of fifty-six, the Board of Education chose him to succeed Maxwell—a hard act to follow. Interested in vocational training in elementary schools, Ettinger developed programs in the upper grades while consolidating and polishing initiatives that Maxwell had installed. He demonstrated his own interest in progressive practice by personally approving the use of a public school by the PEA for a school-within-a-school progressive experiment under the direction of Elizabeth Irwin in 1922.

Much of Ettinger's attention, however, was directed toward securing sufficient funds to decrease class size and provide adequate housing for overcrowded, old, and outmoded schools. Intense and prolonged quarrels with the Board of Estimate over adequate resources for the schools and constant bickering with the Mayor over keeping top school posts free from partisan taint led to his contract not being renewed in 1924.[11]

Like Ettinger, William O'Shea's career began and ended in New York. Having taught for almost twenty years, he was named principal in 1906. Gradually, he moved through the necessary offices on the trek to the superintendency. At the age of 60, he was selected from among the Associates on the Board of Superintendents to follow Ettinger. The first five years of his tenure continued the pattern laid down by his predecessors: more buildings with larger capacities to house students; adequately trained teachers impartially selected; curriculum expanded and revised to cope with differences among children.

Using the vocabulary of voguish reformers, O'Shea produced annual reports of the school system's achievements that reflected exactly the institutionalization of changes made over a quarter-century earlier. "These schools," O'Shea wrote about elementary schools, "are the front line trenches in the battle for health, for social well-being, and for moral advancement."[12]

District superintendents were required to submit reports with a section labeled "Progressive Steps." Occasionally these reports would include references to classroom activities or projects, flexible schedules, and new curriculum materials. More often, though, "Progressive Steps" for the districts listed new testing procedures, how children were grouped, new services for children, and changes in rules.[13]

If Ettinger left his mark on the system by expanding vocational education, O'Shea left his imprint on courses of study and new programs stressing thrift, citizenship training, and character development. He appeared less interested in bringing classroom practices recommended by the PEA into city classrooms, although he would often borrow reformers' language for his reports. The stormy relationship between the public schools and PEA over Elizabeth Irwin's experimental school at P.S. 41, for example, produced a demand for a formal evaluation of the program. O'Shea's lack of support was evident. The evaluation committee, made up of school staff and PEA appointees, recommended more formal and conventional instruction in basic skills. The PEA pulled out its financial support and eventually the experiment became a private school in Greenwich Village, "The Little Red School House."[14]

The departure of the only formal progressive experiment in the public schools occurred in the midst of the Depression, years which saw retrenchment measures rippling throughout the school system. Class size increased. Fewer teachers were allocated to schools. After-school and summer programs were cut back. The last five years of O'Shea's tenure were marked by earnest efforts to preserve what had been done in earlier years. At the age of seventy, O'Shea retired. The Board of Education again turned to the cabinet of associate superintendents for O'Shea's successor.

Harold Campbell had graduated from the Maxwell Training School in 1902 and began a career as a teacher in both elementary and high schools, receiving his first appointment as a high school principal in 1920. Four years later he was promoted to Associate Superintendent for High Schools and served in that position and that of Deputy Superintendent until the Board of Education again dipped into the pool of associate superintendents for their next school chief. After 32 years in the system, at the age of 50. Campbell succeeded O'Shea in 1934 in the midst of the worst depression ever facing the nation.

Characterized as a "conservative educator" by both newspaper and professional journal, Campbell followed his predecessors' policies, insofar as funds permitted, in trying to reduce overcrowded schools, expand and increase services to children, and differentiate programs for handicapped and gifted students. The pattern laid out by Maxwell persisted, except in one area. Campbell launched a "pedagogical revolution" that became a "key landmark in the triumph of progressivism," according to one historian. In 1934, just a few months after becoming superintendent, he approved the largest experiment ever aimed at determining if progressive teaching practices could be installed in a major urban school system: the Activity Program.[15]

Aside from the PEA's support, there was little public reaction to the Superintendent's decision. Few citizens or school professionals knew Campbell personally or anything substantial about the decision he had made. After all, most New York City teachers seldom saw Campbell, O'Shea, Ettinger, or Maxwell other than in an occasional newspaper photo or as a small, distant figure on a stage speaking to thousands of teachers. Few teachers could have recognized any of them had they visited their classrooms. What teachers did know of their superintendents' presence came indirectly from headquarter's decisions establishing working conditions within which they taught, e.g. class size, double-session schools, revised courses of study, personnel transfers, evaluation ratings—all of which influenced, to some degree, what happened in their classrooms.

Context for Classroom Teaching   Within the classroom, what teachers do can be attributed to their decisions, the influence of the classroom as a workplace, the district setting beyond the school, or some ineffable mix of these variables. In trying to understand teaching practice, I chose those factors, often labeled as working conditions, about which decisions are generally made by others far removed from the classroom. Design of classroom space, how many students and which ones enter class, the required courses of study, district tests, report cards, supervisory rules—all are concrete realities over which teachers are seldom consulted, yet their presence penetrates classrooms daily influencing in large and small ways what teachers do. Consider classroom architecture. It should come as no surprise that the nineteenth-century uniformity, so highly prized by the first generation of progressives, including Maxwell, became embedded in the design of classroom space, C. B. J. Snyder, architect for the New York City Board of Education between the 1890s and the 1920s, created the standardized classroom plan that was used throughout the first half of the twentieth century. Each classroom was built around the seats and desks of students and teacher: 48 permanent desks for grades 1 through 4; 45 desks for grades 5 and 6; and 40 for grades 7 and 8.[16]

Rows of desks bolted to the floor facing the blackboard and teacher's desk made it easier for the teacher to scan the classroom for actual or potential disorder and have students work on tasks uniformly. The arrangement of space discouraged student movement, small group work, or project activities—staple items on the progressives' agenda to modernize instruction. Reformers viewed movable furniture as a basic item, after light and heat, to activity-centered classrooms. Few educators argued that it was impossible to implement progressive methods in rooms with rows of immovable desks, but such seating arrangements proved cumbersome, taxing the ingenuity of teachers in figuring out ways of outflanking this structural obstacle. The problem, of course, was money. Replacing stationary desks with movable ones was prohibitively costly.

The official position of the Board of Superintendents was stated in *The New York Times* in an article written by then Associate Superintendent Campbell in 1930 detailing all the progressive practices then current in the school system.

> As for the movable furniture idea and the substitution of comfortable chairs for the traditional rows of seats, we adopted it long ago in kindergarten and special classes. In most classes, however, particularly when there are thirty to forty pupils, the scheme is not practical. The moving of furniture is creative of noise and confusion. One teacher might want the chairs arranged one way, another teacher another way. Ease is not always productive of attention and concentration.

The clincher argument he cited was the danger of fire. A building in which students were obedient to order and marched in straight lines could be emptied in three minutes.

> Suppose the children were all reclining in easy chairs or wandering about a room filled with movable tables. Could it be done?

Campbell's answer: "Never."[17]

The cost of desk replacement was never mentioned publicly. In the midst of the depression, the capital investment in stationary desks for over 600 buildings was staggering. Yet the issue persisted because it was central to the reform of teaching practices. Compromises were struck. Beginning in 1935–1936, a year after Campbell moved into his new office, the Board of Education approved the Superintendent's recommendation that all *new* elementary school buildings will have 35 fixed seats in rows with additional movable tables and chairs and one or more workbenches to supplement the fixed desks. In 1942, the Board authorized more space in the standard classroom, movable furniture, equipment for library and science corners, and storage space for displays in *new* school buildings.

> The Board of Education has recognized that the standard classroom is no longer just a place to study and recite. It is now regarded as a workshop, a laboratory, a studio, and a place to practice gracious living.

Keep in mind that few buildings met the above standard in 1942. Teachers still worked with children filling up row after row of desks in crowded rooms.[18]

While classes of 50 or more students were common around World War I, class size had been dropping since that time. In 1930, average class size in elementary schools hovered above 38 students. This figure, however, masked significant differences. For example, 17 percent of all elementary classes still had 45 or more students. Within a school, the range varied dramatically. Special classes for "dull" students or handicapped ones were kept around 25 while other classes in the same building would be well over 45. To a teacher in the 1890s facing 75 students daily, the prospect of having only 40 in a class would have been a delight. By the 1930s, however, there was a public commitment and philosophy that expected teachers to provide individual attention to each child.[19]

Given this tenet of progressive belief, how large was too large? Harold Campbell offered one answer in 1935. "It seems," he said, "almost inevitable that with more than 35 pupils of varying personality and capability a teacher can give but scant attention to the individual child." The ideal size for elementary classrooms of "normal children" where one teacher covers all subjects is, he wrote, about 30 children. When the Activity Program for elementary schools began (1934) average class size was 37.8 students. A large class at that time was defined as being over 40 students; of all elementary classrooms 41 percent were large by that standard. By 1942, the Activity Program had been declared a success and extended to all schools. Average class size was 34.4 children with 18 percent of all classes labeled large. In high schools, average class size was 35.4 although the range ran from 30.9 at Benjamin Franklin to 39.8 at Brooklyn Tech.[20]

Space and numbers of children defined critical dimensions of the teacher's daily world. So did the course of study. The Board of Education expected teachers and their supervisor, the principal, to use in classrooms ten syllabi initially printed in the 1896 by-laws of the Board of Education, thereby explicitly telling teachers and principals how important particular content and its organization were. By 1924, there were 26 curricular bulletins and syllabi directing teachers' attention to what should be taught and why.[21]

A district-wide survey of school operations by a group of outside evaluators in 1924 included a report by Massachusetts Commissioner of Education Payson Smith on elementary school curriculum. Smith's report scored the curriculum for its inflexibility and lack of overall aims, its growth by "accretion," without concern for correlation of subjects. The curriculum was overcrowded, he wrote. Too much time was spent on "obsolete and often trifling material;" no guidelines for principals and teachers existed to determine how much content should be taught at each grade level.[22]

The formal responses by District Superintendents varied from passionate defenses of current courses of study to cautious agreement with Smith's conclusions. District Superintendent Taylor attacked Smith's assertions about the supposed inflexible course of study shrinking a classroom teacher's freedom.

> ... a school with fifty or a hundred teachers—many of them inexperienced—cannot afford to permit each teacher to interpret the course of study in a single school. The principal is there to organize, unify, and inspire the teachers in such a way as to realize the aims which she sets up for the school as a whole....

Yet District Superintendent Stephen Bayne, who would later become Associate Superintendent for elementary schools, agreed, albeit guardedly, with Smith's assessment that the curriculum omitted important objectives, grew haphazardly, lacked coherence, and needed periodic revision.[23]

Even though the 1924 survey results and rebuttals from school employees were not published until 1929, Smith's critique triggered O'Shea's appointment of a Committee on the Revision of Courses of Study and Methodology. Copying to some extent what Denver, Colorado had done earlier in the decade, the staff wrote, over a 5 year period (1925–1930), 19 new courses of study, complete with the phrasing and vocabulary of progressive reformers on project methods, individual attention, and pursuing children's interests.[24]

Care, however, should be exercised in predicting classroom practice, as Bayne observed, "by the wording of a course of study," revised or not. Diversity in practice is assumed with almost 30,000 teachers. Once the classroom door closed few principals and supervisors saw what happened or could determine how much teachers used syllabi they knew little about. Did these revised syllabi produce changes in classrooms? Clues to an answer appear in the tests students were given, the report cards they received, the rating sheets used to judge teachers, and the character of supervision that teachers received.

In 1925 for the first time O'Shea ordered the annual testing of elementary and junior high students in composition, arithmetic, spelling, silent reading, and vocabulary. These achievement tests included a great deal of factual knowledge and were linked closely to the revised courses of study. (In high schools the state Regents' academic examinations had been given since 1878.) By the 1930s city educators' views conflicted over classroom impact of these annual exams. At least half of the high school teachers and department chairmen saw these annual exams as hardening certain topics in courses of study, reinforcing drill, memorization and cramming, and having a generally negative impact on what teachers did in their classrooms.[25]

While complaining that in his visits to classrooms he "hears entirely too frequent reference to these examinations," Associate Superintendent of High School, John Tildsley stated bluntly in 1925 that these tests "seem to be necessary as a means of checking upon the work of the schools.... " These exams took the place of school inspection since with "the force at the disposal of this Division, it is impossible to give."[26]

Items on report cards also produce clues of instructional practice. Percentage grades and letters were given to students in subjects. Citizenship marks were also given. The junior high report cards in the 1920s, for example, listed the required subjects of reading, grammar, spelling, composition, arithmetic, history and civics, and geography, with spaces set aside for the final grade, mid-term and final exam marks. Space was provided for grades on effort, conduct, and personal habits. On the high school report card, letter marks were given up to six times a year, three a semester. One high school handbook for students prescribed fifth and tenth week marks; at the end of the fourteenth week exams were given and a week later the final mark was to be entered.[27]

A similar system of letter grades in subjects based upon teacher's judgment of a student's proficiency prevailed in elementary schools until 1935 when the report card was revised to include a number of student behaviors and attitudes (e.g. whether the child works well with others, obeys courteously, is reliable, plays well with others, etc.). This was consistent with revisions then underway in the elementary school program.

In addition to tests and report cards signaling that content, achievement, and fidelity to teacher directions registered strongly, explicit and formal rules also hinted at classroom behavior. During the interwar period principals and supervisors circulated to teachers rules for managing classes and executing lessons. These rules did not describe what occurred in classrooms but they surely defined what supervisors believed "good" teaching practices were.

For elementary and secondary school teachers in diverse subjects, regulations had a similar ring. A sampling:

- 1921—*Evander Childs High School*: For oral work insist on clear speaking. The student should stand erect, with head up, and speak with sufficient clearness to be heard in all parts of the room.

- 1924—*Julia Richman High School*: Organize classes according to regulations.... Do not allow any interruptions of a recitation.

- 1926—*For all elementary and secondary teachers in the Bronx*:
  Size the children and assign seats....
  Make a seating plan of the class. It helps discipline....
  Drill on standing and sitting; on putting the benches and desks up and down noiselessly....
  Place your daily plan, your time schedule on the desk where you can refer to them frequently....
  Keep a strict account of tests, oral work, and other data that will aid in giving the child a just mark on the report card.

- 1930—*Bushwick High School, Math Department:*:
  Plan for Geometry Period
  1. Assignment of new homework
  2. Presentation, development, and application of the new lesson
  3. Blackboard recitations on review of theorems....

- 1932—*John Adams High School, Latin Department*:
  Recitation by pupils should be clear and easily heard in all parts of the room. Remember the placard posted in all rooms, 'Stand Straight! Face the Class! Speak Up!' Don't let pupils talk directly to you; get the audience situation.

- 1939—*All foreign language teachers*:
  Economy in routine demands uniformity. This is particularly true of rising when reciting, going to the front of the room to give an oral reports, etc. Pupils should know what is expected of them....
  Other activities should be carried on by pupils at their seats while board work is being done....
  A few minutes of testing, either oral or written, should reveal whether the aims of the lesson have been achieved....[28]

One of the strongest signals to teachers on what they were to do in class is the evaluation rating and the manner that supervision was implemented by principals, first assistants, district superintendents, and department chairmen. A new rating form was introduced in 1921 to eliminate the many complaints raised by both teachers and principals over the lack of uniformity in ratings and the abuses stemming from "secret reports" on teachers from principals that were used by the Board of Examiners in determining promotions.[29]

William O'Shea, then Associate Superintendent, chaired the task force that drafted the revised form. Eliminated were the letters A, B, C, D to label performance and in its place a two-point scale of Satisfactory or Unsatisfactory was introduced. Space was provided for the supervisor to describe instances of exceptional service and weaknesses. Five teaching areas were identified.

O'Shea wrote the explanation in the handbook for each of the five areas to be rated; teachers received copies of the handbook explaining how evaluation would occur. O'Shea's language resonated with the "New Education." Project methods and pupil activity ran as themes throughout his discourse on appropriate instruction. "We learn to do by doing," O'Shea wrote. "The greatest possible participation of all the children is the real measure of success, and such success," he said, "cannot be attained where the old type of individual question and answer recitation is used too largely."[30]

Among educators, supervision meant more than filling out a form. The essence of supervision, according to New York City officials, was to improve instruction. But supervisors were also required to judge a teacher's performance. The two expectations, then as now, clashed, creating a dilemma each time a supervisor entered a classroom. Dr. Alfred Hartwell, Buffalo superintendent and one of the investigators hired to survey the schools in 1924. saw the dilemma clearly on his visits with principals and district superintendents as they supervised and rated teachers in 16 schools and 50 classrooms.[31]

Hartwell saw that too often supervision and inspection became indistinguishable. He described one visit to a classroom where the district superintendent questioned the teacher in front of the class on her pupils' attendance and what professional courses she had taken. He asked her for the lesson plan book which he examined and found in good order. She was then told to conduct the lesson for the visitors. The superintendent took notes and promised the teacher to discuss them with her the next time he visited. Teachers observed by Hartwell and supervisors were rated on "personality, control of class, self-control, discipline, and scholarship." While he found uniformity in the "recording of ratings" he saw much variation in styles and quantity of supervision. Too many principals and district superintendents practiced supervision, he believed, in a manner that created fear among teachers at the very rumor of a supervisor coming to their rooms. Moreover, too little time was available. District superintendents supervised about 1,000 teachers in 20 to 40 schools, depending upon the district. Two officials that he cited spent twenty minutes to a half hour in each class; they made 400 to 600 visits the previous school year. Principals told him they spent between 20 to 25 percent of their time in classrooms.[32]

Over ten years later a Brooklyn high school teacher wrote that his colleagues often feared a principal or supervisor, as "someone to whom to cater so as to avoid his enmity." He scored principals for failing to reach the ideal: "the supervisor is superior, a sort of expert in the educational process and therefore can help teachers in the dilemmas that confront them." Citing instances of principals with particular instructional passions, e.g. good penmanship, following the time schedule to the minute, poetry and spelling, and using flashcards, he describes how these peculiar notions about teaching infect supervision and make teachers, the writer declared, "timid, easily frightened, scared to have an opinion of their own." The accuracy of the cases the teacher describes is less important than his rendering of the beliefs that teachers held about supervisors.[33]

By describing classroom architecture, syllabi, class size, report cards, written rules, teacher ratings, and supervisory practices in the interwar years I assume that working conditions, the tools available to teachers, and the explicit expectations of their supervisors describe a context that is related to what teachers do daily. Surely something can be learned about how people drive if we have some knowledge of traffic signals, driving conditions, and what good drivers are expected to do on the road, because a linkage exists between how people drive, traffic rules, and road conditions. Similarly, certain contextual conditions helped shape the patterns of instruction, perhaps even reinforcing certain ones, that prevailed in classrooms across the city since the turn of the century. By the early 1930s, what had occurred in New York were changes in syllabi that incorporated progressives' vocabulary and suggested activities for teachers. But the connective tissue of instruction—classroom architecture, class size, report cards, rules, evaluation process, and supervision—hewed closely to prevailing teacher-centered practices.[34]

The Activity Program.   Return now to 1934 when newly appointed Superintendent Harold Campbell approved the largest effort to try out progressive practices in the nation. In describing this six year experiment, a direct examination of teaching across the city will unfold.

Called the Activity Program, the experiment was initially proposed by the Principal's Association to Stephen Bayne, who had just been appointed to head the Division of Elementary Schools. Going up the hierarchy, the experiment was approved at every step. Assistant Superintendent John Loftus, a former elementary principal with a city-wide reputation for installing innovative programs, was tapped to direct the program. Ten percent of all elementary schools (69) were chosen on the basis of being typical for their district and for having positive attitudes toward progressive practices. Over 75,000 students and 2,200 teachers in the 69 schools participated in the Activity Program for almost 6 years. Note, however, that not all classes in a school designated as experimental were involved; the total number of students and teachers in these 69 schools were 90,000 and 2,700, respectively.[35]

What was the Activity Program? While the definition shifted over the course of the experiment, the essence of the massive effort was distilled in a 1940 memo from Loftus and J. Wayne Wrightstone to J. Cayce Morrison, New York State Assistant Commissioner of Education and head of the team that the Board of Education hired to evaluate the experiment. According to the memo, major concepts in the Activity Program were:

- Children and teachers participate in selecting subject matter and in planning activities.
- The program centers on the needs and interests of individuals and groups.
- Time schedules are flexible, except for certain activities . . . which may have fixed periods.
- Learning is largely experimental.
- The formal recitation is modified by conferences, excursions, research, dramatization, construction and sharing, interpreting and evaluating activities.
- Discipline is self-control rather than imposed control. . . .
- The teacher is encouraged to exercise initiative and to assume responsibility; she enjoys considerable freedom in connection with the course of study, time schedules, and procedure.
- Emphasis is placed on instruction and creative expression in the arts and crafts.[36]

In a less sedate description, Loftus, speaking to teachers, said the Activity Program was a "revolt against verbalism, so-called 'textbook mastery' and literal 'recitation.'" Teaching was tailored to each child. The "congenial group" or committee was typical of activity methods as was the "integrated curriculum" (correlated or unified curriculum to an earlier generation of reformers).[37]

The six year experiment stimulated staff development for teachers. In both regular and activity schools, teachers took courses offered by local universities, the Board of Education, and the Principals' Association. Elaborate directions, syllabi, classroom suggestions, and community resources were compiled, published, and distributed to teachers who expressed interest in the Activity Program.

During the life of the experiment students in matched pairs of activity and regular elementary schools took batteries of test. Children, teachers, and administrators answered questionnaires about various aspects of the program. Teams of trained observers using specially designed instruments visited regular and Activity Program classrooms to record student and teacher behaviors.

When the experiment was over in 1941, Loftus's office was inundated with final reports from Activity Schools. Scrapbooks, reports, and photographs spilled over tables and chairs, nearly filling his office. One school sent 46 illustrated reports of projects, each weighing about 10 pounds. Poetry, art, songs, weavings, vases, and hundreds of other examples of student work accompanied the reports.[38]

Before turning to classroom practice, keep in mind that the teachers most committed to the informal curriculum (another phrase for Activity Program) did not follow an activity schedule the entire day. Teachers set aside, at most, three hours daily. Another compromise struck early in the experiment was spending one hour daily for "drills and skills" because of the high mobility of students between schools.[39]

Beginning in the first year of the Activity Program observers went to classrooms and described what they saw both in the experimental and regular classrooms. In a 1941 study of 24 classes in both types of schools, the investigators found that pupils in activity classrooms "spend somewhat less time on the conventional academic subjects and devote more time to arts, crafts, and certain other enterprises (show-and-tell, discussion, student dramatics, etc.)." Yet the researchers also noted that the amount of time spent on formal subjects such as arithmetic, reading, spelling, and what today would be called social studies "is nearly the same in activity and control classes."[40]

The observers recorded whether students worked on tasks in small groups or together as an entire class. They found that the regular classes spent 93 percent of their time in the whole group working on tasks while the activity classes spent 84 percent in the same manner. A paragraph follows these figures trying to explain why the difference "is not as large as one might expect in view of the fact that the programs presumably are quite different."[41]

A related study funded by the Works Progress Administration (WPA) through Teachers College investigated, among other things, what happened in classrooms by observing almost 50 classes and over 2,000 children in 16 schools (8 activity and 8 regular) between 1937 and 1939. While expressing some dismay over how their instruments failed to capture fully the sharp distinctions between classrooms that they saw, they did find that the "average" activity class was different from the "average" control one by:

- more outward appearance of pupil self-direction,
- more diversity and a larger range of (tasks), especially during certain periods of the day.
- more projects of the sort that correlate various enterprises and skills as distinguished from the study of isolated subject matter.
- a considerably larger display of the pupil's handiwork.[42]

The major evaluation of the entire six years occurred in 1940. Commissioned by the New York City Board of Education, national experts in testing, evaluation, and curriculum spent a year interviewing teachers, principals, and headquarter staff. They also tested children. The conclusions of the study were based upon an intensive investigation of 194 classrooms in 28 schools (14 activity; 14 regular) of which 10 pairs had *not* been part of any previous evaluations.

In analyzing the degree of implementation in 100 activity classrooms, the staff found:

- 20% of classrooms where activity procedure was confused and ineffective.
- 38% of classrooms made substantial progress in developing an activity program but still required assistance.
- 42% of classrooms had a well-developed activity program.[43]

In 94 classrooms in regular schools,

> many elements of the activity procedure are observable but poorly practiced due to lack of understanding of objectives or uncertainty as to means. Occasionally, some elements of the activity procedure may well be developed but be so intermingled with the regular procedure as to be disturbing or ineffective.[44]

The study confirmed top administrators' beliefs that New York teachers could implement the best of progressive practices, as defined by these evaluators.

Finally, the survey staff concluded that activity schools had been most successful in getting students to participate and cooperate in groups, encouraging student movement in classrooms, developing positive student attitudes toward school, teachers, and peers, as well as "purposeful, orderly, courteous behavior." Teachers were less successful in developing flexible use of classroom furniture, use of work benches and tools, and reporting to parents.[45]

What also materialized from the study was the realization that the Activity Program penetrated regular schools unintentionally. "Our regular school," the final report observed, "had nearly as much of the activity program as two of the activity schools selected for intensive study. The evaluators found 10 percent of regular classrooms had made "appreciable progress in translating the activity concepts into practice."[46]

The state team concluded that in teaching knowledge and skills, creative work, attitudes, and behavior the Activity Program proved to be as effective as the use of conventional methods of teaching and superior in "educating children to think, improving pupils' attitudes and social behavior." Pronouncing the experiment a success, Morrison recommended that the Activity Program be extended throughout the school system gradually and on a voluntary basis.[47]

An experiment involving over 70,000 students from diverse settings was launched in the midst of the worst economic depression to hit the nation. It received no additional funds for equipment, furniture, or instructional materials and experienced cutbacks in special teachers, while class size increased. A high annual turnover of students, teachers, and supervisors occurred—principals changed in 45 of the 69 schools. If school officials felt some justifiable pride in carrying out the effort, of making chicken salad out of chicken feathers, it seems, in retrospect, a sensible feeling given all the difficulties facing them.

On January 20, 1942, six weeks after the United States entered World War II, Harold Campbell approved the gradual extension of the Activity Program to all elementary schools.

Determining the extent that progressive practices, including the Activity Program, were implemented in over 35,000 classrooms by 1940 is difficult. A few years earlier, then Associate Superintendent Campbell, asked the question: "To what extent has the New York City school system made use of the so-called 'new' educational techniques and ideas of the progressive educationists as exemplified by the child-centered school?"

His answer: A great deal.

His evidence:

- Pupils managed clubs in high schools
- Students revised civics textbooks in eighteen schools
- Some elementary schools had miniature municipal governments and officials
- The socialized recitation was practically universal; pupils take charge of the class and conduct recitations
- More and more project work was being done every year
- 500 schools had savings banks
- 100,000 children enrolled in homemaking, cooking meals, and acquiring housekeeping skills[48]

Except for two items that dealt with instruction in the classroom, the other items were organizational and curricular changes engineered by central administration and implemented by principals, all of which were easily monitored since they were observable. Not so for socialized recitation and projects.

A decade later, Joseph Loftus estimated that activity methods were used in 25 percent of all city elementary schools "in some degree," he said. The estimate was no more than an informed guess since no one had visited all teachers to ascertain whether such methods were, indeed, practiced and to what extent. Furthermore, many concepts about child-centered classrooms, project methods, even the word "progressive," were interpreted differently by both professionals and laymen. Left to the teacher was a great deal of discretion for selective implementation, e.g. one teacher lets a class elect officers without changing any portion of her instructional repertoire; another teacher sets aside 2:30–3:00 each day for students to work on anything they please and calls that an activity program, etc.[49] Given these obstacles, one can only pursue hints or occasional indicators of larger impact over a two decade period.

Some schools, like islands in the midst of an enormous lake, remained untouched by the ideology of the progressive movement and the Activity Program. In 1942, for example, 3 Harlem schools with 6,000 pupils became the site for a project to improve both instruction and curriculum in the first grade. When the support team from central headquarters arrived, they found classrooms, curriculum, and time schedules for each subject. Teaching practices were unmarked by any of the ferment occurring elsewhere in the city. First grade teachers were familiar with progressive language but demonstrated no evidence of modified classroom practice.

Over a two year period, the Research Bureau's attention, modest resources, and staff development altered the traditional classroom, curriculum, use of time, and instructional practice sufficiently to make the target primary classrooms activity-oriented. How many of the other 700 elementary schools in the city were like these 3 in 1942, I cannot say. But exist they did.[50]

Consider also the sizable number of teachers who were opposed for either philosophical or other reasons (a common argument given by many teachers was the great amount of extra work it took) to the activity program. The Morrison evaluation of activity and regular schools sampled teacher opinion after six years of the experiment. They found that 36 percent of teachers in the activity schools *preferred* the regular program; in regular schools 93 percent, unsurprisingly, favored the conventional program. A considerable number of teachers, then, found the experiment lacking because they believed that classroom activities concentrated on whole group instruction, little student movement, and question-answer format were better for them and their children. In comparing the supposed benefits of the Activity Program, these teachers remained convinced of the rationality, if not effectiveness, of conventional instruction.[51]

High Schools

Turning to the high school, there is evidence that some schools initiated a highly touted innovation, contract teaching (the Dalton Plan). As early as 1924, 11 high schools reported that some teachers in each school were using individual contracts with students as a way of diversifying the course of study. Teachers submitted articles to *High Points*, the journal written by and for high school teachers in the system, on how they modified the Dalton Plan for their classrooms. But these references number less than a handful.[52]

In 1935, Teachers College professor Thomas Briggs sent a graduate student into 21 New York City and suburban high schools to "observe the work of the best teachers of any subject." Principals selected the 104 teachers the observer visited. Based upon these narratives, Briggs found 80 percent of the teachers "teaching from the textbook." The remainder had classrooms where pupil participation in discussions and panels occurred and substantial linkage between current events and subject matter were made. About 65 percent of the classes used "conventional procedure of questions by the teacher on an assignment with answers by the pupils or of specific directions followed by board or seat work." In the use of traditional recitation, 80 percent of the teachers were observed practicing it.[53]

Another example of high school instruction is an actual transcript of a demonstration lesson in an American History class at Washington Irving

High School in 1940, witnessed by a teacher, principal, and department chairman from three other high schools. The subject of the 40 minute lesson was the railways of the nation. The 35 students had been assigned 2 pages in the text and excerpts from the *American Observer*, a newspaper published for high school students.[54]

The transcript carries 96 entries, 31 for the teacher and 65 for students. Of the 31 teacher entries, 26 were questions, many married to long explanations. The 65 student responses were paragraph length in the transcript indicating that ample time for expression was permitted. The lesson included a discussion of a graph on railroad statistics, one student who copied the class's responses to a question on the chalkboard, and the teacher writing other points on the board.[55]

The three observers agreed that it was an excellent lesson and that the teaching was first rate. They viewed it as an exceptional instance of a socialized recitation, with student participation dominating discourse. The teacher channeled content into leading questions and periodic summaries, revealing the deft touch of a solid professional, according to the observers. They were impressed with the way students rose from their seats to answer questions, the extent of student talk, the teacher calling on each student by "Miss" rather than the first name, and the comfort students and teacher felt with one another.[56]

Such individual cases help. Yet more descriptions of what teachers did would add much to what is currently available. In a small effort to increase data on teacher practice, I located 152 descriptions and photographs of classrooms during the interwar period. The Appendix contains my rationale for looking at classrooms the way I do and the methods I used to categorize data. Included there are also some cautions on using these data. Table 2.1 describes the specific categories that were included for each teaching pattern. Figures 2.1 and 2.2 consolidate the data for patterns of instructional practice in New York City.

The data I collected from 152 classrooms support the survey results, evidence drawn from contextual conditions, and evaluations of the Activity Program. No more than an extimated one of four elementary and, even a lesser fraction of, high school teachers adopted progressive teaching practices, defined broadly, and used them in varying degrees in their classrooms. The dominant mode of instruction remained a combination of teacher-centered and mixed patterns. Nonetheless, there is considerable evidence that teachers incorporated student-centered practices into their repertoires, particularly in elementary classrooms.

Why did a considerable minority of New York City elementary teachers adopt some progressive practices while fewer of their colleagues in high school chose such approaches? Although I can only speculate at this point, let me suggest some plausible answers. An obvious reason is that the Board of Education and Superintendent Campbell endorsed the experiment and directed that it get underway in elementary schools. The

Table 2.1   Patterns of Teaching: Dimensions

Classroom instruction was divided into five dimensions: classroom arrangements, group instruction, classroom talk, class activities, and student movement. For each dimension, there were specific behaviors that could be located in descriptions and photographs. If found, they were coded and counted. The patterns, classroom dimensions and specific behaviors follow:

	Teacher-Centered	Mixed Pattern	Student-Centered
CLASS ARRANGEMENT	• Movable desks and chairs in rows facing teacher's desk and/or blackboard	• Movable desks and chairs in hollow-square, horse-shoe, etc. • Up to half of class arranged at desks and chairs facing one another.	• Students sit at tables or clusters of desks facing one another • No rows
GROUP INSTRUCTION	• Whole class • Teacher works with individual student while rest of class works at desks	• Teacher works with small groups • Teacher varies grouping: whole, small, and individual.	• Class divided into groups • Students engaged in individual and small group activities
CLASSROOM TALK	• No one in class talking • Teacher talking • Teacher–led recitation/discussion	• Student reports, debates, panels, dramatizations • High frequency of both teacher and student instructional talk	• Student–led discussion or recitation • Students talking in groups or with individuals
CLASS ACTIVITIES	• Students working at desks • Teacher talking (lecture, explaining, giving directions, reading to class, etc.) • Teacher checking work • Students taking test, watching film, listening to radio, etc. • Teacher–led recitation/discuss.	• High frequency of activities that indicate both teacher–and student–centered behaviors	• Class in small groups • Students work individually and in small groups • Students lead discussions/recitation • Students working on projects/centers
STUDENT MOVEMENT	• No movement at all • Student needs permission to leave seat	• Less than five students away from desks	• Six or more students away from seats at one time • Students move freely without teacher' permission

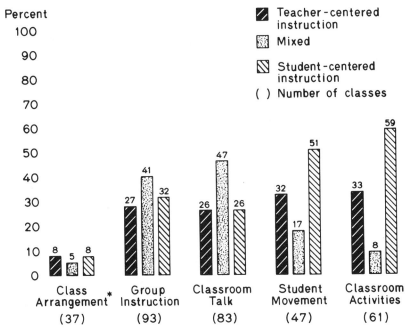

* 79% of all desks were stationery.

Figure 2.1 Patterns of Instruction in New York City Elementary Classrooms, 1920–1940.

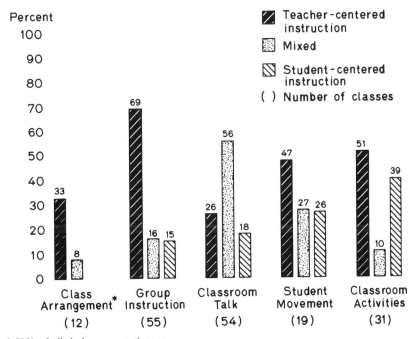

* 59% of all desks were stationery.

Figure 2.2 Patterns of Instruction in New York City High School Classrooms, 1920–1940.

Activity Program in an Elementary School, 1935 (*New York City Public Schools, 37th Annual Report*, All the Children, *1934–1935, p. 12*).

New York City Elementary School, Fourth Grade Class, 1943 (*Office of War Information, Library of Congress*).

administrative hierarchy, organizational machinery, and limited resources were mobilized to implement the program in 10 percent of the schools. That the Activity Program varied within the target schools and that regular schools outside the venture introduced elements of the program is less important than the simple fact that a formal stamp of approval from headquarters permitted advocates at 110 Livingston Street, principals, and teachers to press forward knowing that their efforts were consistent with what the Board and Superintendent wanted.

But I do not believe this entirely explains the differences in elementary and high school classroom practices that the descriptions and graphs reveal, since there was a great deal of ferment in high schools over introducing student-centered practices. Campbell had directed the high school program prior to his promotion. Issues of *High Points*, the journal for city high school teachers, documented the debates over progressivism in classrooms and show-and-tell instances of teacher innovations. Another reason, then, one that is less obvious but nonetheless deserves some consideration, is the structural differences in content studied, instructional time spent with students, and differences in expectations between the lower and upper grades. Such differences are often ignored because they are taken for granted as permanent features of the school terrain.

Children in elementary grades learn fundamental verbal, writing, reading, and math skills. Content is secondary and often used as a flexible vehicle for getting at those skills. Subject matter is relatively unimportant, especially in the lower grades. But in the last year or so of elementary school, and certainly in the secondary school, not only are more sophisticated skills required of students but these skills are hooked directly into complex subject matter that in and of itself must be learned. Literary criticism, historical analysis, solving advanced math problems, and quantatitive analysis in chemistry all require knowledge of complicated facts and their applications. High school teachers dispense knowledge; subject matter, it seems, drives methodology in the classroom. Skills are far more potent organizers of classroom tasks than subject matter.

Also in elementary schools, student and teacher contact time differ sharply from the high school. The self-contained classroom remains the dominant form of delivering instruction. Generally, teachers spend five or more hours with the same group. They see far more of a child's strengths, limitations, capacities, and achievements than a high school teacher who sees 5 groups of 30 students less than an hour a day. In terms of simple contact, the elementary teacher sees a class of 30 children nearly a 1,000 hours a school year; a high school teacher sees any one class (of the 5 he or she teaches) at most, 200 hours during the year or about one-fifth of the time that elementary colleagues spend with pupils. Contact time becomes an important variable in considering issues of grouping, providing individual attention, varying classroom tasks and activities, and rearranging furniture. In elementary schools, the *potential* to make changes in these

The Writing Lesson (*New York City Public Schools, 42nd Annual Report*, All the Children, *1939–1940, p. 3*).

The Answer (*Office of War Information, Library of Congress*).

and other areas is present just because the teacher has more contact time with the same children; such potential is absent for 30 students within a 50-minute period. Whether such changes occur in the lower grades, is, of course, an entirely separate issue, but the structural difference in time allocation allows for possible changes in elementary classrooms.

Finally, in elementary classrooms, especially in the primary grades but still apparent in the upper three grades (4–6), external pressures from accrediting associations, college entrance requirements, and vocational choices are missing. In high school classroom, strong pressures from Carnegie units, College Boards, Scholastic Aptitude tests, Advanced Placement, certifying agencies and other external constraints push teachers to complete the textbook by June, drive students to prepare for exams, seek jobs, and take the proper courses for graduation. While similar pressures exist in elementary grades, particularly the press to get children ready for the next grade, the pressures seldom pinch as they do in the higher grades. Slack time is available in elementary schools. Flexible arrangements are more evident. Grades can be combined; groups within a class can include a range of ages and performance. Retaining a student for another year, while uncommon, occurs more frequently in elementary than in high schools. These three structural differences—emphasis on subject matter, contact time, and external pressures—may well account for why changes occurred with more frequency in elementary schools than in high schools.

Related to this last point are two further speculations. Because high schools in the 1920s and 1930s became increasingly harnessed to vocations and professional careers, elementary schools became less pressured to deal directly with vocational training. Notions of play and creativity and individual development became more acceptable, especially in the primary grades.[57]

Also high schools staffs at this time were predominately male and elementary classrooms were overwhelmingly staffed by women. Child-centered progressivism, drawing on nineteenth century idealism about the child, seemed more attuned to women and the lower grades than to male teachers hired to prepare young men and women for college and jobs.[58]

This issue of differences in the degree that elementary and high school teachers adopted student-centered techniques will arise again in both Denver and Washington, D.C. in these two decades. Turn now to Denver, a school district 2,000 miles away from New York City with less than 5 percent of its students.

DENVER

When Mira Scott Frank's children went to school and moved through the grades, she baked cookies, wrote letters, met with teachers and principals,

Donald Healey Reciting in Latin Class at Fort Hamilton High School, Brooklyn, New York (*New York City Public Schools, 43rd Annual Report,* All the Children, *1940–1941, p. 36*).

chaired parent meetings, and worked at a score of tasks that active PTA mothers do as they serve in local and district leadership posts. In 1939 Frank was elected to the Board of Education and served 12 years. Since the 1920s, she had worked with parents and school professionals. At the Valverde School dedication in the Spring of 1951, she spoke passionately about a school system that had come under attack from groups outside Denver for its progressive practices.

> Over the years, because Denver's system had been recognized as an outstanding one, it has been chosen as one of the few cities to participate in national studies for the improvement of education. There has been much criticism of late leveled at so-called "progressive education." This has been a form of propaganda. Denver's educational system is its own. It has never been an importation from outside. True, in 1934, we participated in the Eight Year Study, sponsored by the Progressive Education Association.... But everything done in that study was originated in Denver. What was good we retained; what was unsatisfactory was discarded some years ago.[59]

Board member Frank's defense of Denver's progressive practices was accurate: no school programs and directions were forcibly or even subtly grafted onto an unwilling or unaware school district. Even before Frank's tenure on the Board. Denver welcomed with gusto progressive practices brought by former high school principal Jesse Newlon and the young men he hired after he became Denver's superintendent in 1920.

In the years after Newlon moved into his offices at Fourteenth and Tremont, Denver newspapers, businessmen, and city officials boosted the school system's growing national reputation. A headline from a local newspaper, "Denver Leads Way in Progressive Education," would cause no historian to blink twice since such articles were common in the *Rocky Mountain News* and the *Denver Post*. But to see such an article in the *Taxpayers' Review* complete with three photographs, was a surprise. Its appearance suggests that the ideas of Jesse Newlon and his successors found an enthusiastic response even among citizens normally vigilant about anything that might increase school expenditures. Progressive ideas introduced by Newlon were adopted quickly as a local product.[60]

Frank's memory of the Eight Year Study was also accurate in linking the experiment in five Denver high schools to the cycle of curriculum revision that, again, Newlon had introduced in his first term as school chief. What Frank neglected to mention was how fortunate Denver was in its continuity in top leadership. Between 1920 and 1940, four superintendents served the Denver schools: Jesse Newlon, A. L. Threlkeld, Alexander Stoddard, and Charles Greene. Except for Stoddard who served less than two years, Newlon's influence extended over the entire period, since he hired Threlkeld as assistant superintendent in 1921 and Greene as the first Director of Research in 1923. Threlkeld succeeded Newlon and served a decade; after Stoddard's brief term, Greene, who had been Threlkeld's assistant superintendent since 1933 and who had headed up the Eight Year Study in the Denver schools, assumed the superintendency in 1939, holding the post until 1947. The chronology is useful in underscoring a continuity in leadership that the city schools enjoyed as it moved through two decades of boom, depression, and a second world war.

Superintendent Jesse Newlon was an outsider. Born, reared, and educated in Indiana, Newlon taught high school and began his career as an administrator in 1905 when he became principal of the Charlestown, Indiana high school. Moving through principalships in Illinois and Nebraska with time out to earn a master's degree (1914) from Teachers College he became superintendent of the Lincoln, Nebraska, schools in 1917. After three years there he was appointed to Denver's top post.

Threlkeld, who served as Newlon's assistant and deputy, worked as superintendent in three small Missouri towns for a decade before Newlon asked him to come to Denver. While assistant superintendent, Threlkeld also earned a master's degree at Teachers College in 1923. After Newlon's departure to head Teachers College's Lincoln School, Threlkeld maintained the directions laid down by his colleague, elaborating and amplifying certain elements as the Depression buffeted the Denver schools. His

10-year superintendency was the longest since Aaron Gove's 30 year stint that spanned the turn of the century.

Both Newlon and Threlkeld believed in the progressive doctrine of social efficiency and scientific management. They blended administrative progressivism with clear pedagogical views on the pivotal role of the teacher in instructional and curricular decision making and the importance of having flexible, activity-centered schools that linked daily life to what students learned. For two decades these two men built both physically and organizationally a school system that grew from almost 33,000 students in 1920 to over 45,000 in 1937. More important, they helped make Denver a national pacesetter for city school systems in curriculum revision and teacher participation in making instructional decisions.

Their stature as school leaders who not only used the buzzwords of the day but also implemented efficient school management, continuous revision of the curriculum, and progressive school practices was noted by their peers when Newlon was elected National Education Association President in 1925 and when Threlkeld became President of the Department of Superintendence in 1936.[61]

Continuity in top leadership is one thing; what happened in classrooms as a result of decisions aimed at improving instruction and curriculum is another. The usual help that historians get from previous studies of a school system is limited in Denver. If New York City schools intimidate researchers with their size and complexity, at least it was surveyed and evaluated repeatedly. But not Denver where the scale, a city of 250,000, is well within the grasp of most historians. In 1916 Franklin Bobbitt, Charles Judd, Elwood Cubberley, and a flock of professors, graduate students, and practitioners studied the schools. A quarter-century later when the Eight Year Study's results were released, all Denver secondary schools were included because they had joined the experiment as a group. Nothing else. This restricts the evidence that can be gained from external sources on teacher practice.

In order to determine what occurred in classrooms, I will review the contextual conditions within which teachers worked, describe two major interlocking experiments that stretched over the entire interwar period, and analyze the data I collected from 133 Denver classrooms.

The District Setting

Newlon came to Denver less than two years after the Armistice and four years after the 1916 survey. That survey revealed old, overcrowded schools with cramped, dimly lit classrooms. Because of the war, few expenditures for new buildings or renovations were authorized. By 1922 a concerted campaign to pass a major bond referendum succeeded. With these funds and judicious use of money in the annual operating budget, 17 elementary,

5 junior high and 3 senior high schools had been built by the time Newlon left for New York City. Before the full force of the Depression hit, Threlkeld saw 12 more elementary and 2 junior high buildings go up. So between 1920 and 1931 over half of the elementary, 7 of 8 junior high schools and 3 of 5 senior highs were constructed. This massive construction of new buildings and expansion of the junior high program over a decade also brought movable furniture, lunchrooms, libraries, gymnasiums, and ample outdoor recreation space for both elementary and secondary schools.[62]

New classrooms were built to hold 38 students although by 1923 a definition of classes that were small (below 30), medium (30 to 40), and large (over 40) had emerged. By that year, 60 percent of all elementary classes were between 30 and 40 students; 13 percent had over 40 and, surprisingly, 27 percent of all elementary classes had less than 30 students. But by 1934, large classes had jumped from 13 percent to 33 percent and elementary classes below 30 students had shrunk from 27 percent to 3 percent. Thus 64 percent of all classes were between 30 and 40 students. At the junior and senior high school, headquarter administrators tried to keep class size in the middle range. They succeeded and even saw one of every three high school classes with less than 30 students; 20 percent of the classes mostly in nonacademic areas (e.g. music, art, physical education) had more than 40 students.[63]

That few administrators and teachers complained publicly about class size may be due to Denver's position in having smaller classes at all levels than comparably sized systems elsewhere. Class size, which was a perennial issue in New York City, failed to surface in Denver as an abrasive item between school officials, parents, and teachers.[64]

Nor were courses of study a target for discontent. The ideas Jesse Newlon brought to Denver and translated into an ongoing program were simple, clear, and potentially effective in altering teacher behavior. In a 1916 paper he wrote when he was serving as a principal, he laid out concepts he executed five years later in Denver.

> When a group of teachers has worked upon this problem (making curriculum) during a period of two or three years, has carried on a series of investigations, has debated the issues pro and con in departmental meetings, in committee, and in faculty meetings, and has finally evolved and adopted a set of curriculums, and has determined upon the character of courses to be offered, that group of teachers will teach better and with more understanding and sympathy than they could ever otherwise teach.[65]

Teacher participation in curriculum revision was uncommon. The practice in New York City and elsewhere was to state goals, including guidelines for content selection or actual subject matter, designed by central office administrators with some help from a few carefully chosen teachers. After the course of study was completed, perhaps even reviewed by another group of teachers, the document was revised, printed, and delivered to each principal for use in the school. Supervisors might meet with principals to explain the new arithmetic or geography course; thereafter the principal was expected to see that teachers used the new documents. Sometimes, after a number of years, the syllabus would be reviewed and updated; sometimes not.

Newlon proceeded differently. He wanted widespread, active teacher involvement in determining what should be taught because he believed that such participation produced better trained teachers far more able and enthusiastic to conduct a classroom that is "more natural, more vital, and more meaningful to the students than it has ever been." Also, he might have added: more progressive.[66]

The process that teachers went through, he believed, was just as, if not more, important as the course of study in its final version. Anyway, Denver administrators reasoned, if teachers and the specialists they hired designed an inadequate syllabus it would be quickly identified as such and within a short time revised again, since both Newlon and Threlkeld directed that curriculum revision be a continuous, not a onetime, process. That the process had a fair chance of succeeding, apart from the novelty of letting teachers participate in developing the ideas they were expected to teach, was due to a factor that neither top executive mentioned in their effort to upgrade teacher performance through curriculum revision: the high level of education among Denver teachers. By 1931, 54 percent of Denver elementary staffs had four or more years of college education; in comparable size cities elsewhere only 22 percent had a similar level of schooling. For senior high school teachers 95 percent were college graduates; in New York City, only 69 percent had earned their bachelor's degree.[67]

Between 1920 and 1930, Newlon and Threlkeld supervised the work of over 700 teachers and principals organized into 37 committees led by teachers. These committees revised 35 courses of study at all school levels. In Newlon's words, curriculum and instruction "must grow from the inside out." By 1927, a novel, widescale involvement of teachers making curriculum kept the promise Newlon made.[68]

For those teachers who revised courses of study in the large, airy rooms set aside for them in the new downtown administration building, more than miles still separated what they produced from the classrooms of their fellow teachers. Unlike their colleagues in other districts, however, top Denver officials gave an unusual amount of thought to implementation of teacher-designed syllabi. They were especially keen on developing organizational mechanisms that would turn curriculum revision into a tool for changing teacher practices. Newlon and Threlkeld felt that the planning of syllabi by teachers was an effective, inexpensive way of increasing their knowledge and bringing them in touch with the current thinking of the profession, i.e. progressive practice. Looking back over a half century, a present-day superintendent would applaud the Denver school chiefs for initiating shrewd implementation procedures to spread new ideas throughout a school system.

The applause would be due for two reasons. First, some superintendents seek both broad and intense teacher involvement, as Denver's school chiefs did, but seldom can mobilize the resources to transform the intention into a carefully designed framework that gives teachers time, aid, and independence. Second, Denver's leadership avoided symbolic or token participation. Teacher involvement is a good example of this.

In 1927–1928 there were 1,400 Denver teachers, of whom 27 percent (376 teachers) served on curriculum committees. They were distributed as follows:

- 10% of all elementary teachers
- 42% of junior high school teachers
- 48% of senior high school teachers[69]

In this process, each school had at least one teacher on a committee. All secondary principals and one-third of elementary principals were in these groups. Also, by 1927, five years after the entire effort had begun, 626 teachers had served on committees. Assuming that a number of teachers had retired, died, or left the system, a rough estimate of between 30 and 40 percent of the entire instructional staff had participated in curriculum revision.

That process included the following:

- Teachers chaired subject matter committees on which principals and central office administrators served.
- Teachers worked during the day; substitutes were hired to replace them on the days they were at the administration building.
- University curriculum specialists worked with teachers; over 30 scholars and practitioners, at the center of a national network of progressive reformers, came to Denver to work with teachers.
- Each committee prepared objectives, selected content, designed instructional methods, including questions to ask, and suggested varied projects and materials that their colleagues might wish to use.
- Committees revised syllabi after initial classroom trials, further comments from teachers, and extended use in classrooms.
- Committees reviewed curriculum test items that were developed by the Department of Measurements for each course of study.[70]

In addition, there were a number of specific procedures targeted on involving teachers who were not on committees. Committee members were expected to report to their principal and staff on the revised course of study. Teachers were asked to complete an assessment form to critique the syllabus after they had used it. Committees used these replies to revise their course of study. After giving students the curriculum tests, teachers submitted suggestions and concerns over specific items to the Department of Measurements.

Coordinating this complex implementation was the newly established (1925) Department of Curriculum Revision. While all of this sounds as cumbersome as changing clothes under water, the various procedures produced overlapping networks of staff members who saw, spoke, and exchanged information with one another, thereby increasing professional contacts and a sense of collegiality while greatly reducing the isolation common to a large school system.

Finally, principals were charged to install the new course of study. Each committee and its specialists briefed principals on the revised course and then principals held meetings with their faculties, gradually introducing the syllabus to the school. The message from headquarters was direct:

> In the installation of new courses the principal must be the leader in his school.... The principal must conduct a program of study and discussion of the new course before it is ready to go into the classrooms of his school.... It is assumed that if a principal takes an unusually long time to get a new course into classroom use he will be able to give good reasons for such delay.[71]

Seldom made explicit in the entire process was a formal commitment to progressive beliefs and teaching practices. Yet the ideas and pedagogy were never far from the directions and suggestions that top administrators made to staff. Content for courses of study was chosen, for example, on the basis of relevance to "life situations," an ambiguous phrase that produced many tortuous discussions among teachers. In home economics, the committee studied the activities girls did at home and chose content and teaching techniques linked to those activities. Similarly, in each of the academic areas, content was selected that teachers believed was both critical and connected to what students experienced or would face. Latin, for example, a difficult subject at first glance to link to "life situations," made the leap in the 1929 Senior High School Courses of Study:

> It gives power in getting the meaning of new words; aids in spelling; and gives a clearer understanding of much in newspapers, magazines, and literature in general.[72]

Newlon, Threlkeld, and advocates of progressivism believed that if content was connected to current and future situations, and students saw those links, their interest would be captured and channeled into productive, imaginative school work. A later generation would call it relevance.[73]

Another progressive approach implicitly embraced in curriculum making was the activity and project method. For content and method, this approach included secondary social science courses, so labeled as early as 1919, many elementary school subjects, and literature courses of study. I say "implicitly" because the charge given to all of the subject matter committees contained no explicit directions as to what goals or methods to pursue. But one didn't have to be an educational weatherman to know what was in the air those years.

By 1927, the Denver curriculum revision effort had gained national attention. Requests for the new courses of study poured in. Newlon and Threlkeld spoke to national groups of professionals describing the Denver experience. City after city, including New York and Washington, D.C., copied, in their own fashion, what Denver did. "A scientific masterpiece," A. E. Winship, editor of the *Journal of Education*, called the new syllabi, comparing them to Horace Mann's Fifth Annual Report. Teachers College professor George Strayer, nationally known expert constantly in demand to direct surveys of school systems (he studied New York and Washington, D.C., in the 1940s), declared that "Denver has made one of the outstanding contributions to education in America through the development of its curriculum."[74]

Threlkeld succeeded Newlon in 1927 and pursued the same practices including curriculum revision. In 1932 the Progressive Education Association's Commission on the Relation of School and College requested that Denver join their national experiment to reform curricula. The Superintendent and Board readily agreed since it fit neatly into their continuous revision effort. To the request for one high school, Denver asked the Commission to include all five high schools in the experiment. The Commission agreed.[75]

The Eight Year Study

In September 1933 the Eight Year Study began in each of the 5 high schools with one class of 40 students who volunteered (parental consent was required), were average or above average in achievement, and, according to their junior high counselors, had the capacity to profit from such an experiment. Each succeeding year another class was added. Over the life of the experiment no school had over 30 percent of the student body enrolled in the program. A later generation would call such an innovation a mini-school.

To teach the experimental classes, principals chose two teachers (one English; one social studies) who also served as counselors for the group. Although the program differed in each high school, the "progressive education" classes, as they were labeled, remained together between one to three hours per day depending on what year of the program they were in. For the rest of their daily schedule, students took subjects with their classmates elsewhere in the school.[76]

The schedule for the handful of classes usually located in a wing of each high school, provided time for key pieces of the experiment. While no two high schools had identical programs, East High School's schedule for 1938 represented the general format and sequence of activities for sophomores enrolled in these classes. (See Table 2.2.)

Table 2.2   East High School's Schedule, 1938

Period	Monday	Tuesday	Wednesday	Thursday	Friday
1					
2	(classes in rest of school)				
3					
4					
5	special interest groups*	free reading	special interest groups	group counseling	special interest groups
6			CORE	COURSES**	
7	pupils dismissed; teachers' conference	lab	lab	individual counseling	lab***

 *   Based upon students' interests in core content, he or she can pursue reading, music, crafts, art, current events, science, dramatics, writing.

 ** Core courses, initially were English and social studies teachers joined later by art, science, home economics, and industrial arts teachers.

*** Laboratories set up in each room offered individuals or small groups time to meet with the core teachers best qualified to help them. For example, a student working on a project could go to science, art, English, or social studies labs.[77]

The number of teachers directly involved with the experiment remained a minority (but an important one) on the faculty. In 1939, for example, there were 12 out of 42 (29 percent) teachers at Manual Training in the program; at North High there were also 12 teachers but this staff was larger (80) and that meant only 15 percent participated. Also, a number of these teachers had also taken part in previous curriculum revision work.[79]

What was the purpose of this experiment? The Commission established by the PEA sought to enliven the high school curriculum and stir independence and imagination despite the strictures that college requirements placed upon the existing curriculum. With the endorsement of most major universities, the Commission chose 30 public and private secondary schools in which Denver, Des Moines, and Tulsa high schools were included. Participating schools were told: forget college requirements; reconstruct your curriculum and tap the imagination and ingenuity of your students and staff.

Because no central direction was given to the five Denver high schools (and the ten junior high schools that joined the experiment in 1938) on what to revise or what methods to use, the first three years saw small groups of students and teachers in each school stumble, innovate, and catch themselves. By 1936, the instructional staff began the task of coordinating basic concepts that were believed to be held in common for high schools. A handbook circulated to staff in that year listed the operating principles and methods to be used by teachers.

- Core teachers are expected to teach the basic knowledge and skills of their fields "insofar as (they) are consistent with teacher-pupil goals."
- Core teachers are responsible for expanding student interests "and for helping them see relationships in all their work."
- Teachers must replace the existing system of grades and punishment with "new drives for learning."
- In choosing subject matter, only content that "assists in the solving of problems and in the meeting of the needs of pupils" is appropriate.
- Pupils and teachers together plan the work.
- Usual subject matter lines "may be ignored."

Team planning, free time for students to pursue interests, study and work in the community, no letter grades, and more operating principles in the Handbook gave guidance to new and experienced teachers in the experiment.[79]

Courses taken by the experimental classes varied. Many were jointly planned; some were not. Some new courses were trendy shifts in title; most were not. After eight years there was little doubt that substantial curriculum revision in content had occurred. ,

Consider the core program at East High School. Gone were the separate courses in English, American and World History, etc. Instead the teachers chose four areas to concentrate upon:

- Personal living
- Immediate personal-social relationships
- Social-civic relationships
- Economic relationships

A sampling of units planned and previously developed by both teachers and pupils that were suggested for use at tenth through twelfth grades were: orientation to the school; understanding one's self; becoming aware of current scene; exploring vocational interests; studying Denver; understanding democracy and the American heritage; studying problems of employment; exploring problems of living in the modern family.[80]

In 1940, the first evaluation report of the Eight Year Study appeared; the experiment was declared a success. Students in these classes, the report stated, did as well in college, and often better than a matched set of students who had completed a conventional program. As intended, curriculum had been revised; students helped reshape courses and their interests were used to explore non-traditional content closely linked to issues that they would face as adults.

Returning to the hurricane metaphor, there is notable evidence of conspicuous, widespread activity occurring at headquarters producing impressive changes in educators' use of language, content in courses of study, teacher professional growth, and the creation of experimental programs within five high schools between 1933 and 1940. The educational hurricane whipped up the surface and stirred the waters deeply. Did the turbulence touch the ocean floor?

The Classroom

The data are limited for Denver. I located 133 classroom photographs and written descriptions for the period. For elementary schools there are 34 classes of which only certain ones provided information for the categories. Figure 2.3 shows the number of classes for each category. (To review these categories, see Table 2.1 on page 62). Because the direction of Denver's curriculum revision and experimentation in the interwar period tilted toward the secondary level,* I will concentrate on what teachers did in high schools. Data on 83 high school classes (see Figure 2.4) will be supplemented by an examination of specific schools.

The dominant teaching pattern within high school was a teacher, more often than not, instructing the whole group with his or her explanations and questions controlling most of the verbal exchanges with students and classroom activities. Even though classrooms contained movable desks and chairs, the furniture was often arranged in rows facing the teacher's desk and blackboard. Also, there were classes, less than 20 percent of the total, that had extensive student involvement in group work, pupil choice of tasks and projects, and freedom of movement.

Compared to the classroom portrait drawn at the turn of the century, movement away from a strict teacher-centered approach is evident in a substantial percentage of classes where student movement occurred. Also in the Mixed Pattern of instruction particular categories reveal teachers using practices that involved students actively in classroom work. Limited as the comparison is, note also that in all the categories high school classes show higher percentages of teacher-centered and lower percentages of student-centered behavior than elementary classrooms, precisely the same pattern as New York City.

By examining particular high schools using the available classroom descriptions, student accounts, and teacher reports, a more complete map of teaching behavior can be drawn. Recall that in no Denver High School were more than one-third of the staff involved in the Eight Year Study. Hence, what "progressive education" teachers did in their classes located

---

* Recall that Newlon and Threlkeld were high school teachers; Newlon was a high school principal prior to Denver; also the bulk of curriculum revision occurred at the secondary level.

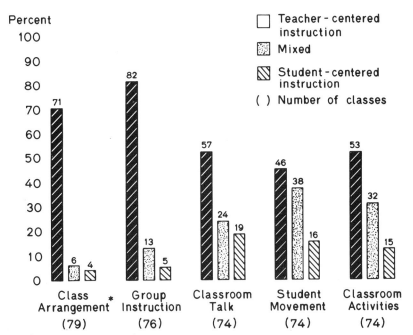

* 19% of all desks were stationery.

Figure 2.3   Patterns of Instruction in Denver High School Classrooms, 1920–1940

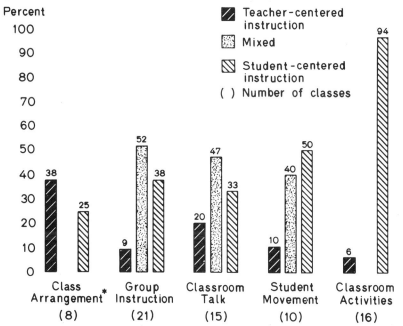

* 37% of all desks were stationery.
† Analysis of sources that produced this percentage revealed that they were either photos from local newspapers that school officials had provided or had suggested to reporters that such photos be taken. This percentage, then, probably overstates frequency of student-centered activities.

Figure 2.4   Patterns of Instruction in Denver Elementary Classrooms, 1920–1940.

in one wing of the building may or may not be what their peers did elsewhere in the high school. I located 20 written descriptions and photographs of experimental classes in the 5 schools between 1934 and 1939. I estimate that these 20 classes represent about one-quarter of the teachers who taught experimental classes during these years.* Fourteen teachers (70 percent) reported or were shown using panel discussions, debates, pupil-teacher planning, and other techniques associated with student-centered patterns of instruction implied in the Eight Year Study. The rest discloses little movement away from the familiar teacher-centered configuration even though they were part of the experimental classes. Read, for example, what Ralph Putnam, East High Latin teacher wrote in an article for Denver teachers in the initial year of the experiment:

> I wish to emphasize ... that nothing very radical is being or will be attempted. We are here to learn Latin and the mastery of Latin will always be our prime objective.

How, then, he asked, did work with 40 "progressive education" students differ from other Latin classes he taught? In reading Caesar's works on the Helvetian War, Putnam said, "the more rapid reading, possible in a special group, enables the pupils to follow more readily the thread of the story and thus to feel the vitality and vigor of the narrative. "Moreover, far more attention can be given to the study of English derivatives and extra reading because the class of 40 had "extra time," i.e. larger blocks of time in class. Putnam's view of covering more material in depth seemed to have been in the minority.[81]

Another view of the core program at East comes from a 1938 report written by tenth graders during the first two semesters they moved through the core classes, labs, special interest groups, etc. A project planned and written by 8 students in diary form, they described what it was like to be in a program with 235 students, 6 teachers, 3 periods a day. As the 235 students moved through the daily schedule they described how they and their teachers planned units, how class members chose activities, pursued their interests independently in core labs, worked in groups on projects, and went into the community on numerous field trips.

October 3, 1938 (second semester of first year in core program).

> We still consider our class very interesting, but we have discovered that it is also quite a bit of work. We must find our references by ourselves, outline our own methods and means of study; use our own initiative throughout our work....
>
> The sixth hour is our regular core period during which we have lectures, reports, motion pictures, or discussions of topics related to our community study. For example, during our study of crime and juvenile delinquency, two films were shown in our classroom. One was a cut from the picture 'Big

---

* Based upon actual counts taken in yearbooks and master schedule of three high schools.

House,' and the other was a picture of gang life among boys. After the pictures, we had a class discussion on topics concerning the films....

On Thursday the seventh hour is used as a laboratory period. Most of the work on our projects is now done in these periods. There are six of them, covering art, history, human relations, social studies, English, and science and statistics.... One girl selected a subject which required interpretation of long tables of statistics. She used several periods in getting help from the math laboratory on interpretation of these tables.

Nine photos of students working at different classroom activities flesh out the student-written narrative. No teachers appear in the photographs.[82]

Another piece of evidence on teaching behavior of those participating in the Eight Year Study comes from surveys in two high schools completed in 1933 and 1940. In the 1933 survey, the first year of the experiment, 16 percent of the participating teachers chose the word "much" (as opposed to "not at all" or "some") to describe the degree of joint planning they did with students in selecting what to study, class activities, individual projects, and evaluation. By 1940, 53 percent checked "much," although it is likely that there was turnover among the teachers in the experiment over the eight years.[83]

Finally, in early 1938, Wilford Aiken, Director of the Eight Year Study, visited each of the innovative programs in Denver's five high schools. He met teachers, students, and headquarter administrators. His report concluded that "a real break with the traditional subject matter" had occurred. Substantial pupil-teacher planning took place. Life in the community had increasingly become a subject of investigation in core classrooms. Moreover, "many of the old recitation techniques are disappearing from the classroom." In some cases, however, the report said that "the socialized discussion that had been substituted for the recitation is being conducted without proper regard for study and research." Bluntly put: "in some classes discussion consists primarily of the pooling of misinformation." Generally complimentary toward the program, the report confirmed that curricular and teaching practices had, indeed, changed.[84]

These fragments of evidence suggest that a majority of teachers involved in the Eight Year Study taught in a manner consistent with the aims of the effort. But not all could drop the baggage of teacher-centered practices, a situation similar to the results disclosed in the formal evaluation of New York City's Activity Program.

After the Eight Year Study final evaluation appeared in 1941, Superintendent Charles Greene, who had led the study as Assistant Superintendent, approved the expansion of the core program to all junior and senior high schools by mandating a three-year course of study and two years of General Education as a requirement for graduation. Using instructional units that had been developed and polished by high school teachers over the previous eight years, high school sophomores spent one-third of their time in General Education classes; the amount of student time in these classes decreased to one period a day when they became seniors.[85]

By 1943, the graduation requirement was reduced to one year, with the five high schools given the option to design their own programs. Shortly after, General Education was transformed into counseling programs. North High School, for instance, had between 15 and 26 teachers out of a faculty of 80 assigned to General Education classes between 1940 and 1943; by 1944 when local option was permitted, General Education as a class assignment for teachers disappeared from the master schedule, replaced by such classes as Diagnostic English, Instructional Communication, and Social Living. At East High School, General Education became a tenth grade course required of all students. The class stressed school and vocational guidance. The General Education teacher was also the counselor.[86]

Following the heated controversy over progressivism in the schools in the late 1940s and early 1950s, a furor that angered Mira Scott Frank, Board of Education member whom I quoted at the beginning of this section, General Education as a course was abandoned three years after Scott left the Board.[87]

The demise of Denver's General Education courses in the 1950s was part of a national reaction to an intense barrage of criticism targeted on public schools that had reputations for being progressive, as defined by these critics. The abolition of General Education, however, should not obscure the classroom changes in curriculum and instruction that had occurred since Jesse Newlon came to Denver in the Summer of 1920. Courses of study, textbooks, and certain teaching approaches changed, although the changes happened differently in elementary and high school classrooms. Although such changes had occurred in New York City at a much slower, very uneven pace, under Newlon and his successors there was a far more systematic and insistent edge to these alterations over the two decades.

One of the reasons for the differences in the pace and intensity of organizational changes that touched a substantial number of Denver classrooms is the remarkable continuity in superintendent leadership; a leadership that shared faith in both progressive pedagogy and the pivotal importance of the teacher—seasoned liberally by the daily realities of schools. These beliefs shaped the general direction taken by Newlon and his successors into the 1940s. Moreover, these top administrators gave much thought to the design and implementation of efforts to alter existing procedures. The curriculum revision program established a pattern of teacher involvement in system-wide policymaking for the classroom. Unusual for its time, the process emerged as a potent, informal introduction of teachers to progressive pedagogy. Because it was highly prized by the top leadership, incentives were embedded into the effort (released time from the classroom, recognition by the School Board, professional growth). Since the venture lasted well over a decade, a substantial portion of the staff were sufficiently touched to consider introducing these ideas into their classrooms.

The evidence reveals that most teachers continued teacher-centered practices. A considerable minority of teachers, however, did adopt, in varying degrees, mixes of existing and new practices. Thus, a top down design of curricular and instructional change, endorsed and generously supported by the School Board and superintendents, wedded to a carefully crafted plan of teacher involvement, influenced classroom instruction— again more in elementary than high school settings.

Yet even in the high schools, the Eight Year Study in Denver was unique. For those teachers who were involved, a minority on each staff, some progressive techniques were put into practice in dozens of classrooms although such practices seldom got past their colleagues' doors. As with New York City high schools, reasons for the seeming invulnerability of these classrooms to student-centered practices may be found in the structural conditions within which teachers worked (5 or more classes to teach a day, meeting with 200 or more students daily, expectations to cover subject matter and prepare students for jobs and college, etc.); or the kinds of persons who enter high school classrooms (trained in subject-matter, mostly male, etc.).

Whatever the reasons, and it is premature to concentrate on any of them now. Denver high schools did introduce to a limited extent pedagogical changes in some classrooms. The Washington, D.C. story contains similar themes identified in both New York City and Denver while revealing some unique to the nation's capital.

WASHINGTON, D.C.

When the present superintendent of schools took office on July 1, 1920, he knew that the administration of the school system involved many difficulties. Superintendents of other cities told him that it was considered by schoolmen one of the most difficult superintendencies in the United States....

Educational progress in Washington is slow because under the present system of educational control and financial support the needs of the school system are allowed to become acute before consideration is given to improvement and relief then comes altogether too slowly....

Failure on the part of the appropriation power to provide money for progressive educational activities makes an educational system unprogressive.... Failure to provide money for adequate salaries means mediocre teachers and ineffective education. Failure to build enough schoolhouses means overcrowded classes, portables, and poorly adapted rented accomodations, and such conditions make impossible the best teaching....[88]

These statements were made to the District of Columbia Board of Education by their new Superintendent, Frank W. Ballou. Within two years of his appointment Ballou bluntly and concisely scored the divided authority of a Board of Education, District Commissioners, and two Houses of Congress that produced the city's reputation as a graveyard for superintendents. Ballou went on to serve almost a quarter-century (1920–1943), the longest tenure of any Washington superintendent before or since.

Born in 1879 and raised in rural upstate New York, Ballou graduated from a state teacher training school and taught in rural schools between 1897 and 1899. By 1904 he had completed a bachelor's degree from Teachers College and decided to move to Ohio, where he earned a master's degree at the University of Cincinnati. While there, he was appointed principal of the University's Technical School and directed it for three years. Switching to the college classroom, he became an assistant professor of education and taught for three years. Returning east, he enrolled at Harvard where he earned a Ph.D in 1914. For his dissertation, he studied how teachers were appointed in urban school systems. The year he received his degree, the Boston school superintendent asked him to head the Department of Educational Investigation and Measurement, one of the few school districts with a research bureau in the nation. For three years his department administered, analyzed, and reported results from various batteries of intelligence and achievement tests. The cutting edge of progressive practice in testing and the use of tests for grouping students within classes and across curricula found Frank Ballou at the right place and time. In 1917 he was promoted to assistant superintendent, and for the next three years helped organize and develop the newest form of school organization—the junior high school. At the age of 41, he applied for the Washington, D.C. position and was named superintendent. Like his Denver colleague, Jesse Newlon, Ballou began his initial three year contract in the summer of 1920.[89]

Within the first decade of his tenure, Ballou had established himself locally as a determined, frank, first-rate administrator unafraid to speak his mind and committed to scientific management as a tool in solving school problems. Nationally, his peers demonstrated their esteem for his talents by electing him President of the Department of Superintendence in 1925. That year he gave an address at the Indianapolis meeting of the NEA on the progress of a science of education since the turn of the century. In Washington he needed every bit of scientific knowledge and talent he possessed.

When Ballou railed at the city's Rube Goldberg governance, his voice joined a growing chorus of criticism against the Organic Act (1906). This law, passed by Congress, created a nine member Board of Education appointed to administer the largest segregated school system in the country. Unlike other big city school boards, the District Board of

Education split its authority (but not responsibility) with three appointed District Commissioners who revised the Board's budget estimates, controlled all expenditures, allocated and audited funds, and purchased school equipment, supplies, etc. In effect, the Board of Education had no independent authority in securing or spending funds, including the purchase of land and the construction of school buildings. Bad as this was from a superintendent's perspective, it became worse when Congress (which appropriated every penny going to the District), in Ballou's words, "reviews, revises, and reduces" the school budget item by item, line by line—first in the House of Representatives, then in the Senate. If the totals between the two Houses differed, a conference committee settled the final amount that went to the schools.

The horror stories of delay, neglect, and confusion were legion to insiders familiar with the byzantine process of securing a budget in the District. In his 1921–1922 annual report, Ballou, using restrained language, detailed all the road blocks he and the Board had to overcome to improve school conditions. To make his case stronger, Ballou drafted United States Commissioner of Education John J. Tigert to testify in behalf of the District schools in the final pages of his report: "... the superintendent is so fettered up with overhead organizations that he is practically impotent, as I see it. I would not take the job at two or three times the salary." Ballou then turned to an "authoritative work on education" prepared by "leading American educators," to describe the organization of the District of Columbia schools. The *Cyclopedia of Education* minced no words:

> Educational conditions in Washington, from an administrative point of view, are among the worst to be found in any city in the Union, and the school system is behind that of cities elsewhere of equal size.... Until Congress can be made to realize that it is incompetent properly to administer such an undertaking and will give to the Board of Education the power and control which should belong to it there is little hope of a good, modern school system for the District of Columbia. The superintendency of the schools of Washington is generally regarded as one of the most difficult and most undesirable positions in the United States.[90]

In a word much loved by superintendents, Washington schools were a challenge. By 1940, when Ballou formally tallied up the achievements of his administration, he was quite proud in listing changes that he had maneuvered through the labyrinth. The conditions he faced in 1920 and the achievements he defined as important in 1940 suggest the roads Ballou traveled in improving a segregated school system in the interwar period.

"School Achievements in Twenty Years," a document Ballou submitted to the Board of Education in 1941, categorized his successes into changes in administration, new buildings, improvements in school organization, and improved supervision and instruction. Out of a 125 page report, 94 pages dealt with streamlining administration, new buildings, and improved teaching conditions (e.g. salaries, retirement, appointments and promotions). Twenty-five pages (20 percent) traced improvements in instruction and supervision. Of these pages, most space was devoted to curriculum revision, expanded testing programs, and new grouping procedures—in that order. No mention of teaching methods, project activities, or any concerted effort to introduce progressive practices into classrooms appeared, although a major change had been announced in 1938 with the Child Development Program. Progressive language, however, popped up in numerous places: the formal statement of philosophy produced by curriculum revision between 1938 and 1940 (printed twice in the report) and a description of what a modern school should be like, sounding almost like it had been lifted from a course description at Teachers College.[91]

The point of all this is to underscore Ballou's aims in administering the District schools. Defining the major issues as the need for more buildings, reorganizing to administer schools efficiently, and navigating the shifting shoals of Washington and congressional politics, Ballou plowed his energies into dragging the system into the twentieth century. A man who believed deeply in the science of education and the necessity for using it to improve schooling, he was cut from the same cloth as those administrative progressives who redesigned school systems throughout the first decades of the century. On instructional issues, his interests inclined more toward expansion of the junior high program, using tests as tools to distribute students efficiently into appropriate groups, and a tightly controlled version of curriculum revision. Closer in spirit to New York City's Maxwell, Ettinger, and O'Shea than Denver's Newlon and Threlkeld and Campbell of New York, Ballou left his marks on the organization. On instruction, his fingerprints were less apparent.

The Setting for Classroom Instruction

A central fact of schooling in the District of Columbia was that there were two separate school systems. In his 1911 report to the Board of Education, Superintendent Alexander Stuart described some of the effects of having a school system segregated by law. With 32 percent of the students attending black schools separate from whites, costs, he pointed out, would be inevitably higher in a dual school system.

> It is obvious that were it not for the exactions of the race question no city of the size of Washington would consider it necessary or wise to maintain two deputy superintendents, two normal schools, two expensive manual training schools....
>
> A study of the location of school buildings shows that to meet the needs of the white and colored children two smaller buildings have been erected in the same (attendance area) which, under other conditions, would have been merged into one larger building at greatly reduced cost....

Repeated examples are found throughout where a class of white children of a given grade is in one building and another small class of colored children of the same grade is in a nearby building....

The same causes explain in part the employment of a number of teachers in excess of most cities where white and colored children attend school together....[92]

Class size is one instance of the impact of segregated schooling. Figures reported by the school district were averages; averages conceal important differences in class size. In 1927–1928, for example, out of almost 1,200 elementary classes, 29 percent contained 40 or more students (about equally distributed between white and black schools). School Board policy was to allocate 40 students per class "as far as practicable." For classes with less than 30 students, there were 18 percent (with 85 percent of those classes containing white students). Thus, 53 percent of the classes had between 31 and 39 students. Still, even these figures mask the differences between black and white classes. In just one decade, differences were marked for elementary classrooms:

	Class Size	
Year	*White*	*Black*
1922	34.3	37.3
1927	34.9	37.9
1932	30.8	36.1

Fifteen years later when Professor George Strayer completed the first comprehensive survey of District schools, the gap had widened: 32.0 for white classes; 39.0 for black.[93]

The buildings and rooms these students and teachers worked in between 8:30 and 2:30 daily changed substantially over the years. Yet even after the major rebuilding campaign Ballou and the Board of Education maneuvered through Congress in 1925, overcrowded, antiquated classrooms remained in far too many buildings across the city, making, in George Strayer's words, "adequate instruction impossible." Over half of the elementary schools were built before 1925. Until the 1940s, classrooms contained long rows of stationary desks which accommodated 40 pupils. "Today (1948) with a recommended maximum class enrollment of 30 in the elementary school," Strayer wrote, "many of these classrooms are still too small and a great many of them are crowded...." Bluntly, Strayer said that the "modern Child Development Program" which the District had launched in 1938, "requires informal groupings of children, floor space for constructive activities, cupboards, storage space for supplies...." Even in the newer buildings existing space was inadequate, according to Strayer.[94]

As classroom space changed slowly, so did furniture. In 1920, almost two-thirds of the desks bolted to floors had been in use since the turn of the

Washington, D.C. Black Elementary School, 1942. (*Office of War Information, Library of Congress*).

century. Between 1920 and 1929, only 200 desks had been replaced. In 1930, the first year of a 5 year program to replace stationary desks with portable ones, 7,000 were replaced. The depression slowed down the conversion drastically. When Strayer's team surveyed classrooms, all elementary schools had installed movable desks and chairs.[95]

Not so for the secondary schools. For those built since 1925 (13 of 19 junior high schools and 4 of 9 high schools) single pedestal desks and other movable furniture had been introduced throughout the 1930s. For Central and Dunbar high schools, constructed in 1916, bolted-down desks sat in rows, class after class, year after year.

While the type of desks were of some importance, what occurred in classrooms often depended upon how teachers allocated time for instruction. For years, teacher received copies of weekly schedules mandating the amount of time they had to spend on each subject. At the secondary school a daily schedule sliced the time into equal segments of 40 to 50 minutes for each subject. Note that in 1927 elementary teachers, unlike their secondary colleagues, had to teach:

handwriting	geography
language (composition and grammar)	elementary science
spelling and word analysis	drawing
reading and literature	music
arithmetic	physical education
history and civics	

For the last four subjects in the second column, special teachers would give lessons once every three weeks.[96]

For each of these subjects a standard time schedule set the expectation for each grade level. Geography was to be taught 10 minutes daily in first grade, increasing to a half-hour in the fourth. Arithmetic was set for 35 minutes daily in the first grade and 3½ hours per day in third and fourth grades, falling to 2½ hours daily in sixth grade. In 1936, another formal time schedule was adopted by the Board of Education that varied the time

Washington, D.C. Woodrow Wilson High School, White, Algebra Lesson, 1943. (*Office of War Information, Library of Congress*).

allotments slightly. When the Strayer team visited schools in 1948, they found that the time schedule adopted 12 years earlier was still being followed, although the Child Development Program, initiated in 1938, called for different amounts of time for clusters of subjects.[97]

Just because a time schedule was approved by a school board did not mean that teachers followed in lock-step the expected standards. Many did not. A number of teachers and principals, how many I cannot estimate, intent upon installing activity programs in their classrooms, departed from the schedule simply because it straitjacketed the flexibility essential for informal classrooms. From a first grade classroom, the teacher–printed daily schedule read:

Our Big Plan Today
1. Look and see our trailer. The boys made it.
2. Let's go for a story ride.
3. Let's read our new story.
4. Let's play hot potato.
5. Have you done a reading card?
6. Let's be happy.[98]

While such primary classrooms used flexible schedules and departed from the approved one, such approaches were uncommon. Teachers, indeed, differed in how much time they spent on reading, arithmetic, and geography but most diverged within a range that was implicitly recognized as reasonable. After all, the organizational signals to teachers and principals were plain. The Superintendent's words accompanying the time schedule available to each teacher left little to interpretation: "Every officer and teacher in the elementary schools shall consider himself governed by this weekly schedule," and principals were expected to inspect teachers' plans to "know that each teacher is observing the distribution of time...." Furthermore, District teachers' instructional day was a half-hour shorter than most districts of comparable size (5 hours compared to 5½ hours) which, I suspect, generated pressure upon teachers to cover the crowded curriculum by following the prescribed time allotments.[99]

The point is that an outdated Board-approved time schedule was ill-fitted for a new program, especially one that was directed toward producing a flexible classroom where teachers and pupils jointly planned tasks. Such a mix–up suggests, at worst, a bureaucratic oversight, or more probably, the existence of mixed feelings toward the new effort. Classroom teachers, less adventurous than some colleagues who leaped upon the progressive bandwagon, would probably think twice before embarking upon a revised time schedule, given the shorter day and directives of the superintendent, especially if their principal lacked enthusiasm for the new venture.

Mixed signals also marked the curriculum revision efforts begun by

Ballou in 1925 and carried forward, fitfully, into the 1930s. As a noted member of the NEA's Department of Superintendence, Ballou served on its curriculum commission and chaired the committee that revised the elementary science course of study written by Washington administrators and teachers. This was published in the 1926 Yearbook of the Department of Superintendence. The course of study was approved by the Board of Education that year.[100]

In the same year, Ballou appointed committees to revise arithmetic, reading and literature, English, and geography courses. At least three major organizational differences separated Ballou from Denver's Newlon and Threlkeld in approach. First, while teachers were assigned to committees, District administrators chaired these groups until the late 1930s when an occasional teacher was chosen to direct a committee's work. Second, the committees began their work after 3:00, on the teacher's time. Third, no specialists were hired to help the committees nor was any training given to committees on how to write objectives or a course of study.[101]

Similarities with the curriculum development efforts in Denver existed, of course. Teachers did participate. Progressive vocabulary and references to activity methods studded the syllabi. In-service education for teachers increased. Networks of like-minded professionals developed. All of this somehow occurred in a slow-motion fashion, unlike the Denver experience. Delays in the production of courses of study were common. Because the work occurred after school hours the process stretched out over years. Finally, teachers began to object to committee work between 3:00–5:00 since other cities provided substitutes to relieve staff from work. Nonetheless, by 1940, 7 elementary courses of study, (19 in the junior high, 4 in vocational schools, and 21 in senior highs) were published, and teachers were expected to use them. Did they?[102]

This question refocuses attention on the classroom. How did District teachers teach? How extensive were progressive practices in white and black classrooms from Anacostia to Georgetown? The conditions described so far suggest some crude boundaries for a few answers. As in New York, but less than in Denver, classroom space and furniture presented more obstacles than opportunities for teachers to use progressive practices. Of course, the physical environment didn't prevent use of small groups, pupil-teacher planning, activity units, and project work, but for those teachers barely willing to experiment, the lack of space and the cumbersome furniture, in addition to difficulties in securing supplies, may well have discouraged them from trying. Also with over 35 students in a class, incentives to work in small groups and with individuals, to prepare extra materials, and to beg for materials, were dulled.

Another constraint was time. Already mentioned was the five hour instructional day in which seven to ten subjects were to be taught. Subtract opening exercises (Bible reading, collecting money, taking attendance) and recess, and add teacher concern for covering the prescribed subjects, particularly in view of an unexpected principal visit, and the results are sharper limits upon introducing new instructional practices.

Another line of reasoning is to ask what organizational mechanisms supported diffusion of progressive teaching practices. Clearly, a curriculum revision process helped, especially as it was wired into a local and national network of similarly inclined professionals. While the District's organizational linkages were hardly as systematic or carefully crafted as Denver's, one would reasonably expect that a number of teachers and principals would have been captured by the child-centered notions embedded in pedagogical progressivism or, already converted, found enough green lights from headquarters to move ahead on their own.

Also teacher institutes, funded in part by private contributions from administrators and teachers, brought locally and nationally known professionals to lecture staff (blacks meeting at Dunbar and whites at Central) on varied topics. Throughout the 1920s teachers heard from W. W. Charters (University of Chicago) on curriculum revision, Florence Bamberger (Johns Hopkins University) on classroom efficiency, Elbert Fretwell (Teachers College) on organizing social activities for junior and senior high schools, Laura Zirbe (Lincoln School, Teachers College) on progressive reading programs. In addition, teachers met monthly, again in separate schools, to study current issues. Often done in a lecture format with either a guest or the assistant superintendent delivering the talk, topics in these compulsory meetings included the activity method, adapting courses of study to projects, and the like.[103]

Another important condition supporting the spread of progressive ideas into classrooms was the teacher's level of education. The assumption was that the higher the level of formal schooling, the greater the awareness of modern trends in education, particularly if the schooling was recently acquired with, therefore, a greater willingness to alter one's teaching behavior. A pinch of skepticism suggests these assumptions are open to debate. School officials, however, implicitly accepted the premise and seldom questioned it. In 1931, 78% of high school teachers had at least a bachelor's degree; 96% of elementary teachers had from 2 to 3 years of Normal School training or a bachelor's. By 1948, 78% of the entire staff were college graduates. Among elementary teachers, more blacks had bachelor's degrees than whites (74% to 61%) while the reverse occurred among senior high teachers (85% of black teachers were college graduates; 93% of whites were). Teachers also reported to Strayer when they last received their professional training. Within the previous five years (1943–1948), 55% of the teachers had taken courses; 29% had taken their last training between 1933 and 1942, and 16% had not taken a course since they had been appointed.[104]

A review of those organizational characteristics that permit and limit the introduction of progressive practices into the classroom offer crude pointers but no direct evidence drawn from classrooms. Let us turn now to teachers in classrooms.

In the Classroom

That black and white teachers used progressive methods to varying degrees is undeniable. A group of black administrators appointed by Assistant Superintendent Garnet Wilkinson to create the Department of Research and Measurement for Divisions 10–13, consisting of all the black schools, was designed and implemented in a 5 month experiment at Mott School and an unnamed "traditional" school in 1924. The aim of the experiment was to compare the effects of progressive education upon both teachers and students. The new approaches used in the 8 grade school included the testing of students, new textbooks, additional materials, and movable furniture for grades 1 through 4. Teachers were encouraged to convert the formal course of study into projects. Mott teachers overwhelmingly approved the experiment, according to a survey: 74% said projects produced superior results with their students; 94% found students' interests in projects superior to usual school work.[105]

Occasional articles in the *Journal of the Columbian Educational Association*, a publication written by and for black educators in District schools, corroborated interest in progressive schooling. Mayme Lewis of Bruce School reported in a 1925 issue the details of her two day visit to the third and fourth grades of Horace Mann, a New York City progressive private school at Teachers College. At the Monroe Demonstration School, an adjunct to Miner Teachers College, a number of teachers, in concert with their student-teachers, introduced and maintained classroom centers, small-group work, joint teacher-pupil planning, etc. Finally, another piece of indirect evidence is the annual exhibit of elementary school activities where black teachers presented projects their classes had produced.[106]

Unfortunately, I have no way of assessing how widespread these practices were in Divisions 10–13. In issues of the *Journal*, for each article describing an activity-centered classroom, three others laid out exemplary lesson plans revealing teacher direction and control at each step of the plan without a hint of student involvement other than answering teacher questions.[107]

A similar problem surfaces in determining the extent of progressive practices in the white schools (Division 1–9). That schools and certain teachers introduced progressive methods in their classrooms goes without question. Articles in national professional journals (*Childhood Education* 1932 and 1933; *Progressive Education* 1936; *Grade Teacher* 1939) featured classes in Petworth and Ketcham schools constructing railroad stations, studying Mexican life, and painting. The *Washington Post* and other local papers carried articles on classroom projects. Julia Hahn, an elementary school supervisor, deeply involved in San Francisco schools' progressive efforts prior to her coming to Washington, worked directly with teachers and wrote articles on the activity movement in District schools. I found it difficult to assess how far these practices had spread in schools and to what extent teachers selected which ideas to convert into classroom techniques.[108]

The only appraisal of the diffusion of progressive methods in the District schools took place in 1948 when George Strayer brought his team to Washington, at the Board of Education's request, to determine, among other things, how much of the Child Development Program had been implemented in classrooms.

The program was equally as ambitious, but far less systematically implemented than either New York City's Activity Program or Denver's Eight Year Study. Ballou's formal effort at installing progressive education contained all the conventional vocabulary about "child-centered activity program" spreading throughout District schools, pushing out the "traditional . . . subject-centered program." Classrooms were to become places where children shared in planning the work, assumed responsibilities for both room and school duties, and studied actively the family, neighborhood, city, and nation. Projects, centers, movable furniture, activity periods, crafts—the often-quoted repertoire that pedagogical progressives sought in public schools—were central to the Child Development Program.[109]

Headquarter's supervisors and principals were charged to establish activity programs in the schools. Some schools, building on the cadré of teachers who had experimented earlier with projects and centers, embraced the Superintendent's charge with great enthusiasm. Most schools, pinned to existing practice, heeded the words of the Superintendent but did not, or could not, apparently institute the entire program.

Strayer's team had, as one of its objectives, the job of assessing to what degree the program, initiated in 1938, had been implemented a decade later. He found "many" classrooms that met both the letter and spirit of the Superintendent's mandate, in spite of numerous and enervating obstacles, errors, and just plain poor judgments made by school officials that either frustrated, or worse, contradicted Ballou's announced direction. Strayer added them up:

- Teachers were not given time or resources to produce new curricula for the new program. This was a "serious error."
- Only one new unit (math) was produced for teachers to use in the new effort in ten years.
- Rooms lacked space, cabinets, equipment; teachers lacked textbooks and instructional materials.
- Short school day

- Large classes
- Teachers lacked preparation for change[110]

Too many teachers held fuzzy notions of what the program was intended to do and what they had to do specifically, i.e. "what am I supposed to do Monday morning?" Strayer divided District elementary teachers into two groups: those with "the child-development philosophy with its emphasis upon the whole child and upon purposive learning" and those with the "traditional" stress upon mastery of facts and skills. As with all such arbitrary categories within the survey, Strayer offered no specific numbers, only such vague words as "many." Hence, determining the spread of the program is difficult.[111]

The closest Strayer came to estimating the diffusion of the program is when he described how four staff members visited all elementary schools, and spoke with teachers, principals, and supervising directors. Based upon these discussions and observations, they rated the schools they saw as Superior, Good, Fair, and Poor. Unlike the Morrison survey of New York's Activity Program in 1940 where observers were trained, scales constructed, verified for validity and reliability, and data carefully sifted, Strayer's team judged a school Superior,

> if the program was designed to fit the needs of the children, the purposes of teachers and pupils were clear, there was a well organized program of child development activities, an effective instructional program dealing with fundamental knowledges, understandings and skills, and a community program which secured the interests and cooperation of parents on the education of their children.[112]

These observers found 19% of all elementary schools Superior; 35.7% Good; 27% Fair; and 18.2% Poor. Only by a courageous inferential leap can one conclude that Child Development Programs existed in more than half of the District schools; that is, by adding those schools rated Superior and Good. Not only would such a leap be courageous, it would be precarious given the multiple and ambiguous criteria observers used, the probable differences among them in making judgments on such loosely defined items and, finally, the obvious fact that within a school, differences among teachers exist as they do between schools, e.g. New York City's Activity Program.[113]

Adding up Strayer's observations of the organizational obstacles to the program's implementation and his statements of how spottily the Child Development Program was executed, the picture that emerges is one of uncertain, unsystematic, and jigsaw implementation in District elementary schools.

Some help in determining the spread of progressive practices comes from the 53 classroom descriptions (of which 20 were elementary classes) I collected for Washington. Figure 2.5 illustrates that student-centered teaching patterns appear in slightly more than one out of three elementary

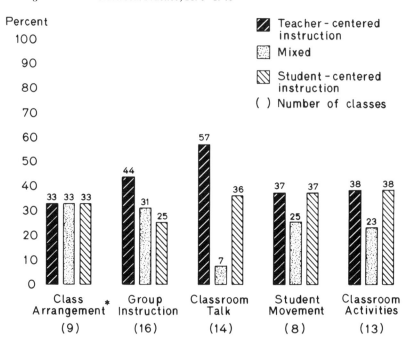

Figure 2.5   Patterns of Instruction in Washington, D.C. Elementary Classrooms, 1920–1940.

classrooms. The numbers, however, are small and offer little more confidence than Strayer's team judgments of individual school quality. Combining the pieces of data, individually flawed as they are, with the contextual conditions described earlier both pieces suggest that progressive teaching practices, as defined by the Child Development Program, penetrated a minority of the District's classrooms, although that minority may be as small as one-quarter or as large as one-third. Equally plausible is the inference that certain progressive practices were adopted to varying degrees by substantial numbers of District elementary teachers, further broadening the number of teachers who expanded their range of techniques. Yet saying all this in careful and conditional language still leaves one fact undisturbed: teacher-centered instructional patterns prevailed in elementary classrooms.

High School Classrooms

Figure 2.6 shows patterns similar to New York City and Denver in that for every category teacher-centered practices at the high school exceed

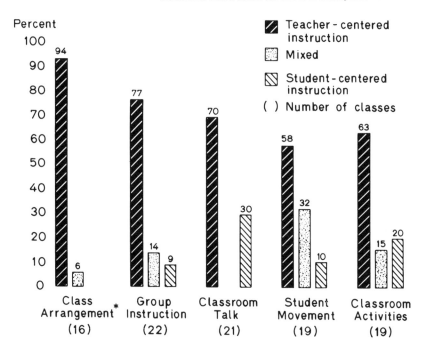

Figure 2.6 Patterns of Instruction in Washington, D.C. High School Classrooms, 1920–1940.

percentages for those practices in elementary classrooms. Drawn from the graph is a profile of a high school teacher teaching four to five classes daily, facing rows of students sitting in desks. Three out of four times, the teachers instructed the entire group, talked most of the time, and permited little student-initiated movement within the room. One way to corroborate that profile is to take a closer look at some District high schools, white and black.

Consider the predominantly academic Central High School. Perched on a hill overlooking the Capitol, Washington Monument, and downtown, Central's reputation for a splendid view of the city began when it opened its doors to white students in 1916. Both J. Edgar Hoover, subsequently Director of the Federal Bureau of Investigation, and Helen Hayes, soon to become a world-renowned actress, were Central students and must have read the student handbooks that described school rules, curricula requirements for graduation, daily schedule, extracurricular activities, and school cheers. In the 1926 Handbook students were told to go to their section (homeroom) for opening exercises by 8:55 a.m. "In classrooms absolute quiet must prevail at this time," the handbook stated, because the students must have the "proper attitude" and "frame of mind necessary to start the day right." At 9:10 the bell rang to start the student's seven period day—"six recitation periods" and lunch. In four minutes, students were to move from one class to another. A rich array of activities was available at the end of the day including the chance to write for the *Brecky*, the senior yearbook, the *Journal*, a literary review begun in 1886, and the *Bulletin*, a weekly newspaper. A glimpse into classrooms appeared in the weekly.[114]

From the *Bulletin*, beginning in 1925 when a section called "Class Notes" began, until 1938 when the column lapsed, students wrote items on what certain teachers did in their rooms. From these "Class Notes" I identified 302 descriptions of teaching activities for 55 English, social studies, science, math, and foreign language teachers. Almost half of the teachers were in the English department; one-quarter in social studies; one-fifth in foreign language and the remainder in science.

Student reporters noted unusual items about teachers' classrooms:

1. Instances of student participation in class recitation.

    November 24, 1925. In Florence Jayne's English class "various pupils, or monitors as they are called, record the attendance, test the rest of the class, read the questions from the true and false tests."

    April 2, 1930. In Alice Clark's Latin class "at each lesson some member of the class acts as teacher.... One of the pupils called on Miss Clark to answer one of the questions."

2. Classroom activities that departed from the routine, e.g. field trips, lantern slides, radio programs, outside speakers, panel discussions, acting out scenes from novels and plays, etc.

    December 17, 1930. Bessie Whitford's sixth period English class debated the merits of high school fraternities.

    October 20, 1932. Mr. DeShazo's third period chemistry class "performed their first experiment by themselves.... They made oxygen and found its properties."

    January 19, 1933. Miss Gill's fourth year French class held "a bridge party with the players speaking only French...."

    March 9, 1933. Alma Boyd's second period English class presented the *Vicar of Wakefield* through a simulated radio broadcast.

3. Unusual class activities where students determined what they study, worked in groups, and created projects.

    March 16, 1932. Students in Ruth, Denham's second period class made replicas of the Globe Theatre—"The theatre will be about large enough to place on a card table."

    February 15, 1934. Freshman Biology students in Miss E. C. Paul's class "are working on projects of practical application. Allowed to pick any topic in which they are interested, some students have chosen dish gardens, sprouting seeds, etc."

November 17, 1938. Florence Jayne's classes "voted for and attained certain changes in the teacher's system of marking."

In analyzing the 302 classroom activities from 55 teachers I found that 15 English and 4 history teachers were responsible for two–thirds of all activities that involved student participation, as reported by the student newspaper—or about one-fourth of the entire faculty in the mid-1930s. Of course, the total sample of teachers is selective, reflecting classes that student reporters heard about, which classes they took, etc. The point is, however, that within this sample there were a variety of approaches among teachers using progressive practices.

Viewed this way, I found that less than 10 percent of all activities reported by students in these classes included joint student-teacher planning, a revised course content related to current and future student needs, students leading a recitation or discussion, and committee work on projects—the usual teaching practices associated with pedagogical progressivism. Activities involving students undertaken by a substantial number of Central teachers stayed within a narrow band, e.g. student reports, debates, acting out scenes, and leading discussions (80 percent)—all were determined by the teacher and linked to required content or text. The evidence is that even among the minority of Central faculty who chose to use student participation to refresh existing content and instruction, the dominant mode of instruction was teacher-centered.[115]

Instruction at Central, then, except for a small group of teachers described in a student newspaper, was seemingly tied to large-group instruction, use of texts, question-answer exchanges initiated and controlled by the teacher, scant student movement and participation—all within classrooms arranged in rows of desks facing the blackboard and teacher's desk.

Travelling down the hill on Thirteenth Street toward the White House, taking a left at O Street, and going another dozen blocks, a visitor would have reached the steps of Dunbar, the black academic high school. In 1870 when it opened its doors to four black students in a church basement, it was the first black high school in the nation. Dunbar moved into a new building the same year as Central did. New or not, compared to Central, Dunbar classes were larger, books were frayed, materials were fewer, furniture was scarred by years of use, and, in the words of a teacher who wrote lovingly of her school, even "the blackboards were cracked with confusing lines resembling a map." Yet this was the school that produced, as Thomas Sowell noted, the first black general (Benjamin O. Davis), the first black Cabinet member (Robert C. Weaver), the first black federal judge (William Hastie), the first black senator since Reconstruction (Edward W. Brooke), and the discoverer of blood plasma (Charles Drew).[116]

Dunbar's purpose was clear: prepare students for college. Drawing from a pool of black students from across the city, the faculty, many of whom had earned advanced degrees from northern and eastern universities, set high standards for behavior and academics. They shared a belief in the "Talented Tenth," a cadré of educated blacks who would provide leadership to the race. Equalling and exceeding whites in knowledge, skills, and gentility was gospel among believers in this faith.[117]

In the 1924–1925 Crimson and Black student handbook, for example, rules for English students were explicit: "Write all lesson assignments in your notebooks. As you have at least three other lessons to prepare daily, do not attempt to trust your memory." For history classes students were warned: "To study history intelligently the student should follow the suggestions of the teacher as to the keeping of notebooks, map work, collateral reports and wider reading." Advice in the form of 12 rules for studying (with *Nihil Sine Labore* as a subtitle) were listed prescribing the kind of light and space at home that would be adequate. Also included were "Hints for Dunbar Boys and Girls e.g. for girls, "silks, chiffons, georgettes, satins have no place in your wardrobe"; for boys, "Wear ties, socks, and shirts of quiet colors. Don't let them be conspicuous and showy. Keep your shoes cleaned and polished." Rules for entering and leaving classrooms were stated with unmistakable clarity: "No talking or unnecessary moving about is to be allowed after the bell has sounded."[118]

The daily schedule of seven periods with bells punctuating changes in classes, except for those occasions when the electric bells broke down, were the same as at Central, although the teacher load and class sizes ran higher at the black than at the white high school. The academic courses of study and texts were the same including the one piece of required work in the senior year that drove students to parody in their yearbooks and literary journals—Edmund Burke's "On Conciliation With America."[119]

What happened in Dunbar classrooms, within a context of clear and precise student expectations for academic work and behavior (and a faculty with a high level of academic training facing, from behind the teacher's desk, classes of 35 or more students 5 or 6 times daily in row after row of bolted-down desks), can only be inferred. Few descriptions of classrooms are available. What these scattered photographs, student newspaper items, yearbook vignettes, and official reports show are instances of project work, student participation in classwork (e.g. reports, debates, etc.) within a larger framework of teacher-centered patterns of instruction.

Harriet Riggs, English and History Department Head for Armstrong and Dunbar high schools, reported in 1920 that in English "the socialized recitation was found valuable in teaching pupils how to think and how to study.... By this method of recitation each child contributed his part and learned to work for the welfare of the group." In all history classes, she continued, "emphasis was placed upon geography and map study. In many classes both teachers and pupils collected pictures and clippings bearing on the subjects studied. Constant effort was made to show the connection of the past and present." Senior English classes of Miss Howard and Mr. Hill did individual projects on eighteenth century England, creating their versions of magazines like the *Spectator*, models of villages, murals, etc. The photographs of English and Spanish classes showed familiar patterns of teachers talking to the entire class; one photograph of a chemistry class shows the teacher conducting an experiment in front of the room and the students standing in a half-circle around him watching. Data are few for Dunbar. Only partial inferences are appropriate given the skimpiness of the evidence.[120]

Until an intensive recovery of more classroom descriptions of Dunbar teachers occurs, little more than informed inpressions can be offered now. These impressions and partial inferences link easily with the patterns revealed at Central High School and the set of other descriptions from high schools elsewhere in the city. As tentative as all this is, a student essay on what happened in 1942 when the electric bells went out of order gives us a peek at the reality that somehow keeps dancing beyond the available evidence.

Clock Trouble

... When the Dunbar clocks are out of order, the efficient school curriculum of Dunbar no longer exists (Long Live Clock Trouble!)

The weary janitors climb the stairs and clang the ancient 'cow bell' which sends children springing from their seats, dashing down the hall, and puffing into their next hour class only to find that the class before has not heard the bell and they will have to return to the class they had left. After they have returned, the teacher proceeds with the lesson just in time to be interrupted by the bell and leave the homework unassigned. (Ah, a good night's sleep for once!)[121]

For the District of Columbia, teacher-centered instruction prevailed in both elementary and high school classrooms. Some progressive practices were embraced by more elementary teachers than their peers in the higher grades, but in numbers that seldom added up to more than one-quarter to one-third in elementary school and no more than one in five high school teachers. This pattern of variation between levels of schooling resembles what appeared in New York City and Denver.

Granted that the pattern was similar, still with the unique stability of Ballou's tenure for almost a quarter of a century, a plausible hunch based upon Denver's continuity in top leadership would be that the pattern might have varied. Plausible it may be but the hunch falls short of being convincing when Ballou's priorities are recalled: new buildings, reorganizing the bureaucracy, the scientific uses of testing, etc. These were the abiding and passionate interests of an administrative, not pedagogical, progressive. The Child Development Program and curriculum revision were adopted but represented no more than symbolic efforts, closer to copy-cat progressivism than a comprehensively developed implementation of current ideas. Continuity may be an important condition for district-wide change in classroom practice, but mild endorsements enhanced by rhetoric with little direct or tangible support for teachers were simply insufficient for District of Columbia teachers to alter their daily routines with children.

How much a role race played in determining classroom practice, I cannot estimate. That race influenced allocation of funds, teachers, and buildings is evident from the data. That the issue of race consumed much time and energy of school officials who worried what Congress, the Commissioners, the Board of Education, and white parents might think of decisions inadvertently made that transgressed the etiquette of race relations is also evident in the sources. That race may have influenced teacher and principal enthusiasm for progressive pedagogy, being more suitable for white middle and upper-class children than blacks who had to exceed whites in knowledge, skill, and moxie in order to survive—a concern voiced among some blacks a generation later over informal education, is only speculation at this point.

What is less speculative, however, is a pattern of mixed forms of teaching that did appear in the three cities. Mixed patterns of teacher- and student-centered instruction mean that a number of teachers constructed hybrids adapted to the classroom conditions they faced, the ideas they found congenial, and the demands of supervisors either urging them to introduce child-centered instruction or to continue traditional practices. Although a small minority of classrooms, these hybrids suggest that teachers, confronting conflicting expectations, developed unique solutions tailored to their settings.

The appearance of these hybrids also suggests a fundamental paradox that dogged the footsteps of both teachers and reformers who tried to transform public schools. For teachers, contradictions multiplied as they tried to resolve the tensions generated by partisans of the "New Education" and the daily realities they faced in their schools. After all, teachers sensed, at some level, that concentration on basic skills, classroom order, and respect for their authority were proxies for what the larger society expected of schools. For those teachers, this dilemma of coping with the complexities of individual choice and expression amidst oranizational demands for children to obey authority, behave uniformly, and acquire a common body of knowledge had to be worked out in each classroom.

Few reformers or school officials knew the difficult choices some teachers had to make when they closed the classroom door. Of course, many, perhaps most, teachers saw no contradictions, felt no tugs, and did what they had always done in their rooms. But in these two decades, the appearance of hybrids—a teacher-centered progressivism—suggests that many teachers began to see a fundamental dilemma in both what they did and what roles they were expected to play.

These contradictions mirror larger ones in the culture: individual concerns versus collective needs of the group; the values surrounding play and leisure time in an achievement-based society that often looks first to the bottom line of the profit-loss statement; the tension between seeking efficiency, getting more bang out of each dollar, and creative self-development. These conflicting values have grown up side by side in our culture and exist uneasily in both public and private institutions.

By opening schools to the debate over what is best for the individual child and a set of prescriptions embedded in pedagogy, a considerable number of teachers discovered their classrooms to be arenas where these values had to be resolved or, at best, maintained simultaneously in some practical manner. Not unlike families today where these dilemmas have to be worked through, teachers a generation ago found varied ways of resolving these contradictions.

I suggest that teachers who constructed classroom tasks containing both teacher- and student-centered approaches were the pathfinders who blazed a trail for later generations of colleagues to follow in coping with conflicting cultural values as they surfaced in classrooms.

That New York City fourth grade classroom of 42 children in 1924 taught by Mrs. Spencer that I described at the beginning of this chapter is one example. She used students as helpers; children coached each other; she permitted children to talk with one another during the arithmetic lesson; she moved around the room aiding individual students; complaints from the class were handled with humor; class activities were varied: games, reading, play-acting whole-class recitation. The instructional climate of the room was both serious and tolerant of individual children. Here was evidence of a teacher encouraging student expression and movement, giving students responsibility, helping individual children, and doing all of this with well-timed dispatch.

Yet in the same classroom, students sat in rows of bolted-down desks; the teacher decided what was to be studied and when; what was appropriate behavior; what class activities were to occur and in what order. The source of all authority was Mrs. Spencer. No pretense or even semblance of student involvement existed except as monitors or helpers to do what the teacher had already decided to do. Teacher rewards and sanctions were clear to the class. Boundaries for individual expression were defined sharply by what the teacher felt was appropriate. Thus, like teachers elsewhere, Mrs. Spencer, eager to try child-centered practices in her classroom, struck a compromise. The results, I believe, were classrooms where contradictory behaviors appeared in an uneasy, often fragile configuration. This paradox of progressivism that grew in the interwar decades is one that has persisted since, creating classrooms where impulses to be efficient, scientific, child-centered, and authoritative beset teachers. Teachers construct patchwork compromises to contain these competing, often contradictory, impulses but (and here I can only speculate) at a cost of leaving within many a vague uneasiness over the aims of teaching, classroom discipline, and relations with students that seldom goes away.

NOTES

1. Agnes DeLima, *Our Enemy The Child* (New York: New Republic, 1925), pp. 21–31. All quotes were taken from DeLima's observation. The classroom setting and description were paraphrased.
2. Tyack, pp. 182–98; Michael Katz, *Class, Bureaucracy, and Schools* (New York: Praeger Publishers, 1971), pp. 117–20; Cremin, pp. 179–239: See also Patricia Graham, *Progressive Education: From Arcady to Academe* (New York: Teachers College Press, 1967), chapter 4; Sol Cohen, *Progressives and Urban School Reform* (New York: Teachers College, Bureau of Publications, 1964), chapters 1–4; C.A. Bowers, *The Progressive Educator and the Depression* (New York: Random House, 1969), chapters 1–4.
3. Graham, p. 46.
4. Graham, chapters 3–4; DeLima, chapters 4, 9; Cremin, pp. 201–34.
5. *Time*, October 31, 1934, p. 31.
6. Historians, however, disagree upon the degree of impact of those progressive ideas targeted on the classroom. Of the dozen historians who have written about progressivism and schools, at least six have dealt with the issue of changes in teaching practice. Lawrence Cremin and Joel Spring assert, for very different reasons, that teaching behavior changed.

    Cremin cites the "Middletown" studies in 1925 and 1935 to illustrate how a conservative strain of progressivism in Muncie (Indiana) classrooms might have been typical of schools in the "pedagogical mainstream." Noting that for every Winnetka there were probably schools "that must have taught McGuffey and little else well into the thirties," he goes on to state that the reformers left unmistakable footprints in classrooms.

    > The character of the classroom changed markedly, especially at the elementary level, as projects began to compete with recitations as standard pedagogical procedure. Students and teachers alike tended to be more active, more mobile, and more informal in their relationships with one another. (pp. 305, 307)

    In *Education and the Rise of the Corporate State*, Joel Spring takes the ideas of Dewey, Kilpatrick, and Colin Scott on group work and traces their direct path into classrooms. Spring isolates specific teaching methods: the "socialized recitation" where students assume the role of teacher and review the lesson by either leading the recitation, developing a group discussion or variations of each; the "project method" put forth by Kilpatrick as an intentional group activity that has a socially useful end; and other methods that generated student group activities in the classroom. To demonstrate impact upon the classroom, Spring cites the abundance of articles on these methods, the books written by advocates of each, and the appearance of courses on these topics in teacher-education curricula. "Group learning experiences in the form of cooperative projects and socialized recitations," he concluded, "prepared the individual to be what David Riesman called in later years 'other directed.'" (Joel Spring, *Education and the Rise of the Corporate State*, Boston: Beacon, 1972, pp. 49–61).

Dissent from these views of reformers' impact upon teaching practice comes from economists Samuel Bowles and Herbert Gintis, and historians Michael Katz, David Tyack and Arthur Zilversmit. In *Schooling in Capitalist America*, Bowles and Gintis argue that a coalition of business leaders and liberal professionals spearheaded successful reforms that changed the public schools' administration and curriculum (for example, the comprehensive high school, standardized testing, ability grouping, vocational education, and the concentrating of authority in school professionals). However, they say, "the schools have changed little in substance" in the exchange between teachers and students. Because pedagogical reformers lacked popular support and avoided criticizing corporate capitalism, Bowles and Gintis argue, they "worked in vain for a humanistic and egalitarian education." No direct evidence of classroom instruction is offered except for what other researchers cited. (Samuel Bowles and Herbert Gintis, *Schooling in Capitalist America*, New York: Basic Books, 1976, pp. 43, 181, 200).

Michael Katz argues in *Class, Bureaucracy, and Schools* that instructional reform stopped at the classroom door because the movement itself was essentially conservative in outlook and aimed at bureaucratic changes. Katz refers also to *Middletown* to support his arguments. He does acknowledge that historians cannot learn what happened in schools by studying what leading theorists wrote and said. Whether teaching changed during the progressive years, he said in 1971, cannot yet be answered by historians. (pp. 113–25)

David Tyack shares a similar perspective on the importance of bureaucracy in explaining the lack of change in teaching practice. He surveyed progressive reform and its consequences, both anticipated and unanticipated, between 1890–1940. Distinguishing among the varied strains of progressivism, Tyack described the success administrative progressives had in changing the structure and governance of public schools. Coalitions of professors, superintendents, foundation executives, and lay reformers, possessing a vision of a "one best system" based upon scientific school management, changed the landscape of American schooling through the strategic use of formal surveys of school systems, writings, conferences, and close contact with different networks of influential educators. Reformers did seek to eliminate inefficient classroom practices such as a uniform course of study, whole group instruction, and formal recitation, according to Tyack. (pp. 126–98) Using more primary sources on schools and classrooms than other researchers of this period, Tyack drew from city school surveys, teacher writings, newspaper articles, and autobiographies to conclude that the dreams of Dewey and his followers about exciting classrooms for children foundered on the very successes of the administrative progressives, especially in the cities.

A gifted teacher in a one-room school house might alone turn her class into Dewey's model of social learning, but changing a large city system was more difficult for Dewey's ideas of democratic education demanded substantial autonomy on the part of teachers and children—an autonomy which...teachers commonly lacked. Predictably, the call for a "new education" in urban school systems often brought more, not less red tape and administration, more forms to fill out and committees to attend, more supervisors, new tests for children to take, new jargon for old ideas. The full expression of Dewey's ideal of democratic education required fundamental change in the hierarchial structure of schools—and that was hardly the wish of those administrative progressives and their allies who controlled urban education. (pp. 197–8)

Arthur Zilversmit is the only historian thus far to focus upon classroom changes in order to determine how widespread progressive practices were in American elementary schools. His verdict: very little.

Zilversmit relied upon three indicators of the acceptance of progressive pedagogy. First, he argued, the curriculum of pre-1940 teacher-training institutions should reasonably mirror the extent of instructional reform since a skilled, alert, and knowledgable teacher is essential to a progressive classroom. Instead, he found in three national surveys of teacher education curricula that progressive ideas had spread minimally through both normal and college training courses of study. Second, Zilversmit investigated classroom furniture. Progressive educators took as a given the importance of movable desks and chairs for flexible seating and work space in classrooms, yet Zilversmit pointed out that in 1934 stationary school desks still accounted for almost 40 percent of *new* desks sold, not to mention those millions of old desks firmly bolted to the floor. A third sign of weak influence on school practice, according to Zilversmit, were the few specialists hired by school systems to promote mental health, i.e. social workers and school psychologists. Mental health of children, the commitment to the whole child, he argues, was a serious concern of progressive educators.

For the classroom itself, Zilversmit relied upon the Regents' Inquiry, an intensive evaluation of New York state schools between 1935–1938. Referring to 2 of the 12 volumes, he quotes extensively from each one's conclusions on the traditional instruction that evaluators found in urban, rural and suburban classrooms across the state. He concludes that the progressive ideas of the child-centered school left few marks on elementary schools. (Arthur Zilversmit, "The Failure of Preogressive Education, 1920–1940," in Lawrence Stone (ed.) *Schooling and Society*, Baltimore: John Hopkins Press, 1976, pp. 252–61).

For those who have written about these years when progressive vocabulary became the accepted language in educational discourse, opinion is divided on the question of impact of progressive ideas on the classroom. The evidence used is sparse, leans heavily upon the *Middletown* research, and refers infrequently to classrooms and schools. Despite the paucity of data on classrooms, historians trying to assess the spread of progressive practices in classrooms often take an all-or-nothing approach, and, except for Zilversmit, ignore the critical point of the extent of penetration. A systematic look at particular districts' schools and classrooms might confirm or refute some of the arguments advanced thus far while suggesting new lines of research and providing a more solid base of knowledge of what teachers did do in classrooms.

7. New York (City) Board of Education, *Thirty-Second Annual Report of the Superintendent of Schools*, (New York: Board of Education, 1930), p. 485; New York (City) Board of Education, *The First Fifty Years: A Brief Review of Progress, 1898–1948* (New York: Board of Education, 1949), p. 86; the last two comparisons with the size of the school system are mine.

8. Cohen, *Progressives and Urban School Reform*; Diane Ravitch, *The Great School Wars: New York City, 1805–1973* (New York: Basic Books, 1974); Diane Ravitch and Ronald Goodenow (eds.) *Educating An Urban People: The New York City Experience* (New York: Teachers College Press, 1981).

9. Cohen, p. 153.

10. On Maxwell as Superintendent, see Samuel P. Abelow, *Dr. William H. Maxwell, The First Superintendent of Schools of the City of New York*, (New York: Scheba Publishing Co., 1934); Selma C. Berrol, "William Henry Maxwell and a New Educational New York," *History of Education Quarterly*, 8 (1968), pp. 215–28; Ravitch, pp. 111–86.

11. *Who's Who in America, 1920–1921*, (Chicago: Marquis Co., 1921), 11, p. 895; *The First Fifty Years*, p. 92; Cohen, p. 110.

12. New York (City) Board of Education, *Thirtieth Annual Report of the Superintendent of Schools*, (New York: Board of Education, 1928), p. 53.

13. See New York (City) Board of Education, *Progress of the Public Schools, 1924–1929*, (New York: Board of Education, 1929); William O'Shea, "What Are The Progressive Steps of the New York City Schools," *Educational Review*, 74 (1927), pp. 99–103.

14. Cohen, pp. 129–32.

15. Cohen, pp. 159–60. While it is beyond the scope of this study, Campbell's embrace of the Activity Program remains an intriguing puzzle that deserves exploration, i.e. why does a Superintendent who characterized himself as an educational conservative in the midst of retrenchment decide to launch the largest experiment ever undertaken in the nation's history to reform the elementary public school curriculum and instruction?

16. C. B. J. Snyder, "A Stupendous Schoolhouse Problem," *American School Board Journal*, 66 (February, 1923), pp. 59–61; also see same journal, volume 65 (October, 1922), pp. 60–1.

17. *New York Times*, May 18, 1930, p. 9.

18. New York (City) Board of Education, *All The Children, 1935–1936* (New York: Board of Education, 1936), p. 120; *All The Children, 1942–1943*, p. 30.

19. New York (City) Board of Education, *Thirty-Third Annual Report of the Superintendent of Schools, 1930–1931* (New York: Board of Education, 1931), p. 615.

20. Harold Campbell, "Class Sizes in New York City," *The School Executive*, 55 (December, 1935), p. 139; *Thirty-Eighth Annual Report, 1935–1936*, p. 83.

21. *Report of Survey of Public School System, City of New York, 1924* (New York: Board of Education, 1929), p. 306.

22. ibid., pp. 1265–92.

23. ibid., pp. 1292–96, 1309.

24. *The First Fifty Years*, pp. 94–5.

25. O'Shea, "Progress of Public Schools," pp. 29–31; *The First Fifty Years*, p. 95; "Report of the Investigation of Regents Examinations by the First Assistants' Committee," *High Points*, 21 (December, 1939), pp. 14–29; "Report of the Regents Examination Committee," *High Points*, 22 (April, 1940), pp. 8–16.
26. *Twenty-Eighth Annual Report, 1925–1926*, pp. 176–7.
27. New York (City) Board of Education, junior high school report card, 1925; *The Handbook of Evander Childs High School, 1927–1928*, pp. 124.
28. *High Points*, 3 (December, 1921), pp. 30–1; *Teachers Manual of Julia Richman High School, 1924*, p. 2; *Practical Suggestions For Teachers*, (Bronx), 1926, pp. 28–31; *High Points*, 12 (October, 1930), pp. 52–5; *High Points*, 14 (April, 1932), pp. 44–8; Theodore Huebner, "Suggested Standards in the Supervision of Foreign Languages," *High Points*, 21, (November, 1939), pp. 7–10.
29. New York Principals Association, *The Principal*, November 14, 1921. (n. p.)
30. New York (City) Board of Education, *The Teachers' Handbook: A Guide For Use in the Schools of the City of New York* (New York: Board of Superintendents, 1921), p. 27.
31. ibid., pp. 22–31.
32. *Survey, 1924*, pp. 841–9.
33. Samuel Tenenbaum, "Supervision—Theory and Practice," *The School Executive*, 59 (March, 1940), pp. 28–9.
34. The comparison with driving and rules for the road comes from Rebecca Barr and Robert Dreeben, "Instruction in Classrooms," in Lee Shulman (ed.) *Review of Research in Education* (Itasca, Ill.: F. E. Peacock Publishers, 1977), p. 114.
35. Arthur Jersild et al., "An Evaluation of Aspects of the Activity Program in the New York City Public Elementary Schools," *Journal of Experimental Education*, 8 (December, 1939), p. 166; John Loftus, "New York's Large-Scale Experimentation With an Activity Program," *Progressive Education*, 17 (February, 1940), p. 117.
36. *The Activity Program: The Report of a Survey* (Albany, N.Y.: State Department of Education, 1941), pp. 20–1.
37. John Loftus, "The Nature of the Activity Program," mimeo, September 9, 1936, p. 2.
38. *The New York Times*, July 9, 1941.
39. Loftus, *Progressive Education*, p. 117.
40. Arthur Jersild, et. al. "Studies of Elementary School Classes in Action," *Journal of Experimental Education*, 9 (June, 1941), pp. 299, 301.
41. ibid.
42. Jersild, December, 1939, p. 196.
43. *The Activity Program: Report of a Survey*, p. 47.
44. ibid., p. 41.
45. ibid., p. 53.
46. ibid.; Also see Ralph Tyler, *Perspectives on American Education* (Chicago: Science Research Associates, 1976), pp. 36–7.
47. J. Cayce Morrison, "The Curriculum Experiment With the Activity Program: Its Implications for the Further Study of Education," in *New York Society for Experimental Study of Education Yearbook* (New York: Thesis Publishing Co., 1943), p. 28: *All the Children*, 1940–1941, p. 62.

48. *The New York Times*, May 18, 1930, p. 9.
49. ibid., February 16, 1940, p. 2. Also see the use of the word "progressive" in Superintendent O'Shea's *Progress of the Public Schools, 1924–1929*.
50. New York (City) Board of Education, *Exploring a First Grade Curriculum*. (New York: Bureau of Reference, Research, and Statistics, 1947), Forword pp. 1–7, 86–90.
51. *Activity Program: Report of a Survey*, p. 143.
52. See, for example, "An Experiment With the Dalton Plan in the Wadleigh High School," *Survey*, 1924, pp. 205–7; *High Points*, 9 (March 1927), pp. 26–7.
53. Thomas H. Briggs, "The Practices of Best High School Teachers," *School Review*, 43 (December, 1935), pp. 745–52.
54. Benjamin Rosenthal, "A Case Study of a Lesson in American History," *High Points*, 22 (November, 1940), pp. 21–39.
55. ibid.
56. ibid., pp. 31–9.
57. Marvin Lazerson suggested to me this line of reasoning. Also see David K. Cohen and Barbara Neufeld, "The Failure of High School and the Progress of Education," *Daedalus*, 110 (Summer, 1981), pp. 76–7.
58. Joseph Kett pointed out this line of argument to me.
59. Mira Scott Frank, "Dedication of Valverde Elementary School," mimeo, 1951, n.p.
60. *Taxpayers' Review*, October 12, 1934.
61. *Who's Who in America, 1936–1937*, 19 (Chicago: Marquis Co., 1937), p. 1814; Denver Public Schools, "Classroom Interests," April 21, 1936, p. 3; A. L. Threlkeld, "Dr. Dewey's Philosophy and the Curriculum, *Curriculum Journal*, 8 (April, 1937), pp. 164–6.
62. School District of Denver, *Twenty-Eighth Annual Report of Superintendent of Schools, 1930–1931* (Denver, Colorado, 1931), p. 45; *Thirty-Eighth Annual Report, 1940–1941*, p. 63; *Twenty-Sixth Annual Report, 1928–1929*, pp. 33–6.
63. *Twentieth Annual Report, 1922–1923*, p. 64; Denver Public Schools, *School Review*, June, 1934, p. 3.
64. U.S. Office of Education, *Statistics of City School Systems, 1933–1934*, Bulletin, 1935, No. 2 (Washington, D.C.: Government Printing Office, 1936), p. 6.
65. Jesse Newlon, "The Need of a Scientific Curriculum Policy for Junior and Senior High Schools," *Educational Administration and Supervision*, 3 (May, 1917), p. 267.
66. ibid., p. 266.
67. Denver Public Schools, *Denver Program of Curriculum Revision*, Monograph No. 12 (Denver Board of Education, 1927), pp. 17–21; Jesse Newlon and A. L. Threlkeld, "The Denver Curriculum Revision Program," in National Society for the Study of Education, 26th Yearbook, *Curriculum-Making: Past and Present*, Part 1, (Bloomington, Ill. 1926), pp. 231–3.
68. *Denver Program of Curriculum Revision*, p. 14; Newlon and Threlkeld, p. 232.
69. *Denver Program of Curriculum Revision*, pp. 22–7.
70. ibid., p. 28.

71. ibid., pp. 30–1.
72. Denver Public Schools, "General Information and Courses: Senior High School Courses of Study," 1929 (Denver, 1929), p. 28.
73. Newlon and Threlkeld, p. 235.
74. Denver Public Schools, *School Review*, March, 1929, p. 2.
75. *Thirty Schools Tell Their Story*, 5 (New York: Harpers and Brothers, 1942), p. 146.
76. See chapter on Denver schools in *Thirty Schools*, pp. 146–212 and Harold Spears, *The Emerging High School Curriculum* (New York: American Book Co., 1940), pp. 243–73.
77. Spears, pp. 268–9.
78. Denver Public Schools, "North High School Master Schedule, 1938–1939;" also the 1938 and 1939 *Thunderbolt* and *Viking*, student yearbooks for Manual training and North High Schools, respectively.
79. Denver Public Schools, "Handbook for the Application of Progressive Education Principles to Secondary Education," mimeo, September, 1936, pp. 45–46, 50.
80. H. H. Giles et al., *Exploring the Curriculum* (New York: Harpers and Brothers, 1942), 2, pp. 320–8.
81. Denver Public Schools, "Classroom Interests," January, 1934, p. 11.
82. East High School Core Classes, "Our Education," 1938, pp. 12–13.
83. *Thirty Schools*, p. 182.
84. C. L. Cushman, "Conference Appraises Denver Secondary Program," *Curriculum Journal*, 9 (November, 1938), pp. 316–7.
85. *Thirty Schools*, p. 210.
86. North High School, "Master Schedule," 1938–44, mimeo; East High School, "History of East High School," 1948, pp. 112–3.
87. Denver *Post*, October 13, 1954, p. 25.
88. District of Columbia, *Report of Board of Education, 1921–1922* (Washington, D.C.: Government Printing Office, 1922), pp. 96, 97, 103.
89. *Who's Who in America, 1936–1937*, 19 (Chicago: Marquis Co., 1937), p. 230.
90. *Report of Board of Education, 1921–1922*, p. 137.
91. *Report of Board of Education, 1929–1930*, p. 71; *Report of Board of Education*, "School Achievements in Twenty Years," June 30, 1941, pp. 106–8.
92. *Report of Board of Education, 1910–1911*, p. 35.
93. *Report on Survey of the Public School System of the District of Columbia by the Bureau of Efficiency, 1928* (Washington: Government Printing Office, 1928), pp. 50–5; George Strayer, *Report of a Survey of the Public Schools of the District of Columbia, 1949*, p. 388.
94. ibid., pp. 401–3.
95. *Report of Board of Education, 1929–1930*, p. 107; Strayer, p. 444.
96. Bureau of Efficiency Survey, 1928, p. 69.
97. ibid., p. 70; Strayer, pp. 439–41.
98. ibid., pp. 438–9.
99. ibid., p. 441.
100. Bureau of Efficiency Survey, 1928, p. 94.
101. *Report of Board of Education, 1929–1930*, pp. 79–80.

102. Strayer, p. 409.
103. Amy King, "Evolution of the Study Group," *Journal of the Education Association of the District of Columbia*, June, 1936, p. 28.
104. Strayer, pp. 81–2.
105. *Report of the Board of Education, 1923–1924*, pp. 92–7.
106. Mayme Lewis, "Report of Visit to Horace Mann School, New York," *The Journal of the Columbia Educational Association*, May, 1925, pp. 28–9 and May, 1932, p. 35; Pearl E. Minor, "A Unit in Creative Writing," *National Educational Outlook Among Negroes*, May, 1939, pp. 11–12.
107. See issues of *Journal of the Columbian Educational Association* for July, 1925 and February, 1926.
108. *Washington Post*, April 3, 1938 and October 27, 1940; Julia Hahn, "Some Whys and Hows of the Activity Program," *Childhood Education*, 9 (January, 1933), pp. 206–10.
109. George G. Handorf, "An Historical Study of the Superintendency of Dr. Frank W. Ballou in the Public School System of the District of Columbia" (Unpublished Ed. D. dissertation, American University, 1962), p. 190.
110. Strayer, pp. 427–8, 443–7.
111. ibid., p. 407.
112. ibid., p. 458.
113. ibid.
114. Central High School, *Handbook, 1926*, pp. 43–4.
115. Central High School, *The Bulletin*, all issues from 1925–1938.
116. Mary Gibson Hundley, *The Dunbar Story: 1870–1955* (New York: Vantage Press, 1965), p. 66; Thomas Sowell, "Black Excellence: A History of Dunbar High," *The Public Interest* (Spring, 1974).
117. For background on the concept of the Talented Tenth, see Sowell article for description of its cultivation at Dunbar prior to 1954; also see essay by W. E. B. Dubois, "Talented Tenth," in *Negro Problems* (no editor given) (New York: James Pott Co., 1903), pp. 33–75; and his "Education and Work," 1930, in Herbert Aptheker (ed.) *The Education of Black People* (Amherst: University of Massachusetts Press, 1973), pp. 61–82.
118. Dunbar High School, *Crimson and Black Handbook, 1924–1925*, pp. 11, 15, 47–8, 70, 81.
119. See Eastern High School, *The Easterner*, February, 1921, pp. 8–21.
120. *Report of the Board of Education, 1919–1920*, pp. 372–3; Dunbar High School, *Liber Anni, 1929–1930* (student yearbook); *Dunbar Observer*, January 28, 1932, no page given in student newspaper.
121. Dunbar High School, *The Dunbar News Reel*, April 23, 1942, p. 2.

3

Rural and Urban Schools, 1920–1940

A Hillsdale County (Michigan) teacher in a one-room school wrote her superintendent in 1939 of the changes she had initiated in her classroom since attending a summer session on a scholarship from the W. K. Kellogg Foundation. Leona Helmick reported what she had done at Grubby Knoll School.

School began one September morning. Enrollment was taken. Classes were called by a 'tap' (Children turn in their seats), 'tap' (children rise from their seats), and 'tap' (children pass to front of room where recitation occurred). This same call bell had called classes for fourteen years before this. Exact assignments were given in all subjects, an average of twenty-five classes were called (to recite to the teacher) and by much hurrying, school was dismissed at four o'clock.... We did art work once a week for enjoyment and training....

Now the little bell is no longer used. The children come in large groups and sit with their teacher in a large circle at the front of the room. Here they read and talk as the need may be. Much of the studying is done here. Quick pupils assist slower ones near them. This eliminates walking around. When the group is finished another group comes. Arithmetic is privately worked out at their seats with some drill and blackboard work. Each one working according to his own ability and speed.

Instead of learning a lot of rules in grammar that many of them never understand and others soon forget, we study birds and write stories about them. We publish a bi-monthly paper. In this the children volunteer original poems, stories, and articles....

We still follow the textbook in Geography although we enrich it with units on travel, transportation, special studies of products and places. Last year we did a good unit on Michigan.

I have learned to think of the needs of the pupils.[1]

At just about the same time Helmick wrote her superintendent, *Time* magazine carried on its cover the portrait of Frederick L. Redefer, Executive Secretary of the Progressive Education Association (PEA). Pronouncing that progressive education had "strongholds in the suburbs of greater New York, Chicago, and Los Angeles," the movement was now "predominately a public school affair" even "transforming" major school systems such as Denver, San Francisco, Los Angeles, New York City, and Detroit.[2]

John Dewey, however, writing shortly before his death in 1952, viewed the changes in schools that had occurred as a result of the progressive movement quite differently than *Time*.

> The most widespread and marked success of the progressive movement has been in bringing about a significant change in the life conditions in the classroom. There is a greater awareness of the needs of the growing human being, and the personal relations between teachers and students have been humanized and democratized. But the success in these respects is as yet limited; it is largely atmospheric; it hasn't yet really penetrated and permeated the foundations of the educational institution. The older gross manifestations of the method, of education by fear and repression—physical, social and intellectual—which was the established norm for the educational system before the progressive movement began have, generally speaking, been eliminated.... The fundamental authoritarianism of the old education persists in various modified forms.
>
> There is a great deal of talk about education being a cooperative enterprise in which the teachers and students participate democratically, but there is far more talk about it than the doing of it. To be sure, many teachers, particularly in the kindergarten and the elementary schools, take the children into sharing with them to an extent impossible and inconceivable under the old system....
>
> In the secondary schools,... however, there isn't much sharing on the part of teachers in the needs and concerns of those whom they teach....[3]

Time, Leona Helmick's report, and Dewey's reflections suggest the difficulties of determining the extent to which progressive theory entered even one Hillsdale County classroom. To what extent these ideas turned up in rural and urban classrooms in the two decades between the world wars is one of a number of questions that this chapter will try to answer.

RURAL MICHIGAN CLASSROOMS

Hillsdale was one of seven rural Michigan counties that participated in a three year project aimed at improving rural life through the schools. Between 1936 and 1939, the W. K. Kellogg Foundation provided funds to "give teachers and administrators a clearer understanding of the philosophy, psychology, and procedures involved in the newer concepts of education." Through college extension courses, weekend gatherings at the Foundation's camps, and special summer college courses teachers were expected to carry back to their one-room schoolhouses new skills and knowledge to use as means for improving rural education.[4]

In these seven counties there were over 1,300 teachers working in one-room schoolhouses. Their average level of schooling was two years beyond the high school diploma. In a remarkable document, 193* of these teachers who attended Kellogg Foundation-sponsored courses, workshops, or summer sessions, wrote to Henry J. Otto, consultant to the Foundation, describing "the changes in classroom teaching ... the administrative problems which had arisen in connection with these changes, and the procedures which were used to meet these problems."[5]

The accounts ranged from sheer ecstasy over rejuvenated teaching to an obvious, and almost embarassing, absence of any change whatsoever. In order to assemble a coherent portrait of these rural teachers' class activities, I grouped the reported practices into categories extracted from progressive education literature on appropriate classroom techniques and constructed the following table.

Table 3.1   Reports from 190 One-Room School Teachers in Michigan Who Participated in Kellogg-Funded Activities

Category	Number of Teachers	Percentage
Physical Changes in Room		
a. Remove/modify student desks	32	17
b. Make room home-like, (e.g. curtains, sofa, tables, etc.)	18	9
c. Create centers for students to read, work, etc.	32	17
d. Did at least two of above	19	10
Grouping Changes		
Teachers report combining classes, using small groups determined by ability, individualizing instruction, etc.	40	21
Schedule Changes		
Teachers report any change in daily or weekly schedule aimed at introducing a new practice, different subject, or modified grouping.	37	19
Increased Pupil Participation		
Teachers report change in governance of class with students leading discussion, running clubs, electing officers.	43	23

(*Continued*)

* Because 3 of the teachers were listed as anonymous, I have used 190 reports in all of the analyses.

Category	Number of Teachers	Percentage
Provisioning Teachers report seeking out books, supplies, equipment to satisfy changes made in instruction, curriculum, and other parts of the program.	43	23
Activity Method Teachers report using method, describing projects, and integration of two or more subjects.	80	42
Extracurricular Activities Teachers report initiating clubs (hot lunch, Mothers' Club, 4–H, etc.).	53	28
Changing Report Cards Teachers report using a card that focuses upon child's emotional development and basic subjects; does not use letters A–F	25	13
Making Curriculum Relevant (excluding activity method) Teachers report use of field trips, current events, examples from daily life in instruction, etc.	77	40

Substantial numbers of teachers reported the use of activity methods, including the use of projects to correlate different subjects and efforts to tie curriculum more closely to the lives of children. Fewer teachers reported other changes in how they grouped children, modified the daily schedule, altered report cards, increased pupil participation, and rearranged class space—a pattern resembling teacher selection of classroom practices elsewhere.

Since these figures summarize what individual teachers reported, no sense of how many teachers employed one or more of these practices is conveyed. The table below suggests the breadth of teachers' activities.

No criteria yet exist for determining how many activities and which ones define a teacher as progressive. Aware of all the problems inherent in developing such criteria, I constructed two in order to analyze the data: the number of progressive techniques teachers reported they used and any rearrangement of classroom space. Notions of progressive practice generally included numerous teacher behaviors (grouping practices, student activities, pupil participation, arrangement of space, etc.) Also the tight linkage between use of classroom space and furniture was a commonly expressed and sought after fundamental in building a student-centered classroom.

Almost half of these Michigan one-room teachers reported using only two techniques; one-quarter used four or more practices. Depending upon

Table 3.2   Summary of Teacher Activities

Number of Categories Reported	Number of Teachers	Percentage
0	11	6.0
1	58	30.0
2	36	19.0
3	34	18.0
4	27	14.0
5	9	5.0
6	9	5.0
7	3	1.5
8	2	1.0
9	1	.5
10	0	0.0
11	0	0.0
	190	100.0

how much weight an observer gives to rearrangment of space as a sign of progressive approaches, particularly in these one-room schoolhouses where bolted-down desks were common, of the 51 teachers (27 percent) who used 4 or more new techniques, 2 out of 3 made some change in the room (e.g. created space for learning centers; unbolted desks and put them of skids; placed curtains on windows, installed tables, sofa, etc.). Of the 24 teachers who reported 5 or more new practices, 87 percent had made some physical change in the room.

Such data have obvious limits. The teachers are an atypical sample, only 15 percent of total staff in 7 countries, and these were either recruited to attend or sought out Foundation-supported courses. Moreover, self-reports are selective, lack independent verification, and often suggest efforts to please donors or supervisors rather than offer a realistic assessment of practice. A number of researchers have underscored the irresistible inflation of teacher estimates of their innovativeness. Despite these limits, there are some decided strengths to the data. They yield a glimpse of how progressive concepts get selected and put into classroom practice. Through such varied filters as professors of education, foundation reformers, books, and other teachers, classroom practice changed unevenly among teachers. Second, differing views among teachers regarding progressivism appear.[6]

Alice Dean in Calhoun County, for example, let students work individually one period a day on arithmetic problems, helping one another when necessary. In the last two years, she said, this was "the biggest change in teaching that I have undertaken." Or Leslie Engle, another Calhoun County teacher, reported her new system of recording each student's personal, family, and school information as the sole innovation. Other teachers instituting such changes as a science center, adding tables to a room, setting up a hot-lunch program in the face of a hostile parent community or indifferent superintendent, considered such changes as personal triumphs and, in some instances, viewed themselves as progressive teachers.[7]

Finally, the data make unmistakably clear that some rural teachers who were isolated from one another and received little support from superiors, nonetheless introduced some new practices into their rooms. However, the majority found it difficult to install more than two progressive techniques over a three year period.

RURAL CLASSROOMS ACROSS THE NATION

Was southwestern Michigan a microcosm of rural schools across the country? Yes and no. The "yes" half of the answer comes from abundant evidence that progressive methods appeared in individual rural schools, both newly consolidated and one-room buildings across the country. Highly publicized experimental rural schools garnered national limelight in professional journals throughout the 1920s and early 1930s: Marie Turner Harvey's work at the Porter School in Kirksville, Missouri; Ellsworth Collins efforts in developing the project method in McDonald County, Missouri; Fannie Dunn's work at the Quaker Grove School in Warren County, New Jersey.[8]

There were many less publicized efforts to introduce progressive techniques into Black and white rural schools. Some of these instances were collected in a survey conducted by the Progressive Education Association's Committee on Experimental Schools in 1937. The Committee sent letters to over 300 schools and districts in 43 states. Seventy-eight replied; 44 came from public schools. Of these, rural teachers, supervisors, and superintendents in Connecticut, New York, North Carolina, Arizona, and California reported curriculum revision, integration of various content areas into school-wide programs, activity programs, and other student-centered approaches.[9]

Even less well known are the decisions individual teachers quietly made when they tried different methods at great expense to their salaries and their limited leisure time. Consider Mary Stapleton from Cuttingsville, Vermont.

> In the fall of 1932, I had an enrollment of about 20 pupils in all the grades. My superintendent told me about the Winnetka method (an approach that stresses individual instructional materials matched to differences in pupils) and suggested my reading some books....
>
> During the fall and winter of 1932–33, I did a great deal of research work, and in the spring I developed the technic (*sic*) in spelling.... I divided the words into units of 25 or 30 words each according to (students') grade placement and ability. This method tests the children on words we want them to know before they study them and allows them to concentrate on the words

they miss in the test, rather than wasting time studying words they already know.

This plan in spelling proved so successful that I decided to try to develop arithmetic the next fall.... I collected all of my textbooks together with my state courses of study and divided the year's work of each grade into 8 units, each with 3 or 4 sub-units. The next problem was the development of a set of diagnostic tests covering each detail....

I found it helpful to exchange tests with other teachers. For a small sum I obtained some tests from Winnetka. I cut out examples and problems from old books, pasted them on cardboard and placed them in my files. The last and perhaps the most important job was to supply the children with self-instructive practice material. Printed drill pads in arithmetic and English have been found helpful....

By the end of the year I had fewer failures than ever before. The children had begun to realize the objectives of this instruction and since there would be no repeating of grades, it was up to each to progress at his own rate of speed....

The activity side of the instruction can be worked out effectively in the social studies program.... For example, an activity dealing with Indian life is an opportunity for children from the first to the eighth grades to make a contribution.... The question that confronted me as I worked out my units was: where can I get the materials to construct these activities? The question was answered by appealing to the children.... [10]

The "no" half of the answer comes from numerous state and local studies of rural schooling since 1920. They provide a backdrop against which the rural Michigan data can be compared to determine what teaching conditions and classroom practices were elsewhere in the nation.

Rural schools were diverse. One-room schools in West Virginia hollows, rickety shacks on a scrub brush half-acre on a Mississippi plantation, and a newly plastered room in a recently built Iowa consolidated school merely skim the varied surface of rural schools. In 1920, almost half of all children enrolled in schools attended rural schools, that is, ones located in the "open country," and villages but not places over 2,500 people. For the most part, rural will refer to schools with one or two teachers, village schools and ones consolidated through the closing of nearby one-room buildings. [11]

More often than not these buildings were old, furnished with antique equipment, and isolated. Teachers had little education beyond high school. They were young (median age 21–23), had little experience, and were mostly female. Turnover was high; wages were low. From $300 to $800 per year (1920) for one-teacher schools, depending on the state, wages ran $500 to $700 less for jobs in village and town schools. Class sizes ranged from 20 to 60 students of various ages. Fifteen year olds sat in the back of the room towering over the seven year olds who sat in the front row of double-seat desks. The major difficulty was having many grades in one room, i.e. 30 pupils scattered across 8 grades with the teacher required to instruct in all subject areas for each grade.[12]

Few writers at this time sang the praises of the rural school. Progressive rhetoric and wisdom located the one-room school somewhere between the flintlock rifle and the wooden plow. "Devoted reformers, philosophers, and educators," a U.S. Bureau of Education specialist in rural education wrote, "have been traveling the length and breadth of the land preaching the inefficiency of the little old red schoolhouse." Preaching and consolidation cut into the numbers of such schools. From an estimated 195,000 one-teacher schools in 1917, the number fell to 153,000 enrolling 4,000,000 children a decade later. Still, some states contained many one-teacher schools. In South Dakota, for example, four out of five teachers taught in one-room schools. Half of the teachers in North Dakota did and over 40 percent of the teachers in Iowa, Montana, Nebraska, and Vermont worked in these schools.[13]

What did teachers do all day in these isolated yet densely packed rooms? In the mid-1920s, a Teachers College graduate student surveyed 550 one-room school teachers in 24 states. Verne McGuffey found teachers reporting that they advised the school board on classroom needs (78%), visited parents (78%), provided drinking water (74%), oversaw school toilets (83%), and regulated heat and ventilation (88%). Instructionally,

- 73% taught all subjects in 8 grades
- 82% kept several groups busy while one recited
- 75% presented subject matter in short periods
- 66% planned and executed work with little or no supervision[14]

Look at teaching practices in 18 Pennsylvania counties with mainly rural schools in 1920. Reports came from 62 percent of the teachers in one-room schools. Median age of teachers (of whom 76 percent were female) was 23. Most began teaching at 19. Almost four out of five teachers lacked a high school diploma or any formal teacher training. Class size averaged 26 in the 18 counties with about one-quarter of the teachers reporting enrollments over 35 students. Remember that each class contained students spread over eight grades.[15]

When teachers say how many recitations they had, that is, how many times a day they questioned students in each grade within the class, figures stagger teachers today. One out of four teachers said they had conducted 30 or more recitations a day. The median was 26. Since the school day averaged 5½ hours (330 minutes), apart from recess and lunch, teachers reporting 30 or more recitations met daily for at least 10 minutes with one or more students, dismissed them, met with another group, and so on. Even the State Department of Education's formal course of study recommended 23 daily recitations. All of this suggests the rugged schedule a teacher in a one-room school followed, according to both expectations and self-reports.[16]

Shortly after the Pennsylvania study, Orville Brim, professor at Ohio State University, led a survey team that evaluated Texas rural schools in 1922. Brim examined the published curriculum, surveyed county superintendents and teachers on how the curriculum was used, and, in a step unusual among researchers then and now, trained a set of observers to describe classrooms in 230 rural schools. These one-teacher schools, as elsewhere in the country, contained up to eight grades. Texas teachers, like their counterparts in other states had limited education, received low wages, and faced similar sized classes. In these one- and two-teacher schools the short class period of 2 to 10 minutes, 24 times per day, was described.[17]

What did teachers do in these brief episodes, called recitations? Brim and his colleagues summarized teacher practices:

- Drill   34%
- Formal textbook recitation   27%
- Meaning of text sought   27%
- Discussion of vital questions   4%
- Enjoyment   5%
- Construction work   4%

The textbook was the primary source of the lesson (88%) with little use of current events and children's experience (8%), according to Brim's team. The investigators found that virtually no special work or projects were given to students (found in 3% of classes).[18]

Brim's final summary of what he and his team saw in recitations follows:

> In practically all the work observed, the teacher is concerned in drilling the children upon some facts they are supposed to know or in asking questions that call for textbook answers. Occasions for thinking are few. Little, almost no, attempt is made to enrich a child's life with new interests.... Work does not grip the pupils. They add little to the facts of the lesson.... The teacher then arbitrarily assigns the next lesson in the text without any effort to develop interest or insight. The class is returned to its seat to memorize the text for the next recitation. Here they work blindly or half-heartedly or idly sit, with occasional admonitions from the teacher to study their lessons.

This, Brim concludes, is the picture in "70 to 85 percent of the schools" in all parts of the state.[19]

In other states throughout the 1920s and 1930s the rigors of teaching all subjects to a few students scattered over the grades produced in one-teacher schools the staccato series of brief recitations bracketed by opening exercises, lunch and recess. In North Dakota, to cite an instance, actual daily programs from one-room schools were collected in 1928 for a

Master's thesis. For a school with 24 pupils in School Number Three, Norway District, Traill County, the teacher held 22 recitations, averaging about 15 minutes each between 9:15 in the morning and 4:00 in the afternoon with 2 recesses and an hour for lunch. In the same county, School Number Three in the Belmont District had 13 students. Twenty-one recitations, also averaging about the same time, within the same length school day, were held. For a Cass County school where the new Rural Course of Study was being implemented the teacher's daily program called for 22 recitations, about 15 minutes each, for 19 students although in this case the teacher had grouped students by primary, intermediate, and grammar levels rather than by grades.[20]

One researcher summarized 11 studies identifying instructional problems of over 3,200 rural teachers in over 20 states. All of the studies were based upon teacher reports of their problems. The similarity in problems disclosed by these investigations in striking. The researcher distilled into a list the diverse problems described by teachers. Heading that list was the category of inadequate time. Teachers complained that they lacked time to:

- prepare plans for every subject for all grades
- help individual students
- allow for pupil activities

"There is general agreement in these studies," she concluded, "that the most frequent and most difficult problems of rural teachers are due to the one-room ungraded type of organization...."[21]

Yet ingenuity and persistence in the face of these obstacles turned up, suggesting that teachers, like most other people, did the best they could with what they had. On the ever-present problem of insufficient materials for seatwork, for example, Stella Lucien of Lewistown, Montana described what she did.

> I obtain one copy of Laidlaw's *Silent Reading Seat Work* for each grade. Many of these lessons direct the child to make some article, such as a bird house, a bubble pipe, etc. I cut out such lessons and paste them on cardboard. We then have seat work which may be used over and over without additional cost. We keep them in boxes and use them year after year.

Teacher Ruth Cederburg of Firth, Idaho wrote how she got primary students to be neat.

> I tacked a strong string across the front of the room; on this I fastened a balloon in front of each row of desks. Each evening before dismissal, aisles and desks were examined. If every child in a row had tidy desks and clean aisles the balloon in front of that row remained up. But if a single child had an untidy aisle or desk the balloon was taken down and remained down the following day. It was not long before every balloon remained up.[23]

RURAL BLACK SCHOOLS

None of these studies mention specifically black rural schools. Plagued by the same working conditions described before, untrained, poorly paid teachers with little formal education, teaching with few books and materials, faced the same structural problems that affected how they taught: pupils of different ages spread over eight grades, mandates from school board and superintendent to cover all subjects, and insufficient time to do everything.

Fisk University sociologist Charles Johnson directed the 1924 survey of Louisiana black schools. His team found the same dreary catalogue of problems in their visits to 132 one- and two-teacher schools familiar to informed observers of rural schools in other states. A typical situation in these schools, representing 65 percent of all black schools in the state, according to Johnson, was captured in a description of the Shelton School in a Delta parish in eastern Louisiana.

Approaching the church in which the school was housed, the field workers saw two small privies surrounded by thick Delta mud next to the front entrance. Inside the school 60 students spanning 7 grades sat next to one another on long wooden benches, fidgeting while they listened to an overweight teacher talk. Because of the chill in the morning air, there was much shifting around to allow students to get closer to warm areas near the small stove in the back of the room. No ventilation in the room stirred the air except for the draughts that came through the many cracks in the floor and walls. Smudged darkly with smoke, the walls held kerosene lamps. One of the lamps hung from an equally dark ceiling. Just above the pulpit, at the rear of the room, a washstand stood with a cracked pitcher. The room was crowded.

The visitors watched the teacher pass out two half-sheets of paper to each pupil saying, "It's got to do you all day, so be careful with it." She looked at one observer and said: "We don't have no pencils; we don't have no books; we don't have anything." She looked back at the class and began giving out assignments in history and spelling, grade by grade, to the restless but quiet students.

> Take pages 45 to 50, seventh grade. Sixth grade take pages 20 to 30. Now read this and tell me what you read when I come back....
>
> All right, fourth and fifth grade, spelling. The first word is *correspond*. It means to write people. Second, *instrument*—something you use. Do you know any *instrument* you'd like to play? Come on, talk up. Do you have a speller, Fred. No? Well, just sit and listen. You'll just have to do without. Third, *examination*, sometimes we have *yes* and *no*—that's examination. Fourth, *tennis*—that's a game. Fifth, *ninety*, counting from one to ninety. All right, that's your spelling. Use them in sentences.

The teacher, walking around the room with a switch in her hand, then moved to reading for the lower grades. She read a single line from a book and the children repeated the line. She completed the lesson in that manner.[24]

Johnson also offered a portrait of a one-teacher school that, in his judgment, "stands in sharp contrast to the mass of one-teacher schools in the state." The Brooks School, a tiny white-washed frame building on a cleared plot of ground in East Feliciana Parish, received a team visitor the week before Christmas. On a table in the room was a class-built scene of the manger and the Christ child. The work table in the rear and the book shelves along the side of the room were covered in bright red and yellow oil cloth while the shelves in the rear of the room contained water glasses individually labeled for the students. The room was spotless.

As one group of children sat in their seats making gifts for a party, another group stood at the work table making "favors" with scissors, paper, and paste. The teacher moved from group to group quietly listening and giving advice when asked.

The class had just completed a unit on cotton. The teacher who had worked on a farm had shown pictures of the various stages of cotton production and actual plants. The class had gone through the process from seed to clothes with all the grades, using arithmetic and reading where appropriate. In the first grade she used flash cards marked COTTON and related words. In second and third grades, pupils made sentences about the plant, and in sixth and seventh grades they wrote short stories. On many occasions, the visitor was told, all of the children participated in discussion. Even with all of the grades and subjects to cover, the teacher moved the class through the subjects in an orderly manner, the team worker reported.[25]

The Brooks School was an exception. Of 100 teachers, 75 had never done a unit that included a project or similar activity. The 25 teachers who reported that they had done projects listed Indian life, gardening, products of Louisiana, health, sewing, cooking, and life at home. Student participation in school governance was nonexistent: of 132 one-room schools, 115 teachers either said they had no student government at all or did not respond.[26]

PHOTOS AND WRITTEN ACCOUNTS OF RURAL CLASSROOMS

This coarse-grained picture of black and white rural schools began with Hillsdale County teacher Leona Helmick and her colleagues in southwestern Michigan who had received some formal exposure to progressive methods of teaching. I had asked whether these one-teacher schools were a microcosm of the rest of the country. Criss-crossing the country, a number of state and national studies suggested yes and no answers. There were numerous instances of progressive practices but they seemed to be tiny coral reefs in a vast ocean of teacher-centered patterns of instruction.

The final data that I offer are 103 classroom descriptions (excluding the 190 rural Michigan teachers) I collected from 32 states in every region of the country. (See Figures 3.1 and 3.2.) Does this data converge with or contradict the diverse studies already reviewed?

While the 103 photos and written accounts differ from the sources used in the studies of rural schools described above they, nonetheless, display a rough symmetry with that data. Teacher-centered patterns of instruction register strongly; student-centered practices scale no higher than 40% with most falling 25% or less. Very few of these 103 teachers tried projects or centers; they show up in less than 10 percent of the elementary school classrooms. Progressive practices, as defined in these categories, existed in rural classrooms nationally but were probably a minority.

One curious note is the high percentage of group instruction and class activities in the mixed pattern of teaching. Half of the teachers used a blend of large and small group instruction accompanied by work with individual students; almost half of the classrooms had activities where a mix of student-centered and teacher-centered approaches occurred. Compared to the other settings, these percentages are high and may stem from factors within the rural classroom unlike any faced by teachers in city schools. With students spread among several grades in one room, for example, teachers would generally call upon a few students to recite near the teachers' desk, leaving the rest of the class to work on different assigned tasks until they were called to the recitation bench. Students working in groups and helping one another in one-room schools, then, may explain why practices in ungraded rural schools varied from those in graded urban schools.

The dominant patterns of instruction were teacher-centered and mixed—similar to, but not identical with, configurations that surfaced in the three cities. A later generation of reformers interested in constructing student-centered classrooms would look beyond the staccato recitations, rote instruction, poorly trained teachers, inadequate school rooms, and poverty wages of the 1920s and 1930s and see embryonic child-centered settings. Rural one-room teachers used mixed forms of grouping because students spread across eight grades required varying amounts of attention. To latter-day reformers this became individual instruction. Children helped one another with assigned lessons while the teacher listened to students recite at her desk. This helping behavior would come to be labeled "cross-age tutoring." The content of the curriculum would draw from rural concerns and daily life, a linkage that subsequent school reformers would admire. The family-like atmosphere of .the schoolhouse, where a school trustee was someone's uncle or the teacher a cousin of a child in the class, was exactly the climate that reformers sought to create decades later for large urban, graded schools.

Such classroom conditions in rural communities did create rough-hewn, atheoretical versions of some progressive practices. Indeed, some

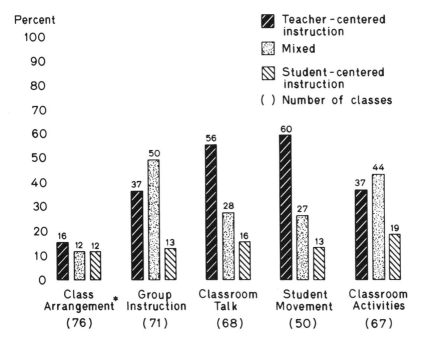

Figure 3.1   Patterns of Instruction in Rural Elementary Classrooms, 1920–1940

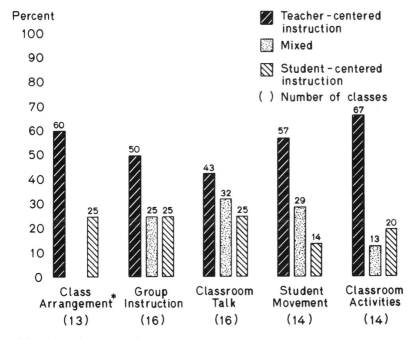

Figure 3.2   Patterns of Instruction in Rural High School Classrooms, 1920–1940.

teaching approaches grew naturally from the classroom as a workplace. Overwhelming many of these natural practices in most one-room school-houses, however, were traditional parent attitudes that reinforced part-time schooling, instruction in those basic skills that they had learned as children, and the ways that their teachers had handled classes; moreover, untrained and inexperienced teachers constructed classrooms where frequent and brief recitations drawn from inadequate textbooks narrowed student responses into what could be recaptured by rote—all of which were enforced by a birch sapling discipline. Few reformers recalled these realities and measured them against their enthusiasm for selected items in the one-room school.

PREVALENT TEACHING PRACTICES:
RURAL AND URBAN

So far I have tried to reconstruct teaching practices at the turn of the century and between World War I and II in three cities and rural schools. Now I turn to teaching practices that were prevalent nationally in the interwar period. A look at schools beyond the three cities I have described sets the stage for a summary of the similarities and differences that I found in both rural and urban schools played against a national backdrop. This summary is contrasted with teaching practices in 1900 to determine what changes, if any, had occurred in classrooms by World War II.

In examining evidence of what teachers did in their classrooms, I will concentrate on those teaching activities that were clearly targets for change: formal recitation, whole group instruction, the teaching of separate subjects, and lack of student activity or movement in the class. It is appropriate now to summarize the data drawn from classroom descriptions on group instruction, classroom activities, and student movement in the four settings. (See Figures 3.3 to 3.6.)

Recall that the teacher-centered pattern for group instruction included teaching the entire class as a unit, while a student-centered pattern referred to dividing the class into small groups and individual work. The mixed pattern described teachers who used varied grouping techniques ranging from teaching the whole class to independent work. Elementary classrooms in Denver and New York City showed the least amount of whole group teaching and the highest amounts of work in small groups. In these city high schools the favored grouping was the entire class, although percentages for rural classrooms were lower. Similarly, urban high school teachers infrequently divided their classes into groups while rural teachers showed a slightly higher percentage than their urban cousins in using small groups for instruction, although the number of teachers is small.

What emerges in these graphs are divergent patterns in grouping

Crossville, Tennessee,
One-Room School, c. 1935
(*Farm Security
Administration, Library of
Congress*).

White Plains, Georgia,
One-Room School, 1941
(*Farm Security
Administration, Library of
Congress*).

Questa, New Mexico, First
Grade, 1943 (*Office of War
Information, Library of
Congress*).

Breathitt County, Kentucky, Big Rock School, 1940 (*Farm Security Administration, Library of Congress*).

Williams County, North Dakota, 1937 (*Farm Security Administration, Library of Congress*).

Gee's Bend, Alabama, First Grade, 1939 (*Farm Security Administration, Library of Congress*).

Grundy County, Iowa, One-Room School, 1939 (*Farm Security Administration, Library of Congress*).

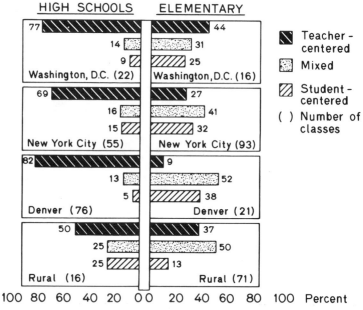

Figure 3.3   Instructional Grouping Patterns in Four Sites, 1920–1940.

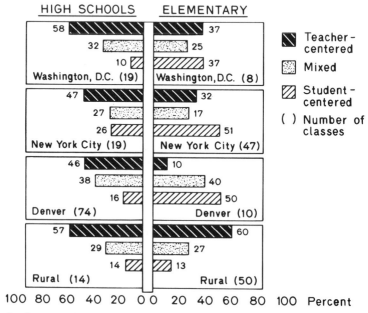

* Analysis of sources that produced this percentage showed that the activities came from photographs from local papers that school officials had provided to reporters or from newspaper articles that described activities, mostly of the project variety. This percentage, then, probably overstates the frequency of student-centered activities.

Figure 3.4   Class Activity Patterns in Four Sites, 1920–1940.

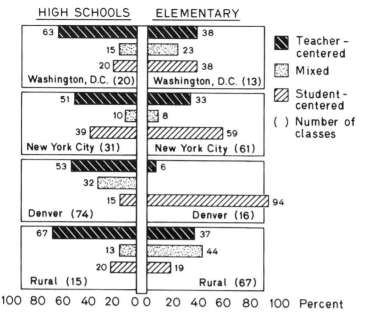

Figure 3.5 Student Movement Patterns in Four Sites, 1920–1940.

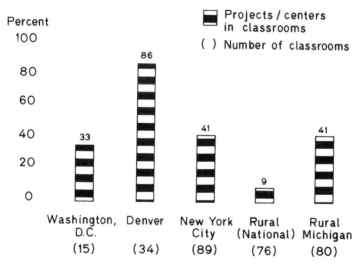

* Analysis of sources that produced this percentage revealed that project/center activities came either from photographs from local newspapers that school officials had provided (or suggested to reporters) or from newspaper articles specifically on such projects, e.g., Indians, Mexico, colonial America, building a boat, etc. This percentage, then, probably overstates frequency of projects.

Figure 3.6 Use of Projects/Centers in Elementary Classrooms, 1920–1940.

between elementary and high school classrooms: the incidence of whole group instruction occurred far more in high school than in elementary classes; teaching in small groups took place substantially more often, except in rural schools, in the lower grades than in the high school.

Under "Class Activities," where recitation, discussion, project work, seatwork, and the usual instructional tasks occurred, similar patterns surface. More teacher-centered class activities and fewer student-centered ones turned up in high school than elementary rooms. Otherwise, no clear pattern between and among city and rural classrooms emerges.

For "Student Movement," the same configurations between elementary and high school teachers, except for rural classrooms, appear again. More students move about in lower than upper grades, with Denver and New York classrooms showing slightly higher percentages in both teacher- and student-centered patterns. Finally, the percentage of elementary classrooms that had project work ran highest in Denver, New York City, and rural Michigan classrooms, although Denver's figure is inflated due to the sources used.

These graphs describe frequencies in teaching behavior in almost 300 classrooms. They show general instructional patterns suggesting the extent that student-centered practices surfaced in how teachers organized their classes for instruction, the activities they structured, and the degree of student mobility they permitted. What about specific teaching tactics like the recitation, textbook, activity method, and cooperative planning between teacher and student? There is a small body of evidence describing what teachers did in their classrooms between the two wars that offer some answers to the question.

In the recitation, for example, the teacher asks questions; students recite answers from either a textbook, workbook, blackboard work, or previously memorized content. The familiar pattern of many teacher questions and short answers from students on specific subject matter has been lamented throughout the last quarter of the nineteenth century by both journalists, professionals, and reformers. Romiett Stevens's transcription of lessons in 1908–1911 documented what others had observed. In the decades that followed the publication of her study—I suggest no cause-effect relationship—the formal recitation softened. The gradual penetration of the "socialized recitation," a technique that had the students, instead of the teacher, cover the subject matter through student-led discussions, reports, staging of scenes from novels or plays, panels, and debates. This practice transformed the formal recitation. Verbal exchanges between teacher and students still pivoted on questions asked by the teacher but could slip easily into either a quasi-conversation or shift back toward the formal recitation where the teacher delivered a volley of rapid-fire questions to students who returned the volley with one word answers, followed, in turn by another burst of teacher questions. Students standing at their desks reciting, a familiar image in classrooms for decades had become, by the 1940s, a quaint custom in urban classrooms. Replacing it was the also very familiar image of arm-waving pupils vying for the teacher's attention.

Pedagogical reformers, divided as they were among themselves on what classrooms should be like, probably saw the relaxation of formalism as a plus. But far more was sought in classroom change. The informal recitation was viewed as one of a number of competing activities chosen by teachers that involved students in the life of the classroom. They sought, among other things, small groups working on topics that joined different subjects, joint teacher-pupil planning, explicit links with life beyond the school, and active involvement of students in class tasks such as building replicas, painting murals, and dozens of other activities—all orchestrated by the teacher in a subtle, non-directive way. Studies of teaching practice between the two wars, however, suggest that Vivian Thayer's *The Passing of the Recitation* (1928) was premature and could have been retitled "The Persistence of the Recitation."[27]

Some investigators in these years looked at classroom teaching methods, but of the few who did only a handful counted what they saw. Counting has no special virtue given the varied meanings observers attached to such words as "child-centered," "progressive," and "modern." Hence, in summarizing seven different studies of classroom instruction, I have restricted myself to those studies that were less judgmental, and reported events that were less vulnerable to interpretation. In short, examining only those behaviors that could be seen and counted reduced the risk of misjudging what had occurred in the classroom: groups of students working together; students answering teacher questions; movable or stationary student desks, students giving reports, leading discussions, etc. Even with these hedges, a risk of misinterpretation remains but it is somewhat reduced.

Briefly, I examined studies that investigated 1,625 elementary and high school classrooms in California, Illinois, Indiana, Minnesota, Texas, and Wisconsin in addition to national reports between 1922 and 1940. Reports came from urban and rural superintendents, supervisors, principals, and college professors. Carefully designed instruments were used by trained observers in some investigations and, in others, hastily written impressions and self-reports from teachers formed the basis of the study.[28]

From these 7 studies of 1,625 classrooms, 3 points are clear: first, evidence collected by very different methods from large and small, rural and urban, elementary and high schools, in different sections of the country, shows notable convergence with the data I found independently in almost 300 urban and rural classrooms. Second, the pattern of using the entire class as the primary vehicle for instruction, the question–answer format, and general reliance upon the textbook that Rice, Stevens, and others observed decades earlier seemed undisturbed in the years between the two wars in the nation's classrooms. Third, the core of progressive practices that entered some elementary classrooms was larger than the core of practices that appeared in far fewer high school rooms. Projects, joint student–teacher planning, small group work simply did not appear as often or as in many high schools as they did in the lower grades, at least from the reports of observers who sat in classrooms, from descriptions written by teachers and others, and from photographs.

Yet evidence drawn from principals' and superintendents' reports, shows far higher percentages of certain progressive methods in high school classrooms than suggested above. The congressionally mandated three year Survey of Secondary Education, 1929–1932, for example, produced a massive body of information from 8,600 secondary schools, about one out of every three such schools in the country at that time. On the one item of project methods, 27 percent of the schools said that they used this form of instruction although only 4 percent reported its use "with unusual success." Similarly, for the phrase "Individualized Instruction," 25 percent of the schools checked off the space indicating use. Here again, 4 percent of the schools said they used it "with unusual success." Part of the problem, of course, is what the words mean to the people reporting the practice. If a handful of social studies teachers out of a faculty of 100 in a school of 3,500 students produced a few projects the semester previous to the survey, the principal would report the school as employing this approach. Equally as troublesome in reporting was the ambiguity, if not confusion, of terms like project method. Quite often this and other phrases were indistinguishable (e.g. Dalton method) from one another in school officials' minds. Furthermore, curriculum changes, i.e. revised courses of study, merging of subjects, changing labels and content of conventional subjects, did happen. These alterations often got entangled with descriptions of changes in teaching practice, impulses to be fashionable in joining current reforms, and positive acceptance of those changes by those who responded to the survey.[29]

J. Wayne Wrightstone, New York City school system evaluator and later professor during the surge of interest in activity programs, made this point in a study he did for the General Education Board. He tried to separate what experimental practices high schools had undertaken in the 1930s from other factors. Leaning heavily upon the National Survey, cited above, the Eight Year Study sponsored by PEA, and a network of contacts he had cultivated with high school experiments across the nation, Wrightstone concluded that major strides had been taken in introducing new subjects and content into the high school curriculum, especially the correlation of school subjects. But, he noted, the specific center of gravity in classroom instruction remained pinned to the recitation, textbook, and instruction to the entire class.[30]

SUMMARY

What conclusions can I draw from a study of urban and rural classrooms and an analysis of national studies of the years between the two World Wars about the extent of the spread of progressive teaching practices? Some commonalities emerge from the varied settings and types of data.

1. A core of progressive teaching practices did penetrate a considerable number of elementary schools, but in the districts I examined and the studies I reviewed the number of classrooms so affected never reached anywhere near a majority in a school district. This core of practices—increased levels of student participation through small group work; project activities; more student expression; increased use of varied classroom groupings; increased joining of two or more subject areas; more contacts with community through field trips; and more freedom to move around a room—was unevenly implemented within and across classrooms for only a portion of the school day. I estimate that such teaching practices seldom appeared in more than one-fourth of the classrooms in any district that systematically tried to install these varied elements. Elsewhere, little formal organizational energy was devoted to implementing these practices. The number of teachers adopting this core of practices probably hovered in the range of one out of five to ten elementary teachers. The percentage would run higher if certain practices were counted since teachers were quite selective in what they chose to incorporate into their classrooms. Turning up less frequently in elementary classrooms were other practices such as student decision making on what content to study, the allocation of instructional time, and what activities to choose.

2. In academic subjects at the high school level even fewer progressive practices modified teacher-centered instruction in the interwar period. In a few high school classrooms, scattered and isolated, except for Denver, an activity program, varied groupings, flexible space arrangments, and joint pupil–teacher planning did exist. Few progressive practices appeared in most high school classes. Course content changed, generally in English and social studies. Some loosening of the formalism connected with the recitation occurred with more discussion, student reports, and debates. Traces of child-centered practices could be seen in increased student participation in classroom talk, occasional trips in the community, and subject matter that touched upon student concerns or life outside of the classroom. But the percentage of time allotted to subjects—except for those schools that tried out core curriculum or general education for a part of the school day—remained the same. Even with movable furniture, classroom space often continued to be arranged with the teacher's desk at the front facing rows of tablet armchairs or portable desk-chairs.

3. These reduced cores of practices in elementary and secondary

classrooms became hybrid versions of pedagogical progressivism that appeared similar to (but were, nevertheless, different from) the cluster of approaches reformers dreamed of installing in schools. These forms of teacher-centered progressivism, with varying strains being evident, existed in a considerable number of schools. A public school version of a progressive classroom appeared that had adapted itself to rigorous climatic conditions: classes with 35 or more students; courses of study with skills and content to cover; teachers untrained in the approaches; an unselected, involuntary mass of students; limited space and supplies, and inhospitable furniture. Why particular teaching approaches were embraced and others rejected is a puzzle I will return to in the last chapter.

Enough of the familiar rhetoric and symbolism of progressivism existed in these hybrids for school officials and teachers to drum up enthusiasm for doing the impossible with few resources and to point with pride at the minority of teachers who had incorporated these practices into their daily instruction. Yet the very resemblance between the practice and the dream drove reformers outside the public schools to condemn these changes as only an incomplete replica of the real thing. Whether these hybrids were an improvement for children is an important but separate issue that is beyond the scope of this study. What is evident is that substantial numbers of teachers did, indeed, modify somewhat their classroom repertoires.

4. Where these cores of practice seemed to appear in strength were in school districts where top administrators gave formal approval for the effort, established organizational machinery to carry it out, and persisted in its implementation. Yet even in Denver and New York, these new teaching practices did not penetrate a majority of classrooms. In rural districts where teachers were isolated, possessed limited schooling, and had insufficient books and materials, fewer progressive methods seemed to have spread, except for certain practices that were already indigenous to multi-grade, one room schools, i.e. grouping practices. Islands of progressive practice also appeared in those unique schools that grew out of the persistence and dedication of tireless individuals, e.g. Fanny Dunn.

The one effort to spread progressive approaches into rural schools that I reported offers a glimpse of another way to change practice. The Kellogg Foundation in the mid-1930s used a strategy, shaped by the dispersal of teachers in southwestern Michigan, that concentrated upon the individual teacher. Through extension courses and summers at colleges, some teachers did alter their classroom methods, according to their reports, but in a limited, hopscotch manner. Higher percentages of teachers used projects, for instance, than were reported in other studies and the classroom descriptions I analyzed. More research is needed to trace what happened over the years in teachers' rooms. Such evidence could determine if the changes that occurred in one-teacher schools in Michigan were substantively different from those classrooms where systematic, district-wide implementation occurred and whether such changes endured.

5. The dominant pattern of instruction, allowing for the substantial spread of these hybrid progressive practices, remained teacher-centered. Elementary and secondary teachers persisted in teaching from the front of the room, deciding what was to be learned, in what manner, and under what conditions. The primary means of grouping for instruction was the entire class. The major daily classroom activities continued with a teacher telling, explaining, and questioning students while the students listened, answered, read, and wrote. Seatwork or supervised study was an extension of these activities.

Restrictions on student movement within the classroom loosened somewhat. Teachers permitted more mobility within the class. Movable furniture provided an option for teachers to rearrange desks and chairs into groups although most teachers continued lining them up in rows. Formal recitation, with students rising from their seats to speak, eased. In short, the classroom climate softened sufficiently for teachers and students to cross the formal boundaries that kept them at arm's length from one another.

Looking back to 1900 I can see that some important changes occurred. Even though the teachers in 1940 were not the same as those who taught in 1900 since there were successive generations of teachers entering the classroom, instruction still tilted toward teacher-centeredness. Yet there were substantial numbers of new and veteran teachers in these years who modified their methods in varying degrees that were unapparent in public schools at the turn of the century.

By 1940, alternatives to standard teaching methods were available, widely known, used by a minority of teachers, and considered respectable by professional norms. The narrow range of existing practice had stretched to encompass a larger repertoire, although the implementation of those practices was indeed limited. For every Leona Helmick in Hillsdale, Michigan, there were dozens of other teachers who found such practices too time-consuming, upsetting to existing routines, or too far removed from the conditions they had to face daily. For every Mary Stapleton in Cuttingsville, Vermont who explored the Winnetka approach on her own time, scores of fellow teachers kept their classroom doors closed to such techniques because of the high price in energy that they, and not their superintendent or principal, had to pay in personal time, loneliness that might arise from introducing changes and making oneself different from colleagues, lack of tangible and explicit incentives to make such changes, and uncertainty of whether promised outcomes would indeed benefit children.

Looking back to the early years of the twentieth century, John Dewey observed in 1952 that progressivism had altered the "life conditions in the classroom" and little else in elementary schools, with hardly any change appearing in high school classrooms. He noticed how much more talk there was about change than actual alterations in classroom conditions. He also observed that the "fundamental authoritarianism of the old education persists in various modified forms."[32]

I found much evidence to support Dewey's observations about the extent and quality of the changes that had occurred since 1900. His comments on "fundamental authoritarianism," however, I have yet to consider. Such a remark directs attention to instructional practices teachers introduced into their classrooms and why those practices were selected and not others. Why, for example, did those elementary teachers who embraced some form of progressive pedagogy encourage more movement of students in classrooms, project activities for part of the day, and mixed forms of grouping over other methods such as joint student-teacher planning of what topics should be studied? Or why was it rare that a teacher delegated to students how the daily schedule should be arranged? Teacher-centered progressivism incorporated some new techniques and not others. Perhaps, these hybrids permitted those adventurous teachers who risked introducing some changes into their rooms to pick those practices that did not threaten their classroom authority or school-wide curriculum. Dewey's comment is intriguing because it suggests that the hybrids themselves, the changes that had entered a number of classrooms, may have strengthened rather than weakened the foundations of a teacher's classroom authority. I am uncertain now about this possibility. Examining a subsequent effort by reformers to introduce informal education, containing approaches similar to progressive pedagogy, in the late 1960s and early 1970s may clarify this uncertainty.

NOTES

1. *Changes in Classroom Teaching Made During 1937–1939 in One-Room Rural Schools in the Area of the Michigan Community Health Project* (Battle Creek, Mich.: W. K. Kellogg Foundation, 1940), p. 129.
2. *Time*, October 31, 1938, p. 31.
3. Martin Dworkin (ed.), *Dewey on Education* (New York: Teachers College University Press, 1959), pp. 129–30.
4. Henry Otto, et al., *Community Workshops for Teachers in Michigan Community Health Project* (Ann Arbor, Mich.: University of Michigan Press, 1942), pp. 1, 5.
5. Otto, p. 3; *Changes in Classroom Teaching*, foreword.
6. Hermine Marshall, "Open Classrooms: Has the Term Outlived Its Usefulness," *Review of Educational Research*, 51 (Summer, 1981), pp. 185–6.
7. *Changes in Classroom Teaching*, pp. 50–1.
8. Evelyn Dewey, *New Schools for Old* (New York: E.P. Dutton and Co., 1919); Ellsworth Collings, *An Experiment with a Project Curriculum* (New York:

Macmillan Co., 1923); Fannie Dunn and Marcia Everett, *Four Years in a Country School* (New York: Teachers College, Bureau of Publications, 1926).

9. Report of the Committee on Experimental Schools, *What Schools Are Doing* (New York: Progressive Education Association, 1937), pp. ii, 3–5, 10, 19, 31, 42–3, 50.
10. Winn L. Taplin and Irving Pearson, "Contributions to Individual Instruction" in *Newer Types of Instruction in Small Rural Schools*, Yearbook 1938 (Washington, D.C.: Department of Rural Education, National Educational Association, 1938), pp. 114–5.
11. Department of the Interior, *Biennial Survey of Education, 1920–1922*, Bulletin 1924, Vol. 1 (Washington, D.C.: Government Printing Office, 1924), pp. 125.
12. Department of the Interior, "Status of the Rural Teacher in Pennsylvania," Bulletin 1921, no. 34. (Washington, D.C.: Government Printing Office, 1922), pp. 8–9, 21, 33; *Biennial Survey, 1920–1922*, pp. 143–5.
13. *Biennial Survey, 1920–1922*, p. 127; Fannie W. Dunn, "Modern Education in Small Rural Schools," *Teachers College Record*, 32 (February, 1931), pp. 411–2.
14. Verne McGuffey, *Differences in the Activities of Teachers in Rural One-Teacher Schools and of Grade Teachers in Cities* (New York: Teachers College, 1929), pp. 10–13.
15. "Status of Rural Teacher in Pennsylvania," pp. 18, 33.
16. ibid., p. 20.
17. Texas Educational Survey Commission, *Courses of Study and Instruction*, Vol. 5 (Austin, Tex.: Texas Educational Survey Commission, 1924), pp. 321, 365.
18. ibid., pp. 307, 368, 376.
19. ibid., pp. 378–9.
20. Andrew C. Berg, "A Daily Program for the One-Room Schools of North Dakota" (Unpublished Masters Thesis, University of North Dakota, 1929), pp. 19–20.
21. Julia Uggen, "A Composite Study of Difficulties of Rural Teachers," *Educational Administration and Supervision*, 24 (March, 1938), pp. 195–202.
22. *Grade Teacher*, 48 (October, 1930), p. 159.
23. ibid., (December, 1930), p. 316.
24. Louisiana Educational Survey, "The Negro Public Schools," Section B (Louisiana Educational Survey, 1924), pp. 57–8.
25. ibid., pp. 164–5.
26. ibid., p. 56.
27. James Hoetker and William Ahlbrand, "The Persistence of the Recitation," *American Educational Research Journal*, 6 (March, 1969), pp. 145–67.
28. Rather than analyze the details of these seven studies, I have included tables that capture the data and some narrative describing each one. Citations follow the narrative.

In 1922, a statewide study of Texas schools brought Margaret Noonan, a New York University professor, to the state to direct that portion of the survey examining black and white city schools. An ardent advocate of progressivism, Noonan stated clearly the standards by which she would judge instruction in Texas city schools: presence of group work, joint pupil-teacher planning, evidence of connections between classwork and life outside the school, and "the whole child must be kept in mind."

Trained observers used a list to check off what they saw in teachers' rooms. Many statements were open to broad interpretation by the observer, e.g. "students show enjoyment and appreciation of activity." A few items on the checklist included specific items and behaviors.

Table 3.3 Selected Items Reported in 1922 Survey of Nine Texas Cities, White and Black Schools

Category	White, %	Black, %
Furniture fastened to floor	70	77
Activity suggested by pupil or class	2	0
Pupils at work on same activity	56	42
Pupils at work on group activity	14	22
Pupils at work on individual activity	3	2
Current events discussed	22	45
Pupils moving freely	24	20
Number of classes observed	(176)	(40)

(Texas Educational Survey Commission, *Courses of Study and Instruction*, Vol. 5, (Austin, Tex.: Texas Educational Survey Commission, 1924), pp. 307, 321, 365, 368, 376–9.)

On a larger scale than Noonan, Teachers College professor, William Bagley, conducted a national study on teaching methods in 1930 that summarized results from state, city, and rural surveys between 1900 and 1930. "One who studies such reports over a series of years," he said, "could scarcely escape the conclusion that the work of the typical American classroom, whether on the elementary or secondary level, has been and still is, characterized by a lifeless and perfunctory study and recitation of assigned textbook materials."

To verify the accuracy of these survey conclusions, Bagley wrote to superintendents, principals, local and state supervisors of instruction across the country asking them to use an observation instrument he had developed to describe teaching methods. He received over 500 completed classroom forms from over 30 states unevenly distributed between rural (169) and urban (356), elementary (342) and secondary (183). Acknowledging that observers may have had varied perspectives in describing teachers, he cautioned readers that these observations "cannot be regarded as thoroughly typical of what is going on in classrooms...."

Although some categories were collapsed to provide clarity, the main results of his survey are shown in Table 3.4.

How did Bagley explain the differences between those formal surveys that concluded textbook recitations dominated instruction and these results from professionals who sat in classrooms and found that student-centered practices had penetrated classes considerably, both in city and countryside schools? Was it because school officials responding to a professor wanted "to make as good a showing as possible in the light of contemporary ideals," i.e. progressivism? Or was it because practitioners visiting classrooms for which they were responsible, exhibited a "natural tendency to interpret what they saw as

Table 3.4 Frequency in Type of Recitations and Project Methods Reported by Bagley, 1929–1930, in Percentages

Method		Rural Elem.	Urban Elem.	Rural High	City High
Textbook Recitation		16.6	10.4	28.8	22.5
Individual and Group Work:					
Individual reports		7.3	7.7	10.0	5.5
Group or Committee report		5.0	5.2	1.1	3.1
Individual and group projects		9.0	12.2	5.5	6.0
	TOTAL	21.3	25.1	16.6	14.6
Number of classrooms		(108)	(234)	(61)	(122)

conforming closely with generally accepted standards?" Noting both explanations, Bagley dismissed them and concluded that "contemporary educational theory seems to be affecting elementary-school practice in a fairly profound fashion, and it is apparently not without its influence upon the secondary school." Whether or not a range of 15–25% of individual and group work observed in classrooms is considered "profound" influence, regularities similar to ones I found appear in Bagley's survey. Differences between elementary and high school are evident in levels of recitation and student-centered activities. Also the magnitude of individual and group work is comparable to percentages for student-centered instruction under the category "Class Activities."

(William C. Bagley, "The Textbook and Methods of Teaching," in National Society for the Study of Education, *The Textbook in American Education*, Part 2, (Bloomington, Ill.: Public School Publishing Co., 1931), pp. 10–11, 15, 17–18, 25.)

In 1940, L. W. Krause, a public school teacher, completed a study in 10 Indiana cities of 217 fourth to sixth grade classrooms. Again, much of the instrument he used to assess progressive practice required a great deal of judgment by the observer, e.g. teacher conducted class on democratic principles, children showed signs of self-discipline, teacher encouraged clear thinking. Some items, though, did call for describing the presence or absence of actual activities, reducing somewhat, but not eliminating, the margin for interpretation by an observer. Those tallies are shown in Table 3.5.

For high schools, a number of studies between 1924 and 1930 concentrated on what teachers did and said in their classrooms. Covering all of the academic subjects in large and small, urban and rural, schools these investigators sat in classrooms, recorded, and transcribed notes for almost 600 experienced

Table 3.5   Average Frequency of Selected Items Reported in 217 Indiana
Intermediate Classrooms, 1940

Category	*Percentage*
Movable furniture	46
Several groups of pupils at work	2
Variety of materials present	16
Teacher has a unit of work in progress	1
Students helping to plan work	4

Source: L. W. Krause, "What Principles of Modern and Progressive Education Are Practiced in Intermediate-Grade Classrooms," *Journal of Educational Research*, 35, (December, 1941), pp. 252–4.

teachers in midwestern and California high schools. The results are remarkably akin to the earlier work of Romiett Stevens (1912) in revealing the high level of teacher control over the amount and direction of classroom talk; the narrow margin of time available to students to respond; and how few other activities occurred in the typical 45 minute period.

Between 1924 and 1926, university researchers visited 346 classrooms in the Minneapolis, Minnesota area and found that 4 activities (recitation, supervised study, assignments and tests) accounted for 90 percent of each class period. Recitation consumed an average of 62 percent of class time. Two Northwestern University professors went into 116 Chicago social studies classrooms in 1929 and concluded that "teaching is still largely 'question and answer' recitation." They found that 82 percent of the teachers asked questions, some as rapidly as 150 in a 45 minute period. They were surprised at how few students raised questions (10 percent) during the recitation or offered any comment (8 percent). "The changes," they noted, "being advocated in our methods of teaching are not finding their way into the schools to any considerable extent." In the same year, A. S. Barr sat in 77 social studies classes of Wisconsin teachers, designated as "good" and "poor" by their principals and superintendents. Within a 40 minute period, he found that the teachers asked 93 and 102 questions, respectively, Stenographic records verified that teachers monopolized air time during the class reaching almost 60 percent for the recitation portion of the class alone. He also found eight teachers who used the "problem-project organization or learning by doing." Finally, in 1930, a Stanford student observed 42 English and social science teachers in 5 San Francisco area schools. Charles Bursch found that "class discussion" averaged 59 percent of each class period.

(Leonard V. Koos and Oliver L. Troxel, "A Comparison of Teaching Procedures in Short and Long Class Periods" *The School Review*, 35, (May, 1927), p. 343; J. M. Hughes and E. O. Melby, "A Cross-Section of Teaching in Terms of Classroom Activities," *Educational Method*, 10, (October, 1930), pp. 285–9; A. S. Barr, *Characteristic Differences in the Teaching Performance of Good and Poor Teachers of the Social Studies*, (Bloomington, Ill.: Public School Publishing Co., 1929), pp. 84, 103; Charles W. Bursch, "The Techniques and Results of an Analysis of the Teaching Process in High School English and Social Science Classes" (Unpublished doctoral dissertation, Stanford University, 1930), p. 128.

29. U.S. Office of Education, *National Survey of Secondary Education, Summary*, Monograph No. 1 (Washington, D.C.: Government Printing Office, 1934), pp. 126, 129.

30. J. Wayne Wrightstone, *Appraisal of Experimental High School Practices* (New York: Bureau of Publications, Teachers College, 1936), pp. 21–2, 48–9, 59, 76, 184–5.

31. This estimate is drawn from the following sources: the descriptions and photographs I collected of classrooms instruction; the analysis of 190 teacher self-reports in rural Michigan (1937–1939); classrooms and 55 teachers at Central High School in Washington, D.C. (1925–1938); Joseph Loftus's estimate in New York City at the height of the Activity Program's implementation; and reports from Krause and Bagley who tried to estimate the degree of teacher use of different practices in the 1930s.

32. Dworkin, pp. 129–30.

Part II

Open Classrooms and Alternative Schools: Progressivism Revisited, 1965–1975

4

Informal Education, 1965–1975: New Wine in Old Bottles?

In a North Dakota city of 35,000, a university researcher went to an elementary school of 180 children and interviewed a second grade teacher in 1972.

I : ... To begin with, would you describe for us a typical day in your classroom?

T: ... The morning is spent with children doing the activities they schedule for themselves. We always gather together after lunch in a group and I read to them. At this time, the children also schedule and announce if they are going to put on a play or if they have something to show. We schedule a time for those kinds of activities to occur later in the afternoon. The other children choose whether or not they wish to attend. If they do, they include that in their schedule....

I : Okay. Now I'd like you to describe the classroom....

T: As you come in the door, we have a high shelf area. That is our hospitality counter with our guest book, coffee, juice, and cookies for the visitors and kids. The math center is on the other side of these shelves. There's a bulletin board right there. We have a long combination blackboard-bulletin board at the other end. A typewriter and our creative writing area are in that particular part of the room. Then we have an old trunk. It is our drama trunk and is filled with a variety of hats, dresses, coats, and some props like a cane. Then we have a table six feet in length that has a listening center with records, a View Master, filmstrip previewer, and a reading machine....

We have a large carpeted area that has a davenport, lots of pillows and stuffed animals. Bookshelves are on the sides, kind of a reading center is what you'd call that. Going on, we have a game shelf, then the science center, plant and animal center. Then you'd see the cooking area with recipes written on chart paper of all the things we've cooked over the year....

I : On a typical day in the classroom, how many children would be involved in language arts and reading?

T: The only time we would be working as a whole group would be during sustained silent reading. Reading, though, is a part of each child's daily schedule. During the day when they come to what part of their schedule, they go into the reading center. They would read by themselves, to a buddy, to a tutor, or other adult that might be in the room....[1]

If a time machine could have swept fervent advocates of child-centered practices in the 1920s across decades and sat them down in this second grade North Dakota classroom in the early 1970s, they would have felt far closer in spirit to this primary teacher than to Mrs. Spencer in her 1924 New York City progressive classroom or to Leona Helmick's rural Michigan one-room school in 1938—both of whom tried student-centered approaches. The North Dakota classroom's use of space and furniture, the high level of student participation both in instruction and rule making, the reach of a curriculum that touched both academic and life-like situations, and the signs of student independence reported by the teacher capture an informal, child-centered classroom. This North Dakota teacher was part of a national surge in lay and professional fervor for open classrooms and alternative schooling that an earlier generation might easily have labeled progressive.

But the line of descent in instruction between the 1930s and the 1970s is zig-zag and broken. Three decades separate an activity program classroom in New York City from the above second grade in North Dakota or a core classroom in Denver's East High School in 1936 from a school without walls in Washington, D.C., 30 years later. This educational progress, in the words of Philip Jackson, "could be more easily traced by a butterfly than by a bullet."[2]

THE SETTING FOR INFORMAL CLASSROOMS: THE 1960s

Rather than retrace the post-World War II history of public schools, I will concentrate on those conditions that seemingly led to the brief enthusiasm for informal and alternative schools which peaked in the early 1970s and suggest comparisons with the earlier progressive movement.

In the midst of the media's fascination for informal and free schools, Lawrence Cremin drew parallels between the earlier progressive movement and the then-current ardor for these reforms. He saw two themes in the "new progressive movement" that resonated with the earlier one: child-centeredness and social reform. Locating the rebirth of the child-centered theme in the publication of A. S. Neill's *Summerhill* in 1960, a book that was selling over 200,000 copies annually a decade later, Cremin saw the writings of school critics John Holt, George Dennison, James Herndon, and Herbert Kohl as contributing to the momentum for seeking different kinds of teachers and schooling that would free children's imagination and creativity from deadening routines, tyrannical authority, and passive learning.[3]

At the same time, growing out of the civil rights movement, Cremin pointed out, blacks and other ethnic groups tried to shape schools to fit their aspirations for identity and a sense of community. "We have seen," he commented, "a fascinating interweaving of the child-centered and political reform themes in the literature of the movement, so that open education is viewed as a lever of child liberation on the one hand, and as a lever of radical social change, on the other." Noting differences between the two themes, he found the literature "notoriously atheoretical and ahistorical." Those who established new schools "have not read their Francis W. Parker or their Caroline Pratt . . . with the result that boundless energy has been spent in countless classrooms reinventing the pedagogical wheel." Yet he saw a fundamental similarity in both movements: the tool of reform remains the public school. Even Charles Silberman's *Crisis in the Classroom*, "surely the most learned and wide-range analysis to be associated with the present movement," proposed the open classroom as "the keystone in the arch of educational reform."[4]

Leaning heavily upon Cremin's work on the progressive movement, Vito Perrone, Dean of the University of North Dakota's New School (subsequently renamed the Center for Teaching and Learning) and prominent in the national network of reformers committed to informal education, located the roots of open education in progressivism at the turn of the century. Although he did not distinguish between the social reform and child-centered themes in the surge of interest in open classrooms, Perrone described both. He broadened his search for roots beyond progressivism, locating it in the civil rights movement, as did Cremin, but also in the growing public awareness of government policies concerning air pollution, the environment, and Vietnam that were viewed as mindless, inhumane, and destructive. Moreover, he credited the English primary schools for giving "considerable stimulus," especially after the publication of *Children and Their Primary Schools* (1967), to the practice of informal education in the United States.[5]

Roland Barth's search for the sources of open education took him back to 1961. John Dewey is absent from the index of the book. In that year, William Hull, a Cambridge, Massachusetts private school teacher went to

England to observe and report on the work of primary schools. His enthusiastic words led to a growing number of American educators traveling to see first hand the "Leicestershire plan," the "integrated day," and the "developmental classroom." The Education Development Center in Newton, Massachusetts where Hull worked became a center for the exporting of ideas and materials on English primary schools. Tracing the movement from its early locus in an interlocking network of private schools, foundations, and federally funded curriculum developers fed by Joseph Featherstone's articles in the *New Republic* and the publication of Silberman's *Crisis in the Classroom*, to a broader enthusiasm that included state departments of education, universities, public school administrators and teachers, Barth pointed out the unsystematic, uneven, yet persistent spread of informal classrooms in the country.[6]

Sources for the origin and spread of open classrooms varied, according to these writers. Yet none of the writers discussed the appearance (and disappearance) of curriculum reform. As part of the national wave of change before and after Sputnik, reformers in the 1950s and 1960s generated math, science, and social studies texts and materials that got students to handle Cuisenaire rods and light bulbs, simulate situations, and, in general, behave as scientists. While many of the academics' enthusiastic proponents and participants in the change effort ended up disappointed in the returns that materialized in classrooms across the country, the focus upon children's interests and motivation, and tying content to contemporary concerns anchored in disciplines, echoes earlier generations of reformers.

The tangled threads of social reform, child-centered pedagogy, curriculum change, and self-liberation that marked the progressive movement decades earlier reappeared in the late 1960s. Similar also were the kinds of participants in both surges of reform. The earlier generation of academics, writers, and professional reformers that saw public schools as constraining, ineffectual, and even harmful to children found an echo in the critics of the later period who saw schools and instruction as mindless and destructive.

Contrasts with Progressivism

Beyond these similarities, however, substantial differences separated the two generations of school reformers. By 1940, for example, the varied forms of progressivism had become accepted by most citizens and professionals as the wisest course to follow in public schooling. Administrative progressives had their scorecards to rate scientifically how efficient facility maintenance, business procedures, and new building construction were. Pedagogical progressives had developed an architecture of teaching methodology. Social reformers wrote books that became best sellers among informed educators and dozens of articles in journals.

Progressivism was mainstream. The movement found expression in formal organizations, annual conventions, informal networks of like-minded individuals, journals, teacher-education curricula, and graduate courses of study used to train school administrators. The then-current vocabulary of teachers and officials mirrored the absorption of progressive ideas. To be part of the educational establishment and to be a progressive educator had become synonymous.

Few of these developments marked the nova of informal education. Its eruption was intense and brief compared to the decades that progressive beliefs took to become mainstream. Informal education, I believe, never took a deep hold organizationally among the general ranks of educators. Perhaps the suddenness of its appearance may explain that. Or perhaps the lack of passion among its partisans for formal ties may account for the shallowness of the organizational root system among open classroom enthusiasts. Occasional groups of advocates joined together in efforts to spread ideas and practices, but these casual networks seldom were more than peripheral to the educational establishment. The similarity in impulses and participants, I believe, masks the substantial differences in organizational approaches and the amount of time available to penetrate legions of teachers, administrators, and informed citizens.

Compared to earlier reform efforts, the brevity of interest in informal schooling was astonishing. Generally accepted as beginning in the mid-1960s, by the mid-1970s, concerns for basic skills, test scores, traditional alternative schools, and minimum competencies had replaced open classrooms on the agenda of school boards, superintendents, principals, and teachers. A barometer of the sudden shift in interest is the number of articles referred to in *Education Index* and the *Current Index of Journals of Education*. Between 1969 and 1973, when there was a burst of publications that stretched for pages in these indexes, and 1975–1979, when references had shrunk to a page or two, is one sign of the drop in interest. As brief as this interest in informal education was, no uniformity in definition or practice emerged even in those peak years of 1967 through 1973.

The explosion of articles in newspapers, popular magazines, professional journals, and books—supplemented by television coverage and films—documented the array of differences among and between schools categorized within the broad label of informal education: open classrooms, free schools, open education, alternative schools, school-within-a-school, personalized education, humanistic schools, mini-schools, etc. While most of the classes and schools shared a strong distaste for public schools, often running to revulsion on the part of some critics, most professional and lay reformers believed that public school teaching could improve.

In sharpening the focus, I will concentrate on those efforts to alter classroom teaching practices in public elementary and secondary schools. To be clear about what I mean, I will use informal education and open classrooms synonymously in describing change in elementary schools. At the secondary level, "alternative" will be the preferred term for the range of innovations that spanned the late 1960s and early 1970s. At both levels there were a number of common elements that became targets for classroom reform.

OPEN CLASSROOMS: 1970s

Consider first the open classroom. After the initial surge of fervor for informal schooling ran its course, advocates worried about the headlong rush by school practitioners to freeze into orthodoxy something called an "open classroom." Assumptions about teaching, learning, the nature of the child, and the process of developing an informal setting, they argued, were the essentials—not some product labeled: open classroom. Roland Barth, Joseph Featherstone, Vito Perrone, Charles and Arlene Silberman, Lillian Weber, and others wrote and spoke often about the dangers of missing the fundamental issues in informal education by confusing means and ends or in searching futilely for prescriptions to be grafted onto classrooms. "Tempering a Fad," ran the headline of a *New Republic* article by Featherstone in 1971. "Although there are many prophets rising in the land," he wrote in another article the same month, "there is no educational Gospel." His warning was to no avail.[7]

In 1973, Barth complained that American educators have copied British primary classrooms mindlessly. "We have made a neat package of the vocabulary, the appearance, the materials, and sold it to the schools." Warnings seldom deflected the strong impulse to define what was an open classroom. Those researchers, school administrators, and board members seized by the public and professional passion for informal schools in the early 1970s drew up lists of items that distinguished open classrooms from conventional ones. Some advocates reasoned that there was a risk of making a complex process trivial by such listings, yet, they argued, that risk had to be traded off against offering specific directions for converts to build more informal classrooms. Checklists, diagrams, and ways of assessing the degree of openness began to appear by 1971. Language accompanying these lists warned readers that teachers differed among themselves in implementing these classrooms and that introducing new practices occurred unevenly.[8]

Even with these concerns, writers agreed upon some common elements. The style of teaching in open classrooms was flexible both in use of space and methods; students were involved in choosing activities, the classroom was provisioned with abundant materials that were handled directly by students. Curriculum was integrated—"correlated" to an earlier generation. Grouping for instruction was most often by small groups and individuals, although the entire class would be taught as one when it was appropriate.[9]

Charles Silberman, sensitive to any distillation that might sap the vitality that teachers brought to open classrooms, warned advocates to be cautious. He feared that unthinking, simple-minded true believers in open classrooms would do what drunks had done to alcohol: give it a bad name.

> By itself, dividing a classroom into interest areas (learning centers) does *not* constitute open education; creating large open spaces does *not* constitute open education; individualizing instruction does *not* constitute open education. . . . For the open classroom. . . is not a model or set of techniques; it is an approach to teaching and learning. . . .
>
> Thus, the artifacts of the open classroom—interest areas, concrete materials, wall displays—are not ends in themselves but rather means to other ends. . . . In addition, open classrooms are organized as to encourage
> - active learning rather than passive learning;
> - learning and expression in a variety of media, rather than just pencil and paper and the spoken word;
> - self directed, student-initiated learning more than teacher-directed learning;. . . [10]

The questions asked in previous chapters about the extent of the spread of progressive practices are now appropriate here. In assessing the degree that informal education penetrated classrooms, I will examine North Dakota, a state that tried to reform teaching practices through an ambitious state-wide certification program, New York City, and Washington, D.C.—all centers of ferment in installing open classrooms between 1967 and 1975.

The signs of informal education that I will seek out, unfortunately, will be the very artifacts Silberman warned against. If clusters of desks with students facing one another, learning centers, unimpeded student movement within the classroom, small groups and individual instruction, and student choice of activities are apparent then some indicators of an open classroom are present. These practices will vary from class to class. But, and the exception should be underscored, these outward clues of openness reveal nothing substantial about teachers' views of learning, childrens' development, or concerns for improving student skills. As a behavioral view of the classroom it can be fairly criticized for being narrow and incapable of capturing the holistic qualities inherent to informal education. To such criticisms, I can only say that teachers themselves saw these visible signs as evidence of moving toward informal classrooms and, at the least, such artifacts point to tangible effort on the part of the teacher to incorporate some version of the open classroom that they felt was practical in their circumstances. Finally, I recognize that what I am doing is a primitive reconstruction of a number of key components to classrooms. As crude as it is, such a reconstruction is still a marginal improvement over studying only statements from educational leaders and rhetoric about teacher fervor or intentions.

NORTH DAKOTA

The *Saturday Review, Atlantic, Newsweek, Readers Digest, Life, The New York Times,* and the *Wall Street Journal* within an 11-month period carried feature articles on the new reform sweeping one-room schools, villages, towns, and small cities in the high plains of North Dakota. By 1972, the Public Broadcasting Corporation and CBS had shown documentaries on the state's open classrooms. Hinterland as avante garde reform was too irresistible an angle for the media to ignore. The Carnegie Corporation-sponsored study that Charles Silberman had published as *Crisis in the Classroom* devoted a chapter to boosting the changes occurring in the state. In all of these feature articles, professional journals, and books the University of North Dakota's New School of Behavioral Studies on Education (hereafter called the New School), played a primary role in generating ideas, funds, teacher training, and support for informal education.[11]

To understand how open classrooms took root in a rural, politically conservative state, and found leadership in an institution with a New York-sounding name led by a Michigan educator whom teachers, state legislators, and children called "Vito," requires explanation. The general outline of the story has been told in a number of places. A study in 1967 documented that North Dakota was dead last among all states in level of preparation for elementary teachers—two out of every five lacked a bachelor's degree—and the range of school opportunities available to its grade school children (e.g. few kindergarten classes, special teachers, services for the handicapped, etc.). To upgrade the 40 percent of the teachers lacking college degrees (average age 43), the study staff recommended that an experimental teacher education school be established to train these less-than-degree teachers in ways that would match the circumstances many of them came from: small schools with students scattered over several grades. Chance brought Featherstone's *New Republic* articles on British primary schools to the attention of the staff, who saw a match between informal education and the needs of small, isolated schools in a rural state. The New School, as part of the University of North Dakota, was created not only to certify teachers but to introduce "radical" changes in how teachers taught, their use of the curriculum, and how classroom decisions were made.[12]

Hiring Vito Perrone as the new Dean, sources agreed, provided the ingenuity and emotional electricity to power the infant venture. Perrone hired like-minded teachers, some of whom were knowledgable about English primary schools or had worked at the Education Development Center in Newton, Massachusetts, where materials for open classrooms were developed and published. Perrone criss-crossed the state telling legislators, school officials, teachers, and parents of the virtues of open classrooms and New School interns (young men and women who replaced less-than-degree teachers who then went to the New School to get their degree and certification). Using imagery of rural schools that parents found familiar, especially many grades in one class and close ties to the surrounding community, Perrone and his colleagues promoted informal education.[13]

Between 1968 and 1973, over 50 districts (about 20 per cent of the state total) with 80 schools (enrolling about half of the state's elementary school children) had joined the New School in its venture. The campaign of the New School and other state colleges to aid teachers in earning a degree sharply reduced the percentage of less-than-degree teachers from 59 percent in 1968 to 13 percent in 1973.[14]

Interns introduced open classroom practices in Starkweather, Minto, Devil's Lake, Fort Yates, Fargo, Bismarck, Minot, and Grand Forks. City, town, village and one-teacher school—all were touched directly or indirectly by New School interns or federally funded outreach programs in the initial five years. After 1973, however, federal funding of New School support programs across the state evaporated. Outreach activities dwindled to include only what those motivated and energetic New School teachers did on their own time.[15]

Cautious about freezing open classroom concepts into a gospel, Perrone and his colleagues also knew that parents had to both understand and accept these different approaches to teaching and school life. The North Dakota version of informal education contained the core of approaches found in British primary schools with the addition of areas that the New School stressed, particularly on student involvement in classroom decisions, student interaction used as a way of teaching and learning, evaluation of important nonacademic growth, and parent involvement.[16]

In determining to what extent open classrooms spread in the state, keep in mind that no other state in the nation had embraced as a matter of policy the introduction of open classrooms. The uniqueness and reach of North Dakota's effort prevents comparisions with other states and should be considered in any assessment of implementation. Open classrooms did spread throughout the state in the early 1970s. In Fargo, in 1969, for example, at the request of the superintendent, the New School established a center for interns at Madison, a school with a record of persistently low student performance. The two principals who served Madison between 1969 and 1977 were both affiliated with the New School.

Principal Vincent Dodge described the changes that had occurred by 1973. Walls between classrooms were torn down. Cross-grade teams were organized. Learning centers in math, science, social studies, creative writing, reading, and art—containing individual stations for students— were used to enrich, motivate, and link the community to the school between 30 minutes to an hour per day. In addition, students made tables, chairs, carrels, magazine racks, supply bins, games, and puzzles out of tri-wall cardboard and other materials. Finally, no letter grades appeared

on report cards. Checklists of specific academic skills, cooperative behaviors, and interpersonal skills were sent home twice a year and two
formal teacher-parent conferences were held. In short, this description
includes all the artifacts of open classrooms as well as the spirit of
teacher-pupil planning and decision making, according to the principal.
The *Fargo-Moorhead Forum* ran articles on the Madison, Clara Barton,
Lewis and Clark, and Horace Mann schools describing centers, small
group activities, and freedom of student movement in classrooms. "Fargo
Schools Lead Education Revolution," one headline proclaimed.[17]

Less than a hundred miles north of Fargo, Grand Forks, in the words
of Superintendent Wayne Worner in 1969, had become a "mecca for
innovation." He declared that there is not one school in the district "where
you find 30 students in a box." The Washington elementary school
established a formal relationship with the New School, itself located a few
miles away. Larry Hoiberg, principal of the kindergarten through sixth
grade school of 220 students (1970), described how Washington merged
the "child's school world and his home world." Photographs and narrative
captured small groups, learning centers, students' free movement, and
flexible space arrangments in which New School interns, parent volunteers,
and aides worked.[18]

In another Grand Forks school, Jerry Abbott told how a federal grant
to introduce aides into a newly built school helped create an open
classroom program at the Kelly School. Centers, small groups of students
at clustered desks, individualized reading programs, abundant materials,
and a dozen other outward signs pointed to the presence of on open
classroom and altered teaching practice. "What happens to the traditional
role of the teacher?" Abbott asked. "She is no longer at the front of the
room directing the same...lesson for all children. As the children work in
teams she is free to move among them and to help those who need it."[19]

Elsewhere in the state, visitors and reporters noted the appearance of
informal classrooms in unlikely places. Arlene Silberman followed students around in classrooms in Starkweather (population 250) where the
school of 200 children in grades 1–12 had 4 elementary teachers (all New
School degree candidates) holding classes "more exciting and certainly
more innovative than anything one can find in the Scarsdales, Winnetkas,
Shaker Heights, and Palo Altos of the United States." She visited
classrooms supplied with pegboards, cash registers, and Cuisenaire rods
that were divided into math, reading, science, and art areas. She saw small
groups of students working together, some children by themselves, others
at a table with the teacher, some in corners or sprawled on a carpet.
Classrooms in Edmore (population 405), Lakota (population 1,658), and
Minot (population 33,477) staffed by New School graduates were also
visited. Chapter seven in *Crisis in the Classroom*, based upon Silberman's
research in the state, resonates with the vitality of the informal instruction
she saw carried out in schools across the state. Articles in *Life, Saturday*

Review, newspapers, and New School publications trace the spread of open classrooms in Devil's Lake, Minto, and dozens of other one-teacher and city schools in the state.[20]

The Spread of Open Classrooms

Trying to document the extent that open classrooms in various forms spread through the state or the persistence in these practices over time is more difficult than simply counting instances of such classrooms. Quite similar to assessing the spread of progressivism, the problem is split between determining the degree of implementation among classrooms labeled open and the inevitable variations between classrooms in which informal practices (centers, small groups, etc.) have been used.

The first part of the problem involves using the global construct "open classroom" with teacher reports and direct observations providing the data from which to draw conclusions. Such data are difficult to interpret because of the varied meanings that teachers and observers pack into the phrase "open classroom." As I have already suggested in analyzing progressivism, informal education or open classroom as an unidimensional construct is less useful than a construct composed of varied elements which teachers have selectively and unevenly put into practice.

The second part of the problem deals with the sources of information themselves. Among researchers, there has been a growing awareness that teacher reports of progressive and open classroom practices tend to overestimate what observers in classrooms record. Thus, teacher and principal reports of how much informal practices have spread tend to be inflated. The evidence I have collected on North Dakota is vulnerable on these points.[21].

One way to determine the extent of informal practices in the state is to find out the number of New School interns and graduates that worked in the schools. By 1973, over 500 New School teachers and interns had taken their ideas of open classrooms into 80 schools, or almost 15 percent of the total schools in the state. Whether or not these New School-trained teachers continued their activities over the years is an issue explored in a study completed by a New School researcher in 1975. Through question-naires he compared a sample of 56 New School interns' classrooms with a random sample of 342 North Dakota teachers on a number of dimensions related to informal teaching: the extent that teachers dealt with children individually; the degree to which the teacher centralized or dispersed classroom decision making; different types of classroom activities and tasks; the linkages or integration of these experiences; and the extent that all of the teacher's arrangements and classroom organization contributed to children learning from one another.[22]

The researcher concluded that New School (by this time renamed the

Center for Teaching and Learning or CTL) interns "have classrooms significantly more open than those of teachers in general in North Dakota." While graduates of the New School maintained their commitment to informal education, there was "a tendency for their overall attitude toward open education to moderate."[23]

Although the study is limited, these results compare graduates with typical teachers in the state and indirectly suggest that most teachers did not convert their classrooms into open ones as defined by New School criteria. Buttressing that inference is a small study completed by a University of North Dakota researcher who asked teachers to describe the use of math materials such as fraction discs, Cuisenaire rods, and chips in their classrooms. These materials were common to informal classrooms since they lent themselves to individual and group use by children in centers; hence, the extent of their use becomes a rough proxy for the diffusion of informal techniques. Almost 1,000 teachers (or about one-third of those in the state) from 116 schools replied to the questionnaire. Ninety percent of the teachers reported that they had two or more of these manipulative materials in their rooms. Teacher use of these materials, however, was low. Almost half of the teachers said they used them "a little" and only seven percent said they used them "extensively." Also, the researcher found a strong relationship between materials children handle and the existence of learning centers, that is, the teachers who reported frequent use of rods, chips, discs, and metric materials were also teachers who reported they had learning centers. Of almost 1,000 teachers, 25% said they had learning centers with the highest percentage located at kindergarten (40%) and shrinking until the fifth and sixth grades where 14% and 15% of those teachers reported centers.[24]

The impact of the New School in disseminating ideas and practices about informal classrooms is demonstrable. The Johnny Appleseeds of open classrooms from the New School sowed and reaped across the state. Data, however, show the limited extent and staying power of the changes. Far more needs to be collected, yet what there is suggests that many North Dakota teachers between 1968 and 1975 adopted in varying degrees different versions of the open classroom as defined and altered by the New School and individual teachers.

In 1981, I spent a week in Grand Forks and Fargo visiting 6 schools and observing 63 teachers (or 20 percent of the grades 1–6 staffs in these 2 cities) to see what teachers did in their classrooms. Of the 63 teachers, 8 were New School graduates. I spent time at Madison and other schools that had been sites for interns and university faculty.

Both cities had about a dozen elementary schools with class sizes averaging 25 students. At least one out of every four elementary schools in each city contained open space; that is, large spaces separated by movable partitions, eight-foot high dividers, or homemade walls built from book cases and portable blackboards. In both cities, teachers told me that they were pleased that the central administration was about to act on their requests for walls so that each teacher would have a separate room, including Fargo's Madison elementary school where walls had been knocked down a decade earlier to create spacious double rooms. The teachers I observed had advanced training beyond the bachelor's degree. Rooms were copiously stocked with overhead projectors, sets of books, math and science materials, and equipment. Project activities were evident.

What patterns of instruction did I see while in classrooms of the six schools?

Table 4.1   Patterns of Instruction: Grand Forks and Fargo, 1981

	Teacher-centered Instruction, %	Mixed Pattern, %	Student-Centered Instruction, %	Number of Classes
Class Arrangement	43	30	27	(63)
Group Instruction	62	25	13	
Classroom talk	60	24	16	
Student Movement	37	0	63	
Class Activities	59	30	11	
Classes with One or More Centers ...	....			32.....

Keep in mind that my observations lasted between 15 to 30 minutes per teacher, generally occurred in the morning when elementary teachers concentrate upon teaching basic skills, and involved more than one teacher since in some buildings I could watch three to four teachers work with their classes simultaneously. This manner of observation is akin to a series of snapshots.

The table shows that a majority of the time teachers taught the class as an entire group, talked most of the time, and structured classroom activities that concentrated upon listening to the teacher and working as a class on workbooks or seatwork. More than half the teachers arranged the furniture in ways that encouraged students to talk with one another. Student movement inside the classroom was permitted without seeking permission from the teacher in two of every three classrooms I visited.

Small group and individual instruction and student-centered class activities occurred infrequently.

In almost one-third of the classrooms, there was at least one learning center. Four fifth and sixth grade teachers at Grand Forks' Benjamin Franklin school used a dozen centers for that part of the morning or afternoon when language arts and science was scheduled. They were the exception, however. When I asked teachers how and when they used the centers, invariably the response was: before and after scheduled activities like reading, language arts, lunch, recess, and as either enrichment, a reward for good behavior, or practice of skills already taught. Except for the four teachers mentioned above, centers were used as a periodic supplement to the existing program.

Teachers set aside time for each task in 27 percent of the classrooms where a daily schedule was posted. Of the eight New School graduates teaching in the schools I visited, and I had no way of knowing how typical they were of New School alumni, two used centers extensively for portions of the school day. In the other six classrooms I saw no evidence of centers. Four of those six had daily schedules on blackboards listing the tasks the class would do for the day.

By 1981, elements of open classrooms could be seen in these teacher rooms: student mobility, learning centers, and arrangment of classroom furniture. In organizing the class for instruction through grouping and classroom tasks assigned to students, however, the primary mode of instruction in these 63 classrooms clustered around a variety of teacher-centered practices. This brief glimpse of classrooms in two North Dakota cities less than a decade after an intense effort to install open classrooms in the state had withered suggests what elements of the approach persisted in classrooms and which were less durable. A predominately rural legislature endorsing classroom changes in order to upgrade the state's elementary schools is a substantially different setting for introducing open classrooms in the nation's largest school system.

Turn now to New York City in the 1970s for a look at the uneven enthusiasm for informal schooling that appeared and richocheted like a cue ball between 110 Livingston Street and schools across the city.

NEW YORK CITY

Compare the school system in 1940 with 1980. There were still about one million students in nearly a thousand buildings with over 50,000 teachers. There was still a Board of Education and a superintendent, although the latter's title had been upgraded to Chancellor. When I visited DeWitt Clinton High School bolted-down desks, somewhat scarred, still sat in rows, in classroom after classroom.[25]

Beneath this surface familiarity, however, a number of profound alterations had occurred in four decades to the New York City schools. Consider:

- Wave after wave of newcomers since World War II changed a school system that was predominately white in 1940 to one in which the majority were black and Hispanic, with heavy percentages of poor children from all ethnic backgrounds by 1980.
- One of ten children attended private school before World War II; four decades later, one out of eight attended private schools.
- In 1940, New York City schools were viewed as national leaders in public education. The Activity Program, elite high schools, and high test scores produced much competition for teacher and administrative vacancies. By 1980, filling classrooms with qualified teachers became a major task. Test scores, reported annually now in newspapers, had been in a downward slide for over a decade with just a glimmer of turnaround evident. Retrenchment measures resulting from the city's unprecedented fiscal emergency had driven class sizes up into the mid-30s and low-40s, stripped schools of critical support services, and buried a number of novel efforts to improve schooling. The image of the school system was that of a troubled, chaotic organization unable to cope with the problems at hand.[26]

Signs of those changes in four decades were posted in the number of superintendents that went in and out of the revolving doors of 110 Livingston Street. While 4 school chiefs served the system in the first 40 years of the century, 6 sat behind the top desk in the schools since 1960. State laws had mandated the division of the school system into 31 school districts (kindergarten through eighth grade schools), each run by a community school board empowered to hire and fire its own teachers and administrators. Protracted and divisive teacher strikes and parent boycotts closed schools down numerous times between 1960 and 1970.

What had changed more than anything were public attitudes. Belief in the legitimacy of the school board and staff as guardians of children's intellectual and moral development had eroded. During the post-World War II years confidence diminished in the public schools to do what they were supposed to do. In those years, New Yorkers heard of school officials' corruption in constructing new schools. They saw school boards and superintendents paddling first on one side of the canoe, then on the other side, keeping a straight course but reluctant to deal frankly with the issue of desegregation. They watched the uncertain, if not fumbling, attempts of top administrators trying to wrestle with teacher union and parent activism. And New York parents with children in the schools experienced the results of squabbles between the Board and unions and parent groups in repeated strikes and boycotts that shut schools down for all children— reaching a crescendo of raucous anarchy between 1968 and 1970 when confrontations between union members and community control advocates unleashed racial bigotry, saw parents and teacher-activists arrested, and led to intervention by the State Commissioner of Education and the legislature. Substantial changes in the governance and organization of the entire school system resulted. As the city watched these events unfold, official charges of incompetence, public pleas for improvement, and failed efforts to negotiate differences were displayed in daily newspapers, on nightly television news, and in national journals throughout the 1960s and 1970s.[27]

While intense criticism of public schools was familiar to New Yorkers —recall the 1912 Hanus Report and barrages of charges that Superintendents William Maxwell and his successors absorbed in their tenures— the recent period differed because criticism was somehow accompanied by a erosion of the public confidence in the schools' capacity to improve the lot of children. Within this political context of the late 1960s, open classrooms and alternative schools popped up like mushrooms after a rain.

Adopting Open Classrooms: Rhetoric and Action

A vignette of a school program getting underway one morning in Harlem's P.S. 123:

> At 9:30 A.M. teacher aides and student teachers begin to line the small, L-shaped section of the corridor with tables and chairs. Out of a storage room they bring out boxes full of materials and spread the contents on the tables. There are scales, Cuisenaire rods, water vessels, musical instruments, a dozen different kinds of match puzzles, counting devices, hexagons, trapezoids, animals, clay.... Singly, and in pairs, threes and fours, children filter into the corridor from five classrooms, the doors of which are open and inside which teachers are conducting lessons....
>
> The corridor has become another kind of place. Some children move directly to activities, having learned the corridor's offerings. Others, sometimes with a friend in tow, shop around before settling down to one thing.... At one table a four year old girl is manipulating a game about people, identifying relationships. Behind, a six year old has spread herself on a piece of newsprint on the floor while a student teacher traces her form in crayon, which she will then measure in blocks and hang on the wall.
>
> Other children are pacing off distances, measuring with string.... A few feet away a group of four has been working steadily for an hour weighing shoes....
>
> Children return to their classes, others come out, work continues in all the rooms.... Inside the room, run along formal lines, there is a striking absence of restlessness. Children are hard at work despite the sounds and movements from the corridor. In sharp contrast, a second grade class next door operates informally in small clusters of children.... By 11 A.M. the corridor begins to clear. Materials, tables, and chairs have been returned to their storeroom. Left on the corridor walls are the paper cutouts of children figures.[28]

This description of the first Open Corridor program, as gently and astutely introduced by City College of New York Professor Lillian Weber in 1967, illustrates another variation of informal education adapted to American conditions. Weber had spent a year and a half visiting British primary schools and had written about them.[29]

In 1967 she found an opportunity in P.S. 123 to apply her ideas of informal schooling by placing student teachers there and in nearby schools. In subsequent years, Weber pursued her convictions about the central importance of the teacher as decision maker, teachers joining the program voluntarily, informal classrooms composed of children with different abilities, and deep aversion to labels about openness. Her strategy of change, working as a professor and later as director of a center for informal education—both outside of the school system—was encouraging a series of small changes taken individually and voluntarily by teachers and schools, to produce, over time, a transformed teacher and school. Never, she said, "was it our intention to convince the whole New York City school system that they should go this way. Instead, she wanted "to work in a small way to create an exemplar of what could be possible in the public schools. . . ."[30]

From five kindergarten-second grade teachers in P.S. 123, a network of contacts spread outward in Manhattan until in 1971 ten schools and 80 classrooms were formally linked to Weber's City College Advisory Service to Open Corridors which became the Workshop Center for Open Education. Four years later, an inventory of schools and teachers affiliated with the Open Corridors program listed 17 schools and 156 teachers with almost 4,000 children in classes.[31]

By 1978 when Weber's friends and admirers, including Charles Silberman and Vito Perrone, gathered to celebrate a decade of her investment in informal education, 26 elementary and 2 secondary schools had 200 teachers with almost 5,000 children in open classrooms tied directly to City College. In addition, over a thousand teachers, aides, principals, and parents visited the Workshop Center annually.[32]

Elsewhere in the city, whole schools and individual teachers adopted versions of the open classroom on their own initiative or with the help of other privately and publicly funded groups working out of universities and store fronts. Other teachers, unaware of the innovations or determined to construct a form of open classroom tailored to their style and students, just went ahead and did it. While Herb Kohl and Gloria Channon wrote books about their personal odysseys in uncertainly opening up their classrooms, other teachers wrote of similar journeys—some of them painfully unsuccessful—in Master's theses.[33]

Between 1970 and 1973, national interest in open classrooms surged forward. Locally, a similar welling up of enthusiasm among parents and teachers occurred amidst the heavy emotional fallout from the 1968–1969 school year of three teacher strikes and the creation of over thirty community school districts. It occurred also in the midst of a year-long national search for a person to assume the newly created top post of Chancellor. After Sargent Shriver, Arthur Goldberg, Ramsey Clark, and Ralph Bunche—all national figures—had turned down the Board of Education, Harvey Scribner, Vermont's Commissioner of Education, accepted the post in 1970.[34]

During these turbulent years, the naming of Scribner as Chancellor and the forthright public position taken by United Federation of Teachers' Albert Shanker in favor of informal education intersected neatly for a moment in time, raising hopes for the future of open classrooms in the city. Fifty-six year old Harvey Scribner, former rural Maine teacher and Teaneck (New Jersey) superintendent prior to his stint in Vermont, rang all the bells that informal classroom enthusiasts wanted desperately to hear. His "Vermont Design for Education" (1968) laid out 17 objectives that captured the main tenets of informal education. He quoted John Holt in his speechs. He met with Gloria Channon, a fifth grade teacher and author of a book on her conversion to open classrooms. He drew often upon his experience as a rural teacher who tried to get out of the way of students who wanted to learn, as he often said. "There is no one design of education that can serve the needs of all people," he told a reporter. "We must give children an opportunity to learn in their particular manner," he said, "to proceed at their own rate, to work at their own level. We must give them many alternatives."[35]

Pledging to make decentralization work and to reform schooling in order to produce more choices for students in classrooms and schools, Scribner visited schools, spoke to teachers and administrators frequently, and sought out like-minded people in the city in an effort to build coalitions for change.[36]

Working the other side of the street, Albert Shanker said to a reporter: "We intend to get teachers to read Silberman (*Crisis in the Classroom*) and see him as a hero, a constructive critic." Endorsing the informal classroom as a vehicle for reforming schools, the teacher union president pledged to inform union leadership of the merits of open classrooms, sponsor community forums, and support system-wide efforts in that direction. At a later city-wide meeting of teachers, Shanker urged that parents be permitted to "shop around" to find an open classroom. The new Chancellor and savvy union president publicly supporting informal education was, indeed, a special moment. It lasted no longer than a sand castle in the incoming tide.[37]

Two and a half years into the job, Scribner announced he would leave the post when his contract ended in June, 1973. His explanation: "a widening gap of confidence" between the Board of Education and himself. Trying to reform the New York City schools, Scribner discovered, was akin to trying to turn around the liner Queen Elizabeth II in the East River. By

1973, even before Scribner left, Shanker's public statements on the joys of open classrooms were hard to locate. By 1975, union-supported Teacher Centers largely ignored informal classrooms as appropriate targets for teacher change. Budget cuts, ballooning class sizes, staff firings, shifting teachers to other assignments, increased emphasis on improving test scores, and basic skills instruction replaced talk about reform and informal classrooms.[38]

Spread of Open Classrooms

Why the brief moment of reform hopes disappeared is of much interest to me but of less importance in this study than determining what most teachers did in their classrooms while talk from union leaders and administrators concentrated upon opening up classrooms and alternatives. Evidence that hundreds of teachers began centers, rearranged furniture, provisioned their rooms, taught small groups, and prized student participation has been presented. But there were over 600 elementary schools and over 25,000 teachers. To what extent did elements of open classrooms appear among them? The answer here is similar to the one offered before on progressive practices two generations earlier. Definitions of openness varied; teachers were selective in what they introduced; and the pattern of adoption was uneven in schools—closer to the spattering of ink than an inkblot.

What can be said with a modest degree of confidence is that the spread of open classrooms, however defined and implemented, did not exceed the generous 25 percent of teachers estimated by Loftus to be using activity methods in their classrooms just prior to World War II. Recall that he made his estimate after years of high interest and a six-year formal experiment sanctioned and promoted by the Superintendent and staff that involved over 75,000 children in nearly 70 schools.

Scribner served less than three years; he shaped no explicit and sustained set of policies and organizational procedures; nor did his ideas enjoy widespread support among central administration and middle-level managers. Words were simply insufficient to generate changes beyond 110 Livingston Street. Also, a general political instability pervaded the system with the birth of 30 community school districts coming in the backwash of acrimonious teacher strikes. Thus, no organizational drive for adopting open classrooms existed. Lacking a formal institutional framework that could boost open classrooms, teachers embraced informal practices on an ad hoc basis, finding occasional support in colleges, private groups, or cadres of like-minded individuals elsewhere in the system. How many schools and how many teachers eventually implemented open classroom practices is impossible to determine with any precision since no formal classroom survey was ever undertaken in the 1967–1975 period.

If a survey had been done and it showed that more than one teacher in four or five had maintained an open classroom, even defined broadly, I would have asked for a recount, given the lack of corroborating evidence. The basis for my estimate is narrow, however. While City College, Fordham University, Queens College, Bank Street, and the Creative Teaching Workshop were active in spreading informal classroom techniques, data for the Open Corridors is available and provides some basis for an estimate. In the 17 elementary schools in 1975 where Open Corridors existed there was a total student population of about 13,000 and around 550 teachers. Of that population, over 3,000 students and 150 teachers were part of the program. By 1978, in 26 elementary schools linked with Workshop on Open Education there were 3,900 children and 180 teachers involved in the program. These schools had an estimated 21,000 children and 800 teachers. And this level of involvement was in schools where one would expect diffusion to be contagious since non-open classroom teachers worked next to colleagues heavily involved in the program. No doubt some schools had heavy participation because of the length of time the school had been associated with City College and other schools may have recently joined.[39]

In other schools across the city where teachers lacked outside support from a university or advisers the level of involvement, I would guess, was lower. None of this is to suggest that the influence of the Workshop on Open Education and similar efforts was insubstantial. Teachers trained in Open Corridors took administrative posts throughout the system and worked elsewhere in school programs (e.g. Teacher Centers). Also, when funding was cut for Open Corridors advisers, community boards often found accounts elsewhere in the budget to continue the work of consultants.[40]

Teacher Reports and Direct Observation of Classrooms

Another basis for the estimate comes from the numerous reports I have read of New York City teachers in these years and how they wrestled with the daily issues of steering 30 or more students through a half-dozen subjects in self-contained classrooms. Some of these teachers, intrigued by talk about informal classrooms, gingerly tried some techniques; most seemed too busy, too exhausted, too intimidated by superiors, too intent upon surviving, or simply disagreed with the direction. They hesitated to try out new approaches that required preparation of materials, more contact with children in and out of the classroom, and possibly extra time at home working on classroom tasks.

In the late 1960s, a number of teacher accounts described conditions under which teachers taught and what they did in their classrooms. The school Gerald Levy wrote about in *Ghetto School*, located in a mid-town slum, had 1,300 children and 70 teachers, half of whom were inexperienced and newly appointed. He records passionately and with much disgust how they stumbled through 1967–1968, a year marked by a wildcat teacher's strike, parent action, and administrative fecklessness. Order replaced learning as the primary goal. Except for the kindergarten teacher and one second grade teacher, instruction was a series of mindless routines designed, he said, to keep children quiet and busy at their desks. Reading like a topsy-turvy version of Joseph Rice's dreary chronicles of New York classrooms seven decades earlier, the book portrays both children and teachers with a strong distaste for schools.[41]

Gloria Channon's frank description of how she introduced 22 Harlem fifth graders to an open classroom in 1967–1968 contains unsparing administrative memos and observations drawn from a painful internal struggle to free herself of a mindset that a dozen years in New York schools had imprinted upon her. From the *Staff Bulletin*, a 110 Livingston Street publication, of January 31, 1968:

- During recitation lessons, pupils should raise hands to indicate desire to make a contribution, they should be encouraged to speak in full sentences....
- Pupils must ask permission to go to the bathroom....
- Gum chewing is forbidden anywhere in the school building. The teacher *must* set the example....
- Pupils should empty their desks regularly under the routine supervision of the teacher and everything other than approved books and materials should be discarded on the spot or taken home at 3:00....[42]

Channon observed that by the third grade the New York curriculum "gets whipped into shape."

> Children sit at their desks for hours. Notebooks and textbooks become the main focus of their activity. Lessons are formally organized into spelling, penmanship, reading, composition, and math. Silence and good behavior are at a premium, now as never before.[43]

In another Harlem school of 1,350 children, Donna DeGaetani chronicled her experiences in a building dominated by a principal she feared and where parents were pushing for open classrooms in 1972—her third as a teacher. Her frankness is disarming. DeGaetani described her reactions to a formal observation by her principal.

> Knowing that she was to observe you teaching resulted in such actions as adjusting shades to regulation height, picking up stray pieces of paper...dropped on the floor, bringing your bulletin boards up to date, and prepping the children on their behavior.... I admit I was a coward, cowed by an authority I did not believe in but had not the strength to challenge.[44]

After this principal retired, 4 teachers (of about 30) in grades 1 through 3 opened up their classrooms slowly through centers and activities chosen by students for an hour or so a day. Proud as she was of her progress, the weight of the Metropolitan Achievement Tests bore down on the teacher. "Too often the cloud of achievement tests," she wrote, "pressures teachers into compromises.... I know I will teach my children how to take the Test, although I realize this is basically against what I believe in." Why did she succumb to the presure?

> I do not have the energy nor, at this point, the willingness of fight the system. I know the scores of open education classes in our school will be compared with those of traditional classes. The comparison is itself fallacious. I know that.... But most parents don't. Many administrators don't and the system doesn't.[45]

In a nearby school similar to DeGaetani's, Alicia Montalvo kept a diary of her third year as a primary teacher in 1971–1972. The six other first grade teachers had classes "conducted in the traditional manner. Each child has an assigned seat and all tables face the front of the room." In order to start an open classroom, a "Bank Street" one as she defined it, "I had to get special permission from the principal." Because she often stayed after 3:00—the time in the contract that teachers could leave school—to prepare materials and change centers, the principal called her in to say that she had to leave by 3:30 because no one could be responsible for her after that time. "I really don't know if this whole idea of mine is worth the effort," she wrote in her diary for that day, "Im so disgusted." She got even angrier later in the year when she switched the children from their work with Cuisenaire rods to the conventional way of teaching addition and subtraction after the principal told her that "the children were going to be tested to see whether or not they were learning in the open classroom."[46]

In P.S. 198 (Manhattan), Dorothy Boroughs, fourth grade teacher of 30 students, unlike her colleagues described above, enjoyed an easy-going relationship with her principal. In a unique series of almost a dozen articles for *The New York Times*, Joseph Lelyveld spent an entire school year (1970–1971) periodically visiting Borough's class.[47]

"A brisk, energetic, and strongly committed young teacher who is usually among the first at school to punch in," Lelyveld described Boroughs' as a teacher dedicated to getting children to read at or above the fourth grade level. He described her when she laughed, scolded, pleaded with children, and showered them with a mixture of touching praise and earnest demands. The children responded with openness and seriousness, if not outright affection for their teacher. Students sat at clustered desks facing one another, working individually, in small groups or as an entire class on tasks that the teacher had assigned. High teacher expectations for achievement and behavior were evident daily in a vibrant charm that few children could resist.[48]

Lelyveld also provides a glimpse of some organizational processes that affect how and what Boroughs did. Take, for example, the visit of her supervisor, assistant principal Edmund Fried, to evaluate her teaching of a social studies lesson. Sitting in the back of the room, Boroughs gave him the daily plan composed of the aims, procedures, and activities that she intended to follow as she taught the lesson.

> Miss Boroughs had been worrying about the lesson plan for a week (Lelyveld writes) but had not actually committed any thoughts to paper until the lunch hour that day. Normally she prepares lesson plans to satisfy the demands of her supervisor but never works from them....[49]

After teaching the lesson on explorers, Boroughs brought the period to a close with the question: "why are we studying the explorers?"

> "Because he's here to watch," said Shaun Sheppard knowingly, nodding in the direction of Mr. Fried.
> "Fooled you, Shaun," the assistant principal declared, "I know about them already."
> On his way out, Mr. Fried noted that Pizzaro was the only Spanish explorer mentioned in the text who had not been mentioned in the lesson. He told Miss Boroughs that later on he would go over with her the comments that filled two sheets on his clipboard.[50]

Or consider Boroughs' exposure to the open classroom. In the spring semester she had signed up with a handful of other P.S. 198 teachers to take an after-school course on open classrooms offered by Hunter College. After hearing from her student teacher about three teachers at P.S. 42 on the Lower East Side who had opened up their classrooms without funds or outside help, Boroughs got permission from her principal to spend a morning in these teachers' rooms. The Hunter College class and these visits spurred Boroughs' thinking and a mild rearrangement of furniture into one math corner. When two of the P.S. 42 teachers were invited by the professor to speak to the P.S. 198 class, the principal announced on the public address system that the entire staff of 55 were invited to hear the teachers describe how they opened up their classes. Twelve teachers, most of whom were registered for the class, showed up at the meeting.[51]

Boroughs was interested in an open classroom. "But," Lelyveld wrote, "she seemed uncertain as to how far or fast she herself would move in that direction. By the end of the week, "debate over educational theory had faded. The supreme reality was Spring."[52]

Not far from P.S. 198, poet Philip Lopate worked in P.S. 90 in the early 1970s as a writer charged to help teachers and children to write creatively. Working in a bilingual, experimental school with open classrooms Lopate received advice from a friendly veteran teacher.

> This school may look free and groovy on the surface but don't be fooled, there's a lot of conservative feeling. Nothing from the outside will take root at P.S. 90 unless it's introduced very cautiously and slowly.

After being in the school for awhile, Lopate noticed some classes were mostly white while others were predominately black and Puerto Rican. Denise Loften explained why.

> Denise said the reason for this was that the parents were given a choice at the beginning of the year whether they wanted to place their children in 'open' or 'more formal' classrooms. The white, liberal parents of the Upper West Side tended to select open classrooms. The parents from ethnic minorities opted more for traditional classes, feeling that open education might be soft on basic skills.... [53]

From these teacher and journalist accounts a flavor for the organizational context, not to mention the larger environment outside of the school, suggests that versions of open classrooms spread in a hop-scotch manner, following personal contacts and random information, yet seldom dominating an entire school.

Supporting this observation are limited data drawn from over 30 elementary classroom descriptions from across the city. Figure 4.1 shows that student-centered practices occurred in over half of the classes in furniture arrangement and student movement but in grouping for instruction and classroom tasks in no more than one-quarter of the classrooms did these practices appear. Two items, however, are interesting. The substantial percentages of a mixed pattern that turn up under group instruction

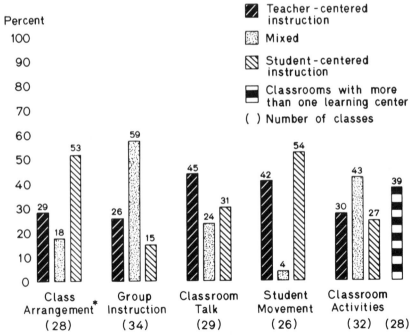

Figure 4.1 Patterns of Instruction in New York City Elementary Classrooms, 1967–1975.

and classroom activities; and the number of classrooms that contained at least one learning center. I have already mentioned the problems accompanying any attempt to determine the spread among teachers of informal practices. These figures support the point that teachers were particular in what they chose to put into practice.

Given the limits to the data I presented, it would still be fair to say that open classrooms, at varying stage of development, dotted the school map of the city in these peak years of interest in informal classrooms. But these dots probably didn't add up to more than one teacher in four or five. What about high schools?

Regular and Alternative High Schools

Alternative schools were not simply the secondary counterpart to open classrooms, although there were similarities. The roots of alternative high schools differed somewhat from the sources of informal education. These roots were located in student protest against university programs, Vietnam, civil rights concerns, and a melange of issues that came together in the late 1960s like metal filings hugging a magnet. Protest filtered down to high schools. Growing disaffection with high school rules and behavior, bigness, conventional instruction, a lack of participation in decisions, and a curriculum viewed as alien to current youth concerns found expression in student boycotts, underground newspapers, drop-outs, and the establishment of private and public alternative schools.[54]

Murray Road (Newton, Massachusetts) and New York's Harlem Prep opened their doors in 1967. Wilson Open Campus School (Mankato, Minnesota) began in 1968, and, a year later, Philadelphia's Parkway program sent students throughout the city to learn. At the height of the movement hundreds of secondary alternative schools had been created by 1972. The mortality rate ran high. Still, by 1975, public alternative secondary schools were a fact of life that most school systems accepted and, in a number of instances, nurtured.[55]

Schools without walls where the city is the classroom, store-front schools, mini-schools within larger conventional high schools, theme or magnet schools (e.g. arts, science, etc.)—all fall under the heading of alternative high schools. I exclude vocational, continuation, and other schools targeted on certain groups of students, most of which were established prior to 1965.

No easy generalization, then, can capture the diversity in these schools. A number of commonalities, however, existed.

- School as community
- Teacher as advisor
- Active rather than passive learning

- Student participation in major decision making
- Needs and experiences of students incorporated into curriculum and instruction.[56]

Varying greatly, individual high schools stressed some of these themes more than others. Nonetheless, in size, climate, teachers advising students, and curricular decision making—particularly in constructing elective courses—and ideological commitment, alternatives differed from regular high schools.[57]

What about instruction? With the individual student, active learning, and curricular choice paramount values in alternative schools, what teaching practices occurred? Most of the research on alternative high schools has concentrated upon issues of governance, curriculum, composition of student body, student-teacher relationships, organizational processes; very little attention has been paid to pedagogy.[58]

What little has been done stresses diversity in teaching methods. David Moore, for example, cites the range of practice that he observed and gathered from the limited research: teacher-directed, programmed instruction, to "relatively formless, collaborative investigations and activities." Discussion is the preferred teaching method, he notes. "Curiously," he writes, "lecturing happens more than one might imagine, but open talk is far more common." Frequent field trips, guest speakers, films, and group work are commonly used, according to Moore. Still "teachers often take the primary responsibility for designing and supplying materials for courses." His interviews with students uncovered that they wanted "instructors to assume that role." Moore notes that there may be less innovative teaching practice in and of itself but the frquency and the mix of these practices "may be new in American education."[59]

Dan Duke visited and studied six alternative secondary schools. In instructional grouping he found mixed ability grouping in all six. Teachers used a variety of classroom groupings, with small group and independent study common to all but one of the schools. When he looked at teaching practices he found that half of the schools had special rooms set aside for students to work with tutors or individually. None, however, had "creative room arrangements," i.e. learning centers, chairs arranged to increase student exchanges, etc. One high school had team teaching and one used older students to tutor younger ones. For student evaluation, three schools used fixed scales that students were measured against; yet far more stress was reported to be on individual, non-competitive grading. In telling parents how students were doing in school, four alternative schools used portfolios of what students had produced and teacher-parent conferences. After reviewing the results and the history of instructional reforms, Duke concluded that "contemporary alternative schools do not constitute a pedagogical revolution."[60]

In New York City, alternative schools became an official plank in Harvey Scribner's platform to improve the city's high schools. Scribner was in charge of over 100 academic and vocational high schools enrolling over 300,000 students in the early 1970s. The academic high schools were large by any standard. Most range from 3,000 to 4,000 students with 175 to 215 teachers on the faculty. Among the smaller schools were the vocational ones which enrolled between 1,500 to 2,000 students; among the larger schools in 1971 were John Jay (Brooklyn) with 5,600 students, Louis Brandeis (Manhattan) with nearly 6,000, and DeWitt Clinton (Bronx), the largest New York high school, with almost 7,000 students—all male. Ethnic composition in the high schools (1971) was:

white	50.9%
black	29.5
Puerto Rican	15.1
Oriental	1.4
other	3.1

Daily attendance for academic high schools was 77 percent of the student body. Almost one of every three students read two or more years below grade level. Yet nearly eight out of ten graduates applied to either junior or four year colleges.[61]

The new Chancellor directed a massive operation. Yet even prior to Scribner's arrival, a number of privately funded store-front schools, established through private efforts, aimed at salvaging able students who had been either pushed out or dropped out of regular high schools. The New York Urban Coalition and the Urban League, using funds raised from banks and corporations, established networks of these schools in low-income minority areas of the city. As the grants ended, the private groups negotiated with the Board of Education to install them in the regular high schools as mini-schools. Such schools had 75 to 125 students with separate staffing and rooms in the main building or in churches and rented facilities nearby, such as Harambee Prep in Charles Evans Hughes High School (Manhattan), Wingate Prep in the school of the same name (Brooklyn), and Haaren High School, itself divided into 14 semi-autonomous mini-schools.[62]

Under Scribner and his successor, these mini-schools and separate alternative schools spread throughout the system so that by 1975 there were 11 alternative schools enrolling 4,000 students and 40 mini-schools in all 5 boroughs of the city with about 6,500 students. In addition there were a number of alternative *programs*, located in schools and central offices, aimed at talented students. The Executive High School Internship program, Erasmus Hall's Institute of Music and Art, and Julia Richman High School's Talent Unlimited program are examples of such programs. By

1976, all of these alternatives, including mini-schools, enrolled almost 15,000 students or about 5 percent of all high school youth.[63]

The range of options, as mentioned earlier, was broad. Most mini-schools were last-ditch efforts to save students from dropping out, to recruit truants back to school and to upgrade marginally academic, but able young men and women who found it difficult to adjust to regular high schools. Small classes of less than 25 students, teachers who listen, make demands, and didn't mind being called by their first names; street workers who would see students at home or at their job: these were elements that characterized many of these mini-schools.[64]

The 11 alternative schools in 1976 included the City-As-School, the New York counterpart to Philadelphia's Parkway program; Harlem Prep; Middle College High School—linked to LaGuardia Community College—and Park East High School, a school initially founded by community groups.[65]

Evidence drawn from journalists who observed over a dozen classes at Wingate Prep, Harambee, George Washington Prep, and Lower East Side Prep suggest a range of teacher approaches well within the mainstream of conventional practice. While classes are smaller and less formal, teaching methods are familiar. A sampling:

- A wide-ranging discussion on the use of drugs, the new state law on punishing drug pushers, and the impact of peer cultures intensely engaged students.
- An English class reading a Dorothy Parker short story about a blind black child spent part of the period moving around the class blindfolded prior to discussing the story.
- Students reading parts in a play written by a contemporary black writer halted periodically for moments of intense discussion between the class and teacher.
- A history class that was a disaster. The teacher lectured, rambled, asked questions and plunged on with answers to her questions; students paid little attention, talked among themselves, ignored teacher warnings. Mercifully, the bell rings.
- A teacher wrote quadratic equations on the blackboard and students took notes silently.
- An astronomy lesson was interspersed with questions and answers on astrology and horoscopes.[66]

One reporter summed up his impressions of classroom teaching in mini-schools: "The classroom instruction and subject matter are not essentially different from what might be found in many conventional high schools." What was different in these alternatives was size of the school, informality in relations between teachers and students, and governance decisions that often involved students.[67]

In Regular High School Classrooms

In the conventional academic high schools, patterns of instruction were like those practiced in earlier generations. I located photographs and written descriptions of 33 teachers in 13 high schools between 1969 and 1975. Spare as the sample is, the convergence in teaching patterns is striking. (See Figure 4.2.)

Teaching the entire class as a group almost always, the teacher talking almost two-thirds of the time, hardly any student movement within the room, and most class activities built around students listening, writing, watching, etc.—this is teacher-centered instruction writ large.

Profiles of two high schools, including extensive classroom observations by *New York Times* reporters offer additional data to the 33 that I collected. Reporter William Stevens produced an in-depth article in 1971

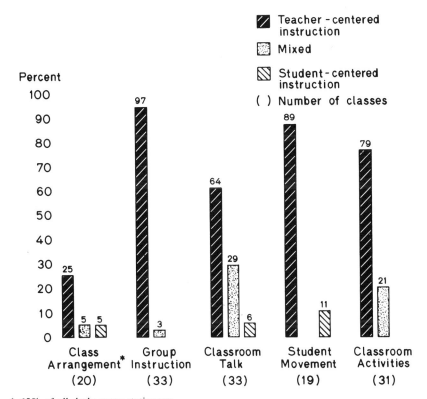

* 65% of all desks were stationary.

Figure 4.2   Patterns of Instruction in New York City High School Classrooms, 1965–1975.

on John Bowne High School (Queens), a school with a faculty of 200 for 3,100 students, of whom 75% went to either a two- or four-year college. Ethnically, Bowne was 65% white and 30% black, most of whom came as a result of a Board desegregation plan.[68]

Stevens sat in classrooms. He contrasted a radio electronics class taught by Physics teacher Norman Hessel, where students individually and enthusiastically built radios piece by piece, and a math class that would give any teacher a sweaty nightmare—students throwing spitballs at one another, playing cards, walking around the room, ignoring the teacher's directions. "This year," Stevens wrote, "Bowne has been preoccupied with how to create more situations like that in Hessel's class and change scenes like those in the mathematics class."[69]

Bowne had nearly 500 classes a day in about 75 different subjects. The day was sliced up into nine 40-minute periods. Solid discussions get going, teachers reported, and the bell cuts them off. While the scheduling of time affects instruction, teachers also pointed out to Stevens that "traditional teaching approaches" drive students into boredom. "If we were ever to teach sex the way we teach other things," one teacher remarked, "it would go out of style." And Stevens, after sitting in a number of classes, said that "the teacher is at the front of the class attempting to interest everyone in the same subject at the same time."

Hard as that is to do, teachers continued to attempt it. The social studies department chairman told Stevens that each lesson is supposed to have a specific objective plus questions that provoke students to think, and participate in classroom discussions. One teacher in that department said that if he had one-third of his class participating, he judged the lesson a success.[70]

Efforts to individualize instruction through independent study and small groups were underway, according to principal Roxee Joly; "our success has been minimal, but not zero." Many teachers, Stevens said, still believe that "a quiet classroom is by definition good."[71]

William Stevens also spent a week shadowing a Harlem ninth grader who attended John F. Kennedy (Bronx), a new (1972) eight-story high school with 1,800 freshmen and sophomores that would grow in enrollment to almost 5,000 as it absorbed more grades. Fifteen year old Natalie Wright was part of the 40 percent of the school that was black. The rest of the school was roughly divided between white and Hispanic students. Stevens' comments and Natalie's observations of her academic classes follow:

- *Introductory Physical Science.* The science teacher paired off students to work on a second run-through of an experiment on the conservation of mass. They heated sealed test tubes of copper and sulphur, weighed, and recorded it. They spent two days on the experiment because the teacher was trying to get the class to graph the results. "Very boring to Natalie." Stevens wrote, because she had learned conservation of mass in junior high school.

- *Algebra.* "Happy class." Natalie worked on polynominal multiplication problems all period as the teacher circulated through the class helping individual students. After Natalie finished, she began helping other students. "I just like it," she replied to Stevens' question about her interest in Algebra.
- *Social Studies.* Natalie is bored on Monday. She couldn't care less about ancient China's civil service system or their scholar-gentry class. On Wednesday, students and teacher got into a lively discussion of civil service, social status, and class mobility.
- *Spanish.* Natalie had failed class in first nine weeks. Teachers were switched. The lesson on Monday was based upon a story of a meeting between a tourist and hotel clerk. Using a "Peanuts" cartoon, the teacher asked questions in Spanish and the class chorused replies.
- *Creative Writing.* Teacher introduced onomatopoeia. Question and answers exchanges occurred after teacher explanation. When teacher asked for examples, class exploded with a "cacaphony of bangs, meows, buzzes, bow–wows, swishes, jingles, moos, oinks.... Much hilarity."
- "2.45 p.m. Bell. Liberation."

Stevens summarized two entire days of classes with the laconic: "Tuesday was the same as yesterday," or "classes were the same."[72]

Except for science, where laboratory work had Natalie and a classmate paired off, the other four classes were taught as a whole group. Discussion or a mild form of recitation were the primary means of exchanging information. Seatwork took up one entire period. Little student movement was apparent, except for science. Each lesson was structured, directed, and moved along by the teacher who covered the content. Teaching through a textbook was common. As another John F. Kennedy teacher put it a few years later, "I have always felt that the best teaching machine is a book."[73]

Stevens' narrative of 2 high schools overlap the 33 descriptions I gathered. Teacher-centered patterns of instruction dominated both conventional and mini-school classes with some variations in degree and frequency of particular practices being evident.

About the time that Steven's account appeared, Scribner had announced his resignation. Within a year Irving Anker, a New York City educator of 38 years service who had risen through the ranks as most of his predecessors, assumed the Chancellorship. Improving test scores and accountability were the new buzz words circulating among insiders in the mid-1970s. Automatic promotions were abolished. Tougher standards for reading performance were instituted before promotion to a higher grade would be permitted. Open classrooms were no longer a hot topic. With the onset of severe budget cuts in 1975, survival replaced talk about reform.[74]

The fiscal emergency that jolted New York like a dash of cold water drove public officials to cut back severely all government agencies, especially the public schools. Teacher layoffs crippled programs. An Open Corridor school (P.S. 84) had 26 of 52 teachers pink-slipped. The ripple effects of layoffs shipped teachers with more seniority to vacancies in schools where teachers with less years in the system, many of whom were black and Hispanic, had been fired. Massive staff dislocation aborted many infant efforts at opening up classrooms. Class size ballooned beyond the contractual limits of 32 and 34 students in elementary and secondary schools, respectively. Aides were let go. Counselors and special teachers were cut. Larger classes and less help added up to further plunges in teacher morale. Not exactly the kind of climate that nourished teacher initiative, risk-taking, putting out extra effort, or a spirit of innovation.[75]

Yet in 1981 P.S. 84, and a number of other elementary schools, with a decade of history in Open Corridors and informal education, still retained those classrooms. While there are fewer teachers and principals than a decade ago, that such efforts survived, indeed, flourished in an indifferent, if not hostile, environment is a testimonial to the tenacity of committed teachers and administrators.

At the secondary level, alternative high schools and mini-schools, also hit hard by retrenchment, survived quite well. In 1979, 11 alternative high schools enrolling almost 5,000 students were still operating, excluding many students enrolled in mini-schools lodged in senior highs (e.g. Seward Park High School, James Monroe High School, Haaren High School).[76]

By the early 1980s, amidst the dominant teacher-centeredness of most classrooms, certain residues of informal schooling persisted across the city. As in the two North Dakota cities I visited in 1981, patterns in classroom variations were evident. Degrees of openness had penetrated considerable numbers of elementary classrooms but far fewer in the upper grades. Let us turn now to Washington, D.C., to see if similar patterns emerged.

WASHINGTON, D.C.

Veteran school-watchers had never seen a year like 1967. In April, teachers voted 3–2 to have the American Federation of Teachers represent them at the bargaining table. Teacher unions had arrived in a non-union town. In June, for the first time in the history of the District schools judicial appointments created a Board of Education with a majority of black members, most of whom actively opposed the policies of Carl Hansen, school chief for nine years. Later in the same month, a year-long, quarter-million dollar study by Teachers College of the entire school system was released. The study severely criticized the Superintendent's policies, the largely ineffective and inappropriate instructional program, and called for an end to the Four-Track system of grouping students.

The very same day, federal Judge J. Skelly Wright rendered a 183-page decision in the *Hobson* v. *Hansen* suit. He ordered an end to the track system, the busing of black children from overcrowded schools to near-empty white schools west of Rock Creek Park, and faculty integration. Within two weeks, the Board decided not to appeal the Wright decision and asked the Superintendent to implement the court order. Instead, Carl Hansen, father of the Amidon Plan, a tightly structured program that placed the teacher at the center of instruction, and the Four-Track system, resigned. Indeed, the events of 1967 shook the D.C. system by the scruff of the neck, unnerving the organization profoundly in the decade that followed.[77]

One benchmark of the subsequent instability is increased superintendent turnover. For almost a half-century (1920–1967), four superintendents served the District: Frank Ballou, Robert Haycock, Hobart Corning, and Carl Hansen. Yet in just over a decade (1968–1980), six school chiefs moved in and out of the large twelfth-floor office in the downtown Presidential Building.

Demography, court decisions, and political change explain the turmoil at the top. The school system had grown from over 90,000 students in 1940 to 150,000 in 1967, of whom more than 90 percent were black. Almost 8,000 teachers worked in nearly 140 schools (1967). Washington was the largest predominately black school system in the nation. Although the *Bolling* v. *Sharpe* decision, the District's counterpart to *Brown* v. *Board of Education*, required desegregation of schools in 1955 when nearly two out of three children were black, whites continued to leave the school system as they had been doing since World War II. As these white students were replaced by newcomers from the South, desegregation generated much attention from the media and civic groups for its symbolic value, but a decade after the *Bolling* there were only 15,000 white children in a school system of 150,000 students, most of whom were caught in a web of poverty. By 1967, other concerns shoved aside desegregation as an issue.[78]

By the late 1960s and early 1970s, educating black children to perform well slowly replaced desegregation as the fundamental issue facing the schools. But the goal's clarity (and its pursuit) often went astray after 1968 when Congress, in the backwash of widespread rioting triggered by the assassination of Martin Luther King, Jr., passed a series of laws that gave pieces of home rule to the District government. In addition, the goal was obscured in the intense efforts of administrators to comply with the judicial decree of the *Hobson* v. *Hansen*, a decision that mandated the transfers of teachers in the middle of the school year to permit equitable allocation of resources to all schools. Such massive transfers of teachers disrupted school programs for the remainder of the school year.[79]

Electoral politics came to D.C. initially with an elected Board of Education in 1968; anything connected with schools became contested items. The new Board's search for a superintendent to replace Hansen produced William Manning from Lansing, Michigan. He lasted less than two years. His successor, a Detroit administrator, became the first black to head a big-city school system in the nation. Hugh Scott, appointed in 1970, arrived just as the School Board independently arranged for Kenneth

Clark (urban schools' critic, psychologist, and member of the New York State Board of Regents) to put his program design to improve district education into the schools. The Clark Plan, an effort that focused the school system's energies on the teaching of reading and improving academic achievement, was handed to Scott to implement. The plan met stiff resistance from the teachers' union because of testing requirements and less-than-subtle hints by school officials that teachers might be evaluated on the basis of test results. Constant bickering between school board members, union threats to strike, and bureaucratic foul-ups over executing the Wright decree buried the plan by 1972 and Scott exited less than a year later. He had lasted less than three years.[80]

Scott's successor, a Chicago school administrator, deeply believed in active citizen participation in the governance and operation of schools, the empowerment of black people, and the positive benefits of conflict. Barbara Sizemore had the two-fold distinction of being the first female superintendent of the district and the first superintendent fired after a public hearing of the Board of Education. Sizemore lasted as superintendent two years.

The swinging-door superintendency halted with Vincent Reed's appointment in 1975. An insider who had risen through the ranks, served as a high school principal, and had been a top lieutenant of the three superintendents that followed Hansen, Reed re-established managerial order to a system that was in profound organizational disarray after the whiplashing of entering and existing administrators. In 1976, he launched a comprehensive program called the Competency-Based Curriculum (CBC). A massive staff development program that trained thousands of staff members how to set lesson objectives, devise instructional strategies to achieve objectives, and assess results of classroom instruction during the year. In-service sessions, three-pound manuals of directions distributed to the instructional staff, elaborate explanations to the public, and tactics to boost staff morale were various strategies used in implementing CBC. A slim majority of the Board approved Reed's direction, including the end of social promotion and the setting of minimal levels of competency that students had to demonstrate before they could be promoted. In 1980, after a number of public displays of Superintendent-Board friction and a deep split in the Board over Reed's plans to create a high school for the gifted and other issues, the Superintendent took an early retirement.[81]

This brief summary of organizational instability at the top between 1967 and 1980 sets the stage for examining what occurred in schools amid turbulent Board-Superintendent politics and the inevitable confusion of green and red lights given to principals and teachers on when to move and when to stop. A snapshot of where the entire system was in 1966–1967 (at the onset of this period of turmoil) comes from the Teachers College study called the Passow Report, after Study Director A. Harry Passow who, with nearly two hundred staff members, conducted the year-long survey.[82]

After two decades under Carl Hansen and Frank Ballou's immediate successors, Passow found the schools in need of fundamental changes if Washington was to create a "Model Urban School System"—the formal title of the study. The shortcomings of the system documented in the 593-page study gave little comfort to Hansen or his supporters when they read it.

- A low–level of scholastic achievement
- Grouping procedures which have been honored in the breach as often as they were observed in practice
- A curriculum which, with certain exceptions, has not been especially developed for or adapted to an urban population
- A central administrative organization which combined over–concentration of responsibilities in some areas, and proliferation and overlap in others

Nor did any of the conclusions on the instructional program throw bouquets at school officials.[83]

Teachers were "inadequately prepared." Pressures to staff classrooms "at all costs" have led the school board to hire hundreds of temporary teachers over the years. "The presence of so many ill-qualified teachers," Passow concluded, "no doubt accounts for the many teachers who, according to classroom observers, are ritualistic, superficial in presenting subject matter, and fearful of the normal activities of teachers."[84]

Curriculum was narrow. Schools "stripped subjects to their most formal and least meaningful aspects." In teaching reading the narrowness reached its peak in a program that "construed reading as word-recognition and word-recognition as phonics, thus turning reading into a program of ritual code-breaking...." Other elementary school subjects "are either given short shrift or detoured into further exercises in reading." Yet test results show "not enough children do, in fact, learn to read well."[85]

Tracking was ineffective. After reviewing student achievement, the numbers of elementary and secondary students that were in the different tracks and what movement occurred between tracks, the task force studying tracking concluded that "there are sufficient inequities, inconsistencies, and inadequacies to warrant its abandonment."[86]

And classroom teaching? Twenty-three experienced teachers and administrators trained in observing classrooms visited 75 teachers in 9 elementary schools selected at random. "The clock seemed to be in charge of the classroom," one observer wrote. Daily schedules set who did what, when, and under what conditions. Lessons—consistent with the Curriculum Bulletin in the Amidon Plan—were similar from one classroom to another. There was little evidence of teachers departing from the spirit of the Plan or daily schedule. "The striking characteristics of these class-rooms," observers reported, "was the quiet and orderliness.... The children seem compliant, obedient, and passive." Time was spent mostly on "drill and reading and phonics, on reading for social studies informa-tion, and on working arithmetic problems."

> The general conclusion to be drawn from these observations is that ... the teachers in Washington have been led ... to place themselves ... in a highly directive role.... the child spent most of his day paying the closest possible attention to his teacher, following her directions, responding to her questions, obeying her rules. The children were not encouraged to talk to one another, either formally or informally....[87]

At the high school level, observations were limited and offered even less comfort to either teachers or administrators.

- *Science:* "In the main, the teachers lecture and the students listen. There was minimal pupil-teacher or pupil–pupil interaction."
- *Social studies*: "In most classrooms, instruction seems to follow a textbook approach...."
- *Foreign language*: "Their training for the textbooks, instructional resources, and the direct method ... needs ... massive upgrading.
- *Mathematics:* "... teachers observed seemed either uncomfortable with the material they were teaching or oblivious to its nuances and implications. Mathematics errors or misconceptions occurred frequently.... Continued organization of large mathematics classes conducted by inept teachers is a questionable policy."[88]

The Passow Study portrayed teaching practices in 1966–1967 at both elementary and secondary levels as mostly teacher-centered. The study also referred to some promising classroom innovations that were underway in individual schools and programs. In the turbulent years following Hansen's resignation and the dismantling of the Amidon Plan and Four-Track system, just at the time when informal education was at the peak of public and professional interest, opportunities surfaced to expand these infant efforts to reform classroom practices. The Model School Division is a case in point.

Model School Division

Located in the Cardozo section of the city, an area labeled for years as a slum by newspapers and reformers, by 1969 the Model School Division (MSD) had been established as a decentralized unit enrolling 19,500 students in 5 pre-schools and 18 elementary and secondary schools, including Cardozo High.[89]

Between 1964 and 1975, MSD was a holding company for almost every single innovation that promised improvement for urban poor and minority students. Established to be an experimental arm for the entire school system, by 1970 (when a program inventory was taken) over two dozen curricular, instructional, and organizational innovations had been installed (e.g. elementary science series, English in Every Classroom, the Madison Math Project, team teaching, nongraded primaries, Language Experience in Reading). Federal, private, and local funds mixed to produce a heady climate resonating with optimism and change in the Cardozo area. With the departure of Carl Hansen, reluctant parent of the decentralized venture, the MSD had even more discretion to innovate.

One showcase effort that brought much publicity while earning the respect of many educators, both locally and nationally, was the Innovation Team. Composed of 15 experienced classroom teachers, the team began operating in 1967 under the direction of Mary Lela Sherburne, who had worked with the Education Development Center (EDC) in Newton, Mass. Its initial task was to begin coordinating the myriad programs that kept spinning out of federal and local reformers' heads and wallets. Beyond coordination, the team was to help classroom teachers incorporate new ideas and materials into their daily practice.

By 1969, when a formal evaluation of the team was completed, the objectives had shifted from conventional in-service training and technical assistance for teachers, toward changing teachers roles, making classrooms more active "where different learning styles, interests, and paces can be accomodated through a variety of materials and techniques, involving teachers in schoolwide cooperative problem-solving and decision making." The team, underwritten, in part, by EDC, had held scores of workshops, visited hundreds of classrooms numerous times—at the request of teachers—and provisioned rooms with new math, science, social studies, and reading materials. In a small, but growing number of MSD classrooms, science and math centers began to appear.[90]

While much of the vocabulary used by team members, the director, and assistant superintendent was consistent with the language of informal education, seldom was there a reference to open classrooms in the MSD. Materials from EDC, using tri-wall cardboard to construct learning centers and carrels, and expanding the teacher's view of the classroom as a place where children actively learn were all part of the approach conveyed by the Innovation Team. Part of the reason may have been that the philosophy of the Team evolved in that direction between 1967 and 1970 and was stated explicitly in the latter year. The convergence of the Team's beliefs in active learning and the teacher's central role as primary decision maker with elements of informal education, however, did not produce large numbers of classrooms packaged and labeled "open" in the MSD. Some did exist, and more were developing by 1970. But the thrust of the Innovation Team was not to copy open classrooms. The Team existed to respond to teachers' requests for help. Moreover, teachers in the

MSD endorsed the team's work, indicating in surveys that the 15 teachers "had contributed to their effectiveness as teachers more than any other source or MSD program."[91]

In 1969, when Russell Cort completed his evaluation of the team, Cort said that "improving performance at the school and classroom levels will take continuous, dedicated, persistent, focussed effort." Within a year, the Innovation Team disbanded.[92]

A new Superintendent, Hugh Scott, stuck with implementing Kenneth Clark's design for academic improvement, saw other uses for the Team; less outside funding produced deficits that the District budget could not absorb, and changes in Team membership help explain the abolition of the Innovation Team. In just over three years, the Team had assembled, worked with teachers, and had been dispersed. The promise of planned changed embedded in the Team slipped away.

Innovation Team members moved on to principalships, central office posts, and some left the system. Mary Lela Sherburne, first director of the Team, and member Olive Covington helped organize the Advisory and Learning Exchange (ALE), a privately funded group of educators interested in establishing and spreading open classrooms in the Washington metropolitan area. Created as a teacher center and support group for those private and public school parents and educators seeking to explore open education and similar approaches, ALE opened its doors in a downtown Washington suite of offices in 1971. By 1974, over 600 workshops had attacted teachers and parents from the D.C. area. By 1981, however, the organization had undergone many changes and support of informal classrooms was no longer its main interest.[93]

Open Classrooms and Open Space

Elsewhere in the city, open classrooms appeared in the early 1970s. Sometimes these were promoted by groups of white parents—as in New York City; sometimes they were installed by eager teachers. In the far Northwest part of the city, for example, at Hearst-Eaton schools, Joan Brown, a new principal (1971) and former Innovation Team member, recruited new teachers enthusiastic for informal education and expected the ones she inherited to open up their classrooms. A summer workshop in 1970 trained 20 teachers to start open classrooms in 12 schools west of Rock Creek Park, a predominately white, affluent area. Parents from schools in the area lobbied school officials for the program. The summer workshop was led by Innovation Team members LaVerne Ford, Mary Alexander, and others.[94]

The Morgan School, the first parent-controlled school in the District, began with open classrooms in 1967 under the aegis of Antioch College. Young teachers, mostly white, and community aides, mostly black, trained to use instructional materials from EDC, divided the school into teams of children by age rather than grades, and embraced informal education. By 1969 Ken Haskins, the first principal, had left and Bishop Reed, head of the Morgan Community School Board, had died. By that time, Antioch College had severed its ties with the school. The few white parents who helped establish the school and negotiated the contract with the Board of Education that gave Morgan its autonomy had also left. A new local Board and principal set specific rules for student conduct, brought back report cards, tested students, and told teachers to stress basic skills and discipline.[95]

By 1970, most of the original teachers and open classrooms had been pushed out of the school. The principal recruited teachers from southern black colleges to replace the ones that had left. In 1971, 17 of 30 teachers in the school were teaching for the first time. When a newspaper reporter visited the school in 1973, six years after it began as a community-controlled school, only two of the primary teachers still maintained informal classroom. Most teachers "ran their classrooms along highly traditional lines and say they are appalled by what they regard as the disorganization and lack of discipline in the classes of some teachers at Morgan." Yet those few open classroom teachers in the school looked forward to the replacement of the old Morgan school with a new open space building in 1974.[96]

Putting up open space buildings, like many efforts in the District requiring money, took much time in properly aligning the Board of Education, District government, and both Houses of Congress in authorizing and then appropriating the necessary funds. As Frank Ballou found out in 1925 when his first building program was finally approved by all the necessary agencies, patience, a sense of the absurd, and a rabbit's foot helped. Often requests submitted in one year would take up to seven years to appear in a document authorizing the Board of Education to proceed with architectural plans already outdated. So it was with the replacement of old, space-poor elementary buildings erected before and during Superintendent Frank Ballou's tenure.

Open space concepts had seized the imagination of school boards and superintendents across the country in the early 1960s. The District was no exception. Requests for open space were submitted and, after lengthy delays, were approved. By the mid-1970s open space schools appeared at both the elementary and secondary levels (e.g. plans for replacing the old Brookland elementary were approved in 1967; the open space school was finally dedicated in 1974; a similar span of time marked the erection of the open space Dunbar High School).

Open space, as an environment, encourages teaming among teachers, varied groupings of children, nongraded arrangements, and diverse uses of space. It is consistent with, but not essential for, open classrooms. Beginning in 1971 when the Ketcham addition opened, each year brought new open space schools until 1979, by which time there were 17, costing $163 million, including the new Morgan school which had been renamed Marie Reed.[97]

In the District, however, open space was wedded to open classrooms. Between 1971 and 1974, in-service workshops for teachers who volunteered to work in open space were held. Six training cycles were sponsored by a federally funded Training Center for Open Space Schools. Few doubted that the British primary school, Lillian Weber's Open Corridors, and informal classrooms, in general, were the models that District school officials had in mind. These goals were pursued seriously. By that I mean that some principals, supervisors, and middle-level managers who shared a passion for open classrooms sought improved ways of training teachers who had volunteered for the new buildings. But no Board of Education nor any Superintendent since Hansen's departure made a public commitment to informal education.[98]

Consider Brookland School. Two years before the new school opened, the principal and members of the six-teacher staff of the "old" school attended workshops, visited open space schools in the Washington area, took courses at D.C. Teachers College, and spent two weeks touring British schools at their own expense. The staff gave workshops to parents explaining open classrooms in open space. The new school opened in 1974 and was subsequently identified as the model open space school for the District schools.[99]

Spread of Open Classrooms

How widespread open classrooms, even broadly defined, were in Washington is difficult to estimate. As in New York City no survey was undertaken after the Passow Report. With 130 elementary schools staffed by nearly 3,500 teachers (1975), signs of diffusion are, at best, blurred. Less than 15 percent of the schools were open space. It would be foolish to assume either that all teachers in open space conducted open classrooms or that open classrooms were located only in open space. There are some clues, nonetheless.

By 1974, in the last training cycle for 200 teachers electing to teach in open space, 28 percent reported they had opened up their classrooms. For over half of the teachers attending the workshop it was their first experience with informal classrooms. The ALE reported in 1975–1976 that over 700 D.C. elementary teachers had attended workshops. There was no indication that the number was cumulative or represented individual teachers. Also consider the 46 classroom descriptions from 23 elementary schools that I gathered from photographs, newspaper articles, published interviews with teachers, and an evaluation report. (See Figure 4.3.) Note, however, that the percentages for student-centered instruction are prob-

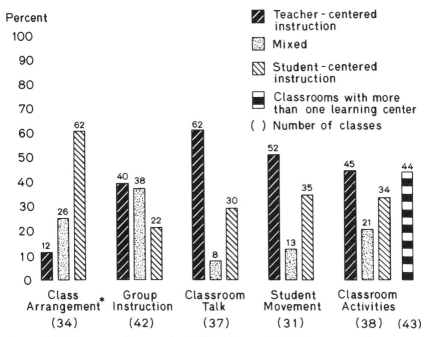

Figure 4.3   Patterns of Instruction in Washington, D.C. Elementary Classrooms, 1967–1975.

ably inflated since, of the ten schools that had learning centers, two— Morgan and Hearst-Eaton—appeared in the narrative. These two schools accounted for almost half of the classrooms that had one or more centers.[100]

A student-centered pattern is strongest in furniture arrangement (62%), learning centers (44%), and students moving around the classroom without asking the teacher's permission (35%). However, when it comes to small groups and individual activities, student participation in classroom tasks and prevalence of student talk the range goes from 22% to 34%— again with the caveat that these figures may be somewhat higher because of the small number of schools, and two schools contributing more accounts than others. Teacher-centered patterns still registered highly; almost half of the classrooms were taught through whole group instruction (40%) and engaged in listening, working at desks, and responding to teacher questions (45%). In over half of the classes, there was little student movement (52%), and in nearly two of every three of these classes, teachers dominated verbal exchanges in classrooms (62%)

What all of these scattered figures provide is a splintered, but nonetheless considered, basis for an estimate of one in four or five D.C.

elementary teachers doing something in their classroom that could be defined as open.[101]

By 1975, interest in open education had flagged considerably. Federal funds for the Training Center had run out. City deficits produced lists of budget cuts, and protracted squabbles occurred between the Board of Education and Mayor over which agencies would bear what portions of the budget cuts. The schools retrenched by cutting aides, staff development, and other services that had nurtured open education. By 1978, a small study that compared reading achievement and other student outcomes in 372 open space and self-contained classrooms found that "the self-contained classroom provided a better learning environment than has the open space classroom." The last nail was pounded home.[102]

More important, however, was the growing concentration on improving basic skills and constant monitoring of progress by tests through initially, the Clark Plan (1970–1973) and, later, the Competency-Based Curriculum under Reed after 1976. Teachers were charged to provide specific and direct instruction in these skills; teachers had to know whether or not students had performed at the appropriate level each day. Testing expanded. Standards for semi-annual promotions were both tightened and enforced. For children who were retained, remedial programs were expanded. While open classrooms are not necessily incompatible with such measures, this direction is far closer in spirit to the Amidon Plan, abolished in 1967, than the child-centered classroom. Many veteran teachers found the structured, teacher-centered approaches called for in the Clark Plan and CBC quite similar to the approach favored by Hansen years before.

The stress upon academic skills through CBC, the reduction of tangible support for open education, and the inherently greater demands that accompany informal teaching may explain the difficulties that principals had, after 1976, in securing volunteers to staff open space classrooms. The jerry-built walls of portable blackboards and book cases that teachers—some of whom were assigned to vacancies in open space schools to replace their less-senior colleagues—threw up around students in of effort to create self-contained rooms within open space may also be explained by the concentration upon academic skills. Learning centers were used less and less.[103]

In 1981–1982 I spent two mornings at Bruce-Monroe and Brookland, both open space schools. Bruce-Monroe, with 525 pupils and a staff of 20, had a principal who had worked with the Innovation Team. The new facility had opened in 1974. At that time, centers on reading, math, science, social studies, and the like dotted each "Learning Community" of three to four teachers, being used often in the course of daily instruction. In 1981, when I walked through the pods I saw a number of centers but they were used sporadically by teachers, usually for practice activities after formal periods on reading, math, and language arts were completed. Aides were no longer present. Special teachers did pull students out of classes for specific instruction.[104]

Of the 7 teachers I observed (14 on staff for grades 1 through 6) only 1 had children sitting in rows of chairs facing the chalkboard; the 6 teachers had students sitting at tables facing one another. Children moved freely as they worked on tasks, asked the teachers questions, etc. Four of the teachers were working with the class as one group; the rest used a mixture of small and large groupings within the two hours I moved in and out of their pods called "Learning Communities." Four of the teachers had on the chalkboards the CBC objective for the day:

- "Circle the beginning sounds."
- "Add and subtract."
- "Review plural endings."
- "Using contractions"

For classroom activities, 5 teachers gave directions to students and the students worked at their desks from 30 to 45 minutes on the same task, i.e. textbook questions, copying from the blackboard. One teacher had the entire class sitting in front of her. She asked questions on math problems of the students, who had texts in their laps, and answered her questions. One teacher had divided her class into at least three groups that worked on different tasks.

Six of the seven teachers had learning centers. They were not used daily. Teachers told me that they were used occasionally as rewards or practice for CBC objectives when scheduled activities were completed.

Also opened in 1974, Brookland had 450 students in kindergarten through eighth grade. Large open spaces with few dividers made up the "Learning Centers" as the grades were called. As with Bruce-Monroe, aides had been cut. Teacher reductions had brought new staff to the school while sending others elsewhere. Art, music, and home economics teachers provided instruction for all grades. Only one classroom center was visible in the entire school the morning I visited.

Of the 9 teachers in grades 1 through 6, I spent 2 hours with 6 of them. Most teachers had their students sitting at round tables, facing one another. Children moved at will in the classroom space. Five of the teachers worked with one group while the rest of the class sat at their tables doing assignments out of texts. One teacher had two groups working on different tasks. In four of the six classrooms where teacher-student exchanges occurred for more than ten minutes, the exchanges were in the teacher question-student answer format with the questions drawn directly from the text or worksheet. On the walls of every classroom were charts listing CBC skills in reading, thinking skills, math, language arts, and so on. Also charts with students' names showing tasks that were completed hung in five of the six classrooms.

Were these classrooms in the two schools open? The space was open. The artifacts were there: centers, flexible furniture arrangement, use of space, and freedom of student movement. Yet teacher direction and centrality were obvious in steering who did what, when, how, and with whom. Student participation was limited to tasks assigned by the teachers. These mixed behaviors resemble closely what an earlier generation of teachers had created: a hybrid, a teacher-centered progressivism.[105]

If informal classrooms, at different levels of development, emerged in elementary schools after 1967, what happened in D.C. high schools in those years?

High School Classrooms

As in New York City and elsewhere in the country, the late 1960s saw university students' protest against their institution's policies and actions spill over onto high schools. Washington shared the same experience with Howard University except that initially, student protests pursued racial issues, especially after the conflagration triggered by the assassination of Martin Luther King in 1968. Development of racial consciousness was the basis of the first public alternative school in the District.[106]

Freedom Annex grew out of the work of a small cadre of Eastern High School students who were dissatisfied with the quality of schooling they received. They designed the alternative school, raised money for it, chose the courses and selected the teachers. Billed as one of the few student-run high schools in the nation, Freedom Annex was supported by George Rhodes, assistant superintendent of secondary schools, and approved by the Board of Education, but no public funds were allocated. Funding came from foundations and other private sources.

Over a hundred students took required courses in the morning at Eastern High School and spent the rest of the school day at a nearby church where they heard lectures and participated in discussion on Black history, Black literature, Swahili, Black art and drama, and community organization.[107]

Two years later, with less than thirty students enrolled, private and foundation grants spent, the school closed its door and boarded up its windows. Eastern High School, with a new principal, had modified its curriculum, instituted a number of changes, and the student leaders who created Freedom Annex had graduated.[108]

An advocate for choices, George Rhodes had been laying the groundwork for other alternative programs sponsored and funded by the School Board since the Freedom School made local headlines. In 1970, Washington's version of Philadelphia's Parkway Program, New York's City-As-School, and Chicago's Metro Program accepted its first students. Called the School-Without-Walls, tenth graders from across the city applied for admission. In addition, Rhodes and his assistants encouraged a group of secondary teachers and administrators to establish mini-schools in five junior high schools. A Literary Arts and Journal Program, where students would spend afternoons producing a city-wide creative arts journal, was established also. No mini-schools, however, were developed at any of the 11 high schools.[109]

As in other cities, there were privately funded alternative schools outside the aegis of the public schools such as the Urban League's Street Academy, D.C. Street Academy, Rap Inc., and other ventures that tried to reduce actual and potential dropouts from District high schools and redirect students into resuming their schooling beyond high school. The School Board did not, as the New York Board of Education had done, incorporate these programs into the alternative school framework that began to evolve in the early 1970s.[110]

By 1981, the School-Without-Walls, the Literary Arts Program, the Lemuel Penn Career Center, the Duke Ellington School of Performing Arts, and the newly established Banneker High School for the Gifted constituted the alternative high school program. Issues of governance, size, and instruction were seemingly subordinated to developing choices for students.

I found no evidence that classroom instruction in alternative schools differed from the range of practices in regular high schools. Class size was smaller. Individual help from teachers was available. Informal relations between teachers and students in the smaller programs did exist. The frequency of small groups and independent work was probably higher in the programs where specific crafts and skills were taught.[111]

In regular high schools, the picture that emerges from Figure 4.4 based upon 86 classrooms (1967–1976) is acutely familiar.

As in New York City, the percentages in each category for teacher-centered patterns shout their uniformity for 10 of the 12 high schools from which these descriptions were drawn. Nearly eight out of every ten high school teachers described in these accounts or caught in photos taught in a stunningly similar fashion. So stunningly, that on a meter of student participation, the needle would have barely moved off zero.

Nothing here contradicts my experience as a social studies teacher and team leader in a teacher-training program for three years (1967–1968 and 1970–1972) at Roosevelt High School. My duties as team leader for groups of interns in the building brought me in contact with many teachers, especially in the English and social studies departments, who I observed briefly and informally. The patterns reported here for high schools elsewhere in the District were similar to what I observed: whole group instruction, little student movement, discussions and informal recitations, assigned seatwork, students at blackboards, occasional student reports and panels. The textbook, chalkboard, durable vocal chords, and a pair of strong legs were the primary teaching tools.

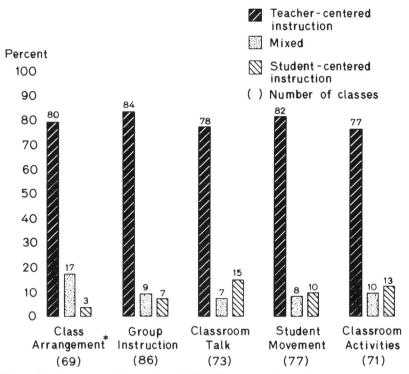

Figure 4.4   Patterns of Instruction in Washington, D.C. High School Classrooms, 1967–1975.

In 1979, Pat Lewis, a *Washington Star* reporter, spent two months in four high schools in the metropolitan area, one of which was Coolidge High School. Sitting in a half-dozen classes, she described two classes in detail. Here is a U.S. history class.

> Fourteen don't answer roll call in room 230 at Coolidge. Ten do.
> "The test is tomorrow. Today I am going to review with you the exact questions on the test." Rita Dinnerstein tells her U.S. History class.
> "What's an act?"
> "A law," someone replies.
> "What was the National Labor Relations Act?"
> No one answers. "It's in your textbook," she says.
> "It is?" someone asks quietly.
> Four students saunter into class eight minutes after it was scheduled to begin.
> "Three tardies are equal to a cut," Dinnerstein yells. "And I've had it."
> "The National Labor Relations Act was passed in 1935. What did it guarantee?"
> Someone answers, "collective bargaining."

There is lots of noise in the hallway. Faces appear in the windows of the wooden door and peer into the classroom.

"What's the difference between industrial and craft unions?"

No one answers.

Dinnerstein raises her voice. "This is a review! We've done this!"

A student in the hallway steps into the room, holding the door open.

"Mrs. Dinnerstein, someone wants to see you."

Dinnerstein marches to the door: "I'm about to explode."

It is eleven minutes after class is supposed to have begun. Dinnerstein steps out into the hallway and comes right back. "You interrupted my class," she tells someone out there.

"What is a union?" she asks her class.

One student reads the answer from his notes. When he finishes, Dinnerstein tells another student, "If you want to play games, feel free to leave."

"Who said I'm playing games?" the student retorts. . . .

"What is a union shop?" she asks.

One girl says the answer quietly.

"I can't hear you," Dinnerstein tells her.

A boy sitting next to the girl repeats the girl's answer for his own. It is correct.

The class is quiet now, 20 minutes after it began. The students are listening. A few know the answers to the questions that Dinnerstein first gave them on Monday. This is Thursday. On Friday, those same questions will be on the test.[112]

The reporter suggests that the class was a disaster in its low level of content, the amount of subject matter covered in a week, and hallway distractions and interruptions spilling over into the classroom. Such vignettes judge implicitly the teacher's performance and give teachers good reason to bar reporters from their classes. Since I have seen Dinnerstein teach I do know that this episode from one class does not in any way capture the overall quality of her instruction. What it does convey is another typical instance of the question-answer format, reinforced by reliance upon the text, and teaching the entire class as one well after interest in open classrooms and alternative schools had ebbed.

The National Picture

Case studies of North Dakota, New York, and Washington, D.C. between 1967 and 1975 established that informal schooling existed in some classrooms and alternative schools developed in the upper grades. How typical were these instances compared to elsewhere in the nation?

In no place could I find a majority of classrooms taught informally, even broadly defined, for any sustained period of time. The largest estimate I came across was drawn from a researcher who claimed that 60 percent of the schools in Roslyn (N.Y.) had at least *one* open classroom.

Takoma Elementary, 1977 (*District of Columbia Media Center*).

Gage-Eckington Elementary, 1977 (*District of Columbia Media Center*).

Winston Elementary School, 1977 (*District of Columbia Media Center*).

The other estimate came from a survey sent by the National Open Education Association in 1974 to superintendents of 153 cities with over 100,000 population. Ninety-one cities (59 percent) responded, meaning that either the superintendent or someone else was delegated the task (Lillian Weber responded for New York City) to complete the questionnaire. The question from which an estimate of the spread of open classrooms was constructed read: "About ____% of the classrooms in my city make substantial use of open approaches to education."[113]

The problems of interpretation packed into the words "substantial" and "open approaches" are no greater than having a central office person, whose interest in informal education is known, make a few inquiries or phone calls to principals he or she knows has such classes and compile the replies into a response of how many teachers were using "open approaches." The mean estimate from superintendents and their designees in the 91 cities was 17%; the median was 10%. Such estimates are, at best, no better than informed guesses, laced with a heavy dose of hope. They are not unlike the predictions of 80 percent of these same administrators who said that in the next 5 years (1975–1980) "open approaches would increase in their cities."[114]

I cite these figures only to underscore how limited the spread of the movement was in public schools by 1974 even when optimism infused

Dunbar High School,
English Class, 1977
(*District of Columbia
Media Center*).

Dunbar High School,
Science Class, 1977
(*District of Columbia
Media Center*).

school officials' statements. Lacking reliable national data on the frequency or spread of open classrooms directs me to sample scattered descriptions, studies, and accounts that have appeared between 1967 and 1975 in order to determine if a fabric can be stitched together that either supports or rebuts the data I gathered thus far.

In the late 1960s, John Goodlad and a team of researchers observed 150 primary grade classrooms in 67 schools in 13 states. They wanted to test whether the widely publicized educational innovations of the 60s—team teaching, ungraded primaries, curricular reform, individualized instruction—had crossed the threshold of the classroom. What they found were "remarkably similar" classroom programs in school after school, irrespective of local differences. The classrooms they observed were marked by:

> ... telling, teachers' questioning individual children in group settings, and an enormous amount of seemingly quite routine seatwork.

The primary tools of instruction were the textbook followed by workbooks and supplementary readings.[115]

The common pattern of instruction in the whole group was question-

and-answer. When the teacher divided the class into groups for reading—a daily activity—one group read to the teacher, one group read independently, and one group did seatwork related to current, previous, or future work. "Rarely," Goodlad wrote, "were children engaged in self-initiated and self-directed small groups or individual activity." The report concluded that in subject matter, materials, and teaching practice the 150 classrooms were "geared to group norms" rather than individual differences. "Judging from our sample," he wrote, "childhood schooling is more vanilla than . . . neapolitan."[116]

Goodlad was disappointed. In looking behind the classroom door, he and his associates found a dreary sameness—"a flatness"—at a level of schooling where promised reforms had a reasonable chance for success. Reforms were "blunted on school and classroom door." His team, interestingly enough, documented repeatedly that teacher reports of how innovative they were contrasted sharply with what observers reported. "Teachers sincerely thought they were individualizing instruction, encouraging inductive learning, involving children in group processes." Observers found that they were not, a finding consistent with results from other researchers.[117]

Examining a similar time span, the National Science Foundation commissioned a survey of research studies in curricular and instructional changes that had taken place in science, math, and social studies between 1955 and 1975. The results, drawn from a synthesis of surveys, classroom observation studies, and other research were remarkably similar for the three subjects.

Math: Summarizing seven studies on elementary and secondary teachers verbal behavior in classrooms between 1968 and 1976,

- The teacher talks about two-thirds of the time.
- Teachers tend to use a direct, rather structured approach.

In classroom practice, Suydam and Osborne cited eight studies (including Goodlad's) between 1959 and 1977, and conclude that:

- Telling and questioning, usually in total-class groups is the prevailing teaching practice.
- Tell-and-show and seatwork at the elementary level with homework-lecture-new homework at the secondary level are the dominant patterns of instruction.[118]

Social Studies: A review of two decades of research including studies in the early 1970s, as with math, disclose a similar pattern that one researcher summarized, almost sadly, as:

". . . the students' social studies classes will be strikingly similar to those that many of us experienced as youngsters: textbook assignments followed by recitation led by a teacher who, in his or her own way, likes students and tried to show concern for them. . . ."[119]

Science: Summarizing nine studies of elementary school science (1963–1976), reviewers found that:

- "There is more use of 'hands on' and laboratory types of instruction. . . .
- "However, a substantial number of teachers do not emphasize laboratory activities. Lecture-discussion is the most common learning activity, followed by student demonstration. Reports and surveys indicate a substantial number of teachers (probably about 30–40%) teach science largely as a reading/lecture class.
- At the secondary level, there is less lecture and more "student-centered activity," than there used to be but "lecture and discussion is the predominant method used by teachers."[120]

Another body of literature that allows a glimpse of existing practice are the studies of failed innovations; that is, descriptions and analyses of individual schools where a systematic and intentional effort to open up classrooms occurred and, for a number of reasons, failed to materialize. Smith and Keith's Kensingston, a pseudonym for a St. Louis area elementary school in the mid-1960s, was expected to be a child-centered, staff-led operation in a new building; Cambire School is another pseudonym for a Boston elementary school in 1966–1967 where Gross and his colleagues documented how an inept administrator and unclear expectations for classroom changes such as student choices, small group work, individual attention, and centers produced an educational disaster; Barth's Attucks-Lincoln program in New Haven (1968–1969) where open classrooms staffed by bright, young, but inexperienced white teachers in a majority black school were, again for a variety of reasons, torpedoed. What all of these studies show is how tough it was to plan and implement changes in teacher's classroom behavior.[121]

A few points are clear. That various stages of openness in classrooms existed and that such informal practices spread among some teachers is, as the evidence I gathered for North Dakota, New York City, Washington, D.C., and scattered sites around the country, undeniable. There was a distinct minority, in a number of instances quite substantial, of teachers, at any given time, in any given setting, involved in restructuring their classrooms to some degree. Yet there also existed, equally as clear, the powerful tug of teacher-centered practices upon most classrooms between 1967 and 1975. Until more data are gathered that would throw the above statements into doubt, an overwhelming majority of teachers stayed within the range that can comfortably be called teacher-centered practices.

SUMMARY

Summarizing patterns of instruction between 1967 and 1975 in three settings at a brief moment of time, when intense and widespread efforts were undertaken to reform classroom teaching, is necessary to determine if what occurred in these places is comparable to what occurred during the years 1920–1940 when the tides of progressivism ran strong in school systems.

1. *Core of Informal Practices.* As with the progressive approaches of a generation earlier, a set of teaching practices that can be labeled informal were evident in a considerable number of elementary classrooms in the three sites from which I collected data. Artifacts of open classrooms were present in learning centers, tables and desks clustered so that students could speak and work together, the increased use of varied groups for instruction, and relatively free movement of students in the class space without securing the teacher's permission. Uneven in development and selective in use, these practices seldom captured more than a fourth of the classrooms in any district, if that many. Even fewer teachers employed other informal approaches such as student decision making on what to study and determining how much time is spent on what topics, or using learning centers as the central vehicle of instruction.

Comparisons between the interwar decades and this period show rough likenesses in the extent of the spread in certain teaching approaches. While there were a few teachers who tried to duplicate the entire panoply of a child-centered classroom, most of the elementary classrooms that showed some evidence of informal practices were selective in what was incorporated into the daily routines. These mixtures of informal and formal practices resemble, I believe, the hybrid forms of teacher-centered progressivism that I described earlier. One major difference, however, was that—unlike Denver and New York City in the 1920s and 1930s—at no site that I studied was there formal school board or superintendent advocacy and organizational mechanisms constructed to implement and incorporate open classrooms into the teacher's instructional repertoire.

2. *Instruction in Regular and Alternative High Schools.* Very little evidence appeared to show that classroom practice in regular high schools varied substantially from that of a generation earlier. While content was revised in subject areas to link it to events in students' lives or heighten interest, and class discussions tended to be quite informal, the basic instructional sequences and patterns reported earlier remained in place.

Even though the number of classrooms was minute, and the methods I used to categorize inexact, the convergence in results is striking—considering that the accounts come from multiple sources and cover diverse settings. In alternative high schools, the categories of instruction, and here the evidence is, indeed, sparse, show no substantial difference in the range of techniques used by teachers, although the frequency of some approaches that involve students, especially in discussions and classroom informality, resemble elementary patterns for student-centered instruction. The picture of high school teaching that emerges from these accounts is unmistakably teacher-centered and remarkably akin to what showed up three to four decades earlier.

3. *Elementary and High School Instruction.* As in the 1920s and 1930s, a higher percentage of student-centered practices entered the lower rather than higher grades. There is some evidence to demonstrate that, in both periods, the extent of student-centeredness peaked in the primary grades and descended until it bottomed out in the senior high school at a fraction of what existed at the elementary levels. In other words, versions of student-centered instruction appeared more frequently in the elementary grades, particularly in the primary years, and virtually disappeared by high school.

4. *Teacher-centered Instruction.* Dominating the classroom were at least two forms of teacher-centeredness. The pure form—whole class instruction, teachers talking most of the time while students listen, limited range of activities done by the entire class at same time, and little student mobility—characterized the high school. Then hybrids of teacher-centeredness emerged with teachers using diverse classroom groupings, allowing more informality in instructional talk, movement, and space arrangements. Student-centered instruction across the major categories captured only a very small fraction of teachers at any given time.

What appeared as a direction by 1940 shows up with more clarity by 1975. Certain child-centered teaching practices became increasingly common in elementary classrooms: flexible seating patterns, student movement within the classroom, and the use of varied groupings. Other practices such as learning centers and small group work show up less frequently but sufficiently to be noted. Looking back to 1900, however, these modest changes give the elementary classroom of the 1970s a decidedly different appearance. But the appearance masks continuities that the limited evidence suggests as remaining quite potent. Teachers continued to monopolize classroom verbal exchanges; teachers determined what activities would occur for how long and who would participate. Working alone at a desk while the teacher either supervised or worked with another group continued as a dominant instructional pattern.

In high schools, pedagogy since 1900 in the five academic subjects altered very little except for the formal recitation. Raising of hands, yelling out of answers, and informal discussion techniques replaced standing at one's desk or in the front of the room to answer the teacher's questions.

Whole group instruction, teacher-controlled classroom talk, little student movement, and little variety in tasks captured the high school classroom in the 1970s.

NOTES

1. Vito Perrone, et al., *Two Elementary Classrooms: Views From The Teacher, Children, and Parents* (Dubuque, Iowa: Kendall/Hunt Publishing Co., 1977), p. 1–20.
2. Philip Jackson, *The Teacher And The Machine* (Pittsburgh: University of Pittsburgh Press, 1968), p. 4.
3. Lawrence Cremin, "The Free School Movement: A Perspective," *Notes on Education*, October, 1973, p. 171.
4. ibid., pp. 2–3.
5. Vito Perrone, "A View of School Reform," in Ruth Dropkin and Arthur Tobier (eds.), *Roots of Open Education in America* (New York: The City College Workshop Center for Open Education, 1976), pp. 186–7; Vito Perrone, "Open Education: Promise and Problems," Phi Delta Kappan Fastback (Bloomington, Ind.: Phi Delta Kappan Educational Foundation, 1972), pp. 10–11.
6. Roland Barth, *Open Education and the American School* (New York: Agathon Press, 1972); Joseph Featherstone, "The British and Us," *The New Republic*, September 11, 1971, pp. 20–5 and "Tempering a Fad," September 25, 1971, pp. 17–21.
7. Featherstone, "The British and Us," p. 20.
8. Roland Barth, "Should We Forget About Open Education?" *Saturday Review*, November 6, 1973, p. 59; for examples of checklists, see New York State Education Department, *Information and Planning Kit for Use in Developing Open Education Programs* (Albany, N.Y.: Task Force on Open Education, 1971); Anne Bussis, et al., *Beyond Surface Curriculum*, (Boulder, Colo.: Westview Press, 1976); for warnings about too rapid an embrace of open classrooms, see Roland Barth's article in *Saturday Review*; Perrone's PDK Fastback; Ruth Flurry, "Open Education: What Is It?" in Ewald Nyquist and Gene Hawes (eds.) *Open Education* (New York: Bantam Books, 1972), pp. 102–10; Charles Silberman (ed.) *Open Classroom Reader*, (New York: Vintage Books, 1973), pp. 297–8.
9. Robert A. Horwitz, "Psychological Effects of the Open Classroom," *Review of Educational Research*, 49 (Winter, 1979), pp. 72–3; Kathleen Devaney, "Developing Open Education in America: A Review of Theory and Practice in the Public Schools" (Washington, D.C.: Department of Health, Education, and Welfare, 1973), pp. 3–5; Perrone, PDK Fastback, pp. 12–21.
10. Silberman (ed.), pp. 297–8.
11. For example, see *Newsweek*, 77 (May 3, 1971), p. 65; Henry Resnick, "Promise of Change in North Dakota," *Saturday Review*, 54 (April 17, 1971) pp. 67–9; *The New York Times*, October 11, 1970, p. 68.
12. Resnick, pp. 67–8; Silberman, *Crisis in the Classroom*, chapters 7 and 11; Vito Perrone and Warren Strandberg, "The New School" in Nyquist and

Hawes, pp. 275–91; The North Dakota Statewide Study of Education, *Educational Development for North Dakota, 1967–1975, An Overview*, (Grand Forks, N.D.: Center for Teaching and Learning, University of North Dakota, 1973), pp. 6–9; Michael Patton, "Structural Dimensions of Open Education" (Grand Forks, N.D.: Center for Teaching and Learning, 1973), p. 7.

13. Patton, p. 21.
14. Kathleen Devaney, "The New School of Behavioral Studies in Education," (Grand Forks, N.D.: Center for Teaching and Learning, 1974), pp. 209, 211.
15. ibid., p. 219.
16. Richard G. Landry, "Comparative and Longitudinal Analyses of Teaching Intern Classrooms on Selected Dimensions of Openness: Third Year (1975)" (Grand Forks, N.D.: Center for Teaching and Learning, 1975), p. 5.
17. Vincent Dodge, "The Fargo-Madison School Program: A Cooperative School–University Effort" (Grand Forks, N.D.: Center for Teaching and Learning, 1974), Item VI, pp. 1–5; *Fargo–Moorhead Forum*, October 4, 1970; October 25, 1970; November 29, 1970.
18. *Grand Forks Herald*, August 26, 1969; Larry Hoiberg, "We're Putting It All Together at Washington Elementary School" (Grand Forks, N.D.: Washington Elementary School, 1971), mimeo, pp. 1–51.
19. *Final Report, Title III, Elementary and Secondary Education Act:* The Impact of the Teacher and His Staff (Grand Forks, N.D.: Grand Forks Public Schools, 1970), mimeo, p. 56.
20. Silberman, *Crisis in the Classroom*, pp. 290–7; Silberman (ed.) *Open Classroom Reader*, pp. 43–52; *Life*, October 1, 1971; *Today's Education*, February, 1973, p. 35.
21. Marshall, p. 180.
22. Patton, p. 7.
23. Landry, p. 14.
24. Ronald Kutz, "An Analysis of the Use of Math Manipulative Materials in North Dakota" (Grand Forks, N.D.: Bureau of Educational Research and Services, 1977), pp. 21, 37.
25. New York (City) Public Schools, *Facts and Figures, 1977–1978*, (New York: Board of Education, 1978), pp. 1, 5, 11.
26. Ravitch, p. 239.
27. For a sampling of the diverse literature written about New York City schools in this decade, see Diane Ravitch, *The Great School Wars*, chapters 23–33; David Rogers, *110 Livingston Street* (New York: Random House, 1968); Miriam Wasserman, *The School Fix, NYC, USA* (New York: Outerbridge and Dienstfrey, 1970); Maurice R. Berube and Marilyn Gittell (eds.) *Confrontation at Ocean Hill-Brownsville*, (New York: Praeger Publishers, 1969); Estelle Fuchs, *Teachers Talk* (New York: Doubleday and Co., 1969).
28. Center for Urban Education, *Open Door: New York City* (New York: Center for Urban Education, 1970), pp. 11–12.
29. Charles Silberman pointed out that in the midst of writing *Crisis in the Classroom* he had met Weber, read her manuscript about British primary schools, and wrote "our work took a new direction. We went off to England to see for ourselves." Ruth Dropkin (ed.) *Changing Schools* (New York: City College Workshop Center for Open Education, 1978), p. 48.

30. Beth Alberty, *Continuity and Connection: Curriculum in Five Open Classrooms* (New York: City College Workshop Center for Open Education, 1979), pp. 6–7; Chitra Karunkakaran, "Life and Work in Several Communities: A Case Study of Open Education," (Chicago: Center for New Schools, 1978), p. 30.
31. David Rogers, *An Inventory of Educational Improvement Efforts in the New York City Schools* (New York: Teachers College Press, 1977), pp. 82–4.
32. Dropkin, p. 51.
33. Some examples of open classrooms across the city are reported in *The New York Times*, January 8, 1973 on P.S. 24 (Bronx) and P.S. 27 (Bronx) in the January 17, 1973 issue; New York (City) Board of Education, *Staff Bulletin* May 15, 1972 on P.S. 92 (Bronx); *United Teacher*, June 25, 1972, pp. 15–16 has a description of P.S. 35 (Queens); *New York Supervisor*, Spring, 1975, p. 19 describes P.S. 13 (Queens). In addition, there are accounts written by teachers such as Herbert Kohl, *36 Children* (New York: New American Library, 1967); Gloria Channon, *Homework* (New York: Outerbridge and Dienstfrey, 1970). Masters theses from teachers enrolled in the Bank Street College of Education detail classroom experiences. See theses written by Donna C. DeGaetani, "Beginning an Open Classroom in a Public School" (1974); Mamie Gumbs, "Humanizing Learning Through Open Classroom Procedures and Self-Discovery Methods" (1974); Helen Haratonik, "A Descriptive Study of an Approach to Teaching Reading in an Open Classroom" (1973); Alicia Montalvo, "Dairy of an Open Classroom" (1972); Helaine R. Meisler, "Educational Change in a School Mandated 'Open' As Seen Through the Eyes of an Advisor" (1977).
34. *The New York Times*, January 8, 1973.
35. *The New York Times*, July 25, 1970; "Vermont Design for Education" in Nyquist and Hawes, pp. 55–62; Joseph Lelyveld, "The More Powerful Man in the School System," *The New York Times Magazine*, March 21, 1971, p. 31; *The New York Times*, July 25, 1970.
36. *The New York Times*, January 30, 1971.
37. ibid., February 7, 1971; December 20, 1970; and January 24, 1971 (a paid advertisement).
38. ibid., January 8, 1973.
39. Edward Chittenden, et al., *First Year Evaluative Study of the Workshop Center for Open Education, City College of New York* (New York: Workshop Center for Open Education, 1973); Dropkin, pp. 51–3.
40. Karunkakaran, pp. 205–7.
41. Gerald Levy, *Ghetto School* (New York: Pegasus Publishing Co., 1970), chapters 4 and 7.
42. Channon, pp. 23–4.
43. ibid., p. 116.
44. DeGaetani, master's thesis, p. 4.
45. ibid., pp. 14, 36.
46. Montalvo, master's thesis, pp. 4–5, 33, 57.
47. Joseph Lelyveld, "Class 4–4: Educational Theories Meet Reality, "*The New York Times*, October 9, 1970, p. 39; November 16, 1970, p. 39; November 25, 1970, p. 39; December 20, 1970, p. 49; January 8, 1971, p. 33; January 16, 1971, p. 31; January 22, 1971, p. 41; February 9, 1971, p. 41; March 11, 1971,

p. 41; May 29, 1971, p. 25; July 1, 1971, p. 49.

48. ibid., October 9, 1970, p. 39.
49. ibid., March 11, 1971, p. 41.
50. ibid.
51. ibid., May 29, 1971, p. 25.
52. ibid.
53. Philip Lopate, *Being with Children* (New York: Bantam Books, 1975), pp. 24, 29.
54. For background to the alternative school movement, I used: Terrence E. Deal and Robert Nolan (eds.) *Alternative Schools* (Chicago: Nelson–Hall, 1978); Dan L. Duke, *The Transformation of the School* (Chicago: Nelson–Hall, 1978); Allan Graubard, *Free the Children* (New York: Pantheon, 1973); Mario Fantini, *Public Schools of Choice* (New York: Simon and Schuster, 1973); Mary Anne Raywid, "The First Decade of Public School Alternatives," *Kappan*, April, 1981, pp. 551–7; David T. Moore, "Alternative Schools: A Review" (New York: Institute for Urban and Minority Education, Teachers College, Columbia University, 1978).
55. Raywid, p. 551; Moore, pp. 21–22.
56. Deal and Nolan, p. 3.
57. Terrence E. Deal and Robert Nolan, "Alternative Schools: A Conceptual Map," *School Review* (November, 1978), p. 33; Anne Flaxman and Kerry Hanstead (eds.) *1977–1978 National Directory of Public Alternative Schools* (Amherst, Mass.: National Alternative Schools Program at School of Education, University of Massachusetts at Amherst, 1978).
58. Mary McBride, "Five Alternative Schools," (Unpublished doctoral dissertation, University of Maryland, 1979); *Harvard Educational Review*, "Alternative Schools," 42 (August, 1972).
59. Moore, pp. 9–10.
60. Duke, pp. 40, 44–6, 51.
61. New York (City) Public Schools, *School Profiles, 1970–1971* (New York: Division of System Planning, 1971), Appendix A, p. 6.
62. Rogers, *An Inventory of Educational Improvement Efforts*, pp. 10–11; Diane Divoky, "New York's Mini-Schools," *Saturday Review*, 54 (December, 18, 1971), pp. 60–7.
63. Rogers, *An Inventory of Educational Improvement Efforts*, pp. 8, 22–5. The schools I deal with exclude Bronx High School of Science, Beach Channel High School, John Dewey High School and others that are city–wide, have themes of special interests, and usually have requirements that students have to meet in order to be admitted. These schools, in the broad sense, are alternatives but they differ markedly from other alternatives in size, ideology, student involvement in governance, etc.
64. *The New York Times*, November 17, 1971; November 1, 1971; July 1, 1975; Divoky, pp. 60–7.
65. Rogers, *An Inventory of Educational Improvement Efforts*, pp. 14–22.
66. Divoky, pp. 60–7; *The New York Times*, November 1, 1971 and July 1, 1975.
67. *The New York Times*, November 1, 1971.
68. ibid., May 24, 1971, p. 33.
69. ibid.
70. ibid.

71. ibid.
72. *The New York Times*, January 8, 1973, p. 57.
73. ibid.; Carol Gladstone, "What Constitutes a remedial Reading Lesson," *High Points* (March, 1975), p. 29.
74. *The New York Times*, December 9, 1973.
75. ibid., September 8, 1975; January 15, 1975; November 16, 1975.
76. New York (City) Board of Education, *Directory of the Public Schools, 1978–1979* (New York: Board of Education, 1979), pp. 5, 27, 39, 51, 122–9.
77. Carl Hansen, *Danger in Washington* (West Nyack, N.Y.: Parker Publishing Co., 1968), pp. 91–106; Larry Cuban, "*Hobson* v. *Hansen*: A Study in Organizational Response," *Educational Administration Quarterly*, 11, (Spring, 1975), pp. 15–37.
78. Hansen, chapters 1–5; Constance M. Green, *The Secret City* (Princeton, N.J.: Princeton University Press, 1967), chapter 13; A. Harry Passow, *Toward Creating a Model Urban School System* (New York: Teachers College, Columbia University, 1967), chapters 2, 4, 5.
79. Cuban, p. 35.
80. Larry Cuban, "Reform By Fiat: The Clark Plan in Washington, 1970–1972," *Urban Education*, 9 (April, 1974), pp. 8–32.
81. *Washington Post*, October 13, 1980, p. C–3; Vincent Reed, "An Introduction to the Competency-Based Curriculum," *Journal of Personalized* Instruction, 3, (Winter, 1978), pp. 199–200.
82. A. Harry Passow, *Toward Creating a Model Urban School System* (New York: Teachers College, Columbia University, 1967).
83. ibid., p. 3.
84. ibid., p. 265.
85. ibid., p. 255.
86. ibid., p. 235.
87. ibid., pp. 275–6.
88. ibid., pp. 295, 305, 312, 322.
89. District of Columbia Public Schools, "Model School Division in a Capsule" (Washington, D.C.: Model School Division, 1969). In 1950, the all-black Cardozo High School moved into the recently closed building that used to house the all-white Central High School.
90. H.R. Cort, et al., *An Evaluation of the Innovation Team* (Washington, D.C.: Washington School of Psychiatry, 1969), pp. 7–8.
91. Cort, pp. 227–8, 240; I also had frequent and sustained contacts with the Innovation Team, its initial director (Mary Lela Sherburne), and Assistant Superintendent Norman Nickens while I directed the Cardozo Project in Urban Teaching—one of two dozen programs in the Model School Division—and later, when I administered the district–wide staff development program.
92. Cort, p. 240.
93. Esin Kaya, "An Evaluation and Description of the Advisory and Learning Exchange, 1973–1974" (Washington, D.C.: Advisory and Learning Exchange, 1974), pp. ii–iii.
94. *Washington Star*, August 16, 1970; Theresa H. Elofson, "Open Education in the Elementary School: Six Teachers Who Were Expected to Change" (Urban, Ill.: Center for Instructional Research and Curriculum Evaluation, 1973), pp. 8–154.

95. *Washington Post*, May 13, 1973, C3.
96. Paul Lauter and Florence Howe, "The Short Happy Life of Adams–Morgan Community School," *Harvard Educational Review*, 38 (Spring, 1968), pp. 235–62; *Washington Star*, March 1, 1970; *Washington Post*, July 6, 1971 and May 13, 1973.
97. *Washington Post*, December 11, 1979.
98. Behavioral Service Consultants, "Final Evaluation Report: Training Center for Open-Space Schools, ESEA Title III Project" (Greenbelt, Md.: Behavioral Service Consultants, Inc., 1974); "Brookland School Plan," February, 1974.
99. "Brookland Plan," n.p.; *Washington Post*, December 11, 1979.
100. Behavioral Service Consultants, pp. 21, 47.
101. District of Columbia Public Schools, *Data Resume Book* (Washington, D.C.: Division of Research and Evaluation, 1976), p. 28, 32; Kaya, p. 9.
102. District of Columbia Public Schools, "Open Space vs. Self-Contained Classrooms" (Washington, D.C.: Division of Research and Evaluation, 1980).
103. *Washington Post*, December 11, 1979; I observed these teacher efforts to close off open space when I visited Bruce-Monroe and Brookland schools in 1981.
104. Notes from my visit; Behavioral Service Consultants, pp. 60, 71.
105. In addition to my observations, reporter Judy Valente of the *Washington Post* wrote a series of articles on second-grade teacher Dorothy Porter of Bruce–Monroe. See October 13, 1980 and May 24, 1981 issues.
106. As in New York City, I exclude continuation schools for potential or actual dropouts (e.g. Spingarn program); the Capitol Page, Duke Ellington School of Performing Arts, Banneker High School for the Gifted, and separate vocational schools. Admission criteria differed markedly in these schools from alternatives I describe as well as other substantial differences in governance, size, etc.
107. *Washington Daily News*, November 14, 1968; *Washington Post*, November 22, 1968.
108. *Washington Post*, November 1, 1970.
109. George Rhodes, Jr., "Action Programs in Progress in the Secondary Schools" Washington, D.C.: District of Columbia Public Schools, 1970), pp. 21–2, 24; *Washington Daily News*, March 9, 1971; *Washington Post*, March 9, 1971.
110. Barbara Sizemore, Superintendent Memorandum to School Board, "Procedures for Alternative Programs," June 19, 1974, p. 4.
111. I had visited the Literary Arts program at the Lemuel Penn Career Center; I had had discussions with teachers at the Duke Ellington School of Performing Arts. Also see *Washington Post*, March 9, 1971.
112. *Washington Star*, December 31, 1979.
113. *The New York Times*, April 20, 1975; *Opening Education*, 2 (Summer, 1975), p. 5.
114. ibid., p. 36.
115. John Goodlad, et al., *Looking Behind the Classroom Door* (Worthington, Ohio: Charles Jones Publishing Co., 1974), pp. 78–9, 81.
116. ibid., pp. 82–3.
117. ibid., p. 97.

118. Marilyn Suydam and Alan Osborne, *The Status of Pre-College Science, Mathematics, and Social Science Education, 1955–1975, Vol. 2, Mathematics Education* (Columbus, Ohio: Center for Science and Mathematics Education, 1977), pp. 54–5.
119. James P. Shaver, et al., "An Interpretive Report on he Status of Pre-college Social Studies Education Based on Three NSF-Funded Studies," in National Science Foundation, *What Are The Needs in Pre-college Science, Mathematics, and Social Science Education?* (Washington, D.C.: National Science Foundation, 1979), p. 7.
120. Stanley Helgeson, et al., *The Status of Pre-College Science, Mathematics, and Social Science Education, 1955–1975, Vol. 1, Science Education* (Washington, D.C.: National Science Foundation, 1977), pp. 31–2, 34.
121. Louis Smith and Pat Keith, *Anatomy of an Educational Innovation*, (New York: John Wiley, 1971); Neal Gross, et al., *Implementing Organizational Innovations* (New York: Basic Books, 1971); Roland Barth, *Open Education and the American School* (New York: Agathon Press, 1972). Also see Robert Herriot and Neal Gross (eds.) *The Dynamics of Planned Educational Change* (Berkeley, Calif.: McCutchan Publishing Co., 1979).

5

Classroom Practice in a School District: Arlington, Virginia, 1969–1980

I first met Carmen Wilkinson in 1975 when in my regulr visits to schools I walked into her room at Jamestown Elementary and was stunned. In my first year as Arlington County Superintendent, I had already seen over 300 elementary open space and self-contained classrooms. This was the only one I had seen that had mixed ages (grades 1 through 4) and learning stations in which students spent most of the day working independently and moved freely about the room; they worked in small groups and individually while Wilkinson moved about the room asking and answering questions, giving advice, listening, and working with various students. Called by parents, children, and staff "The Palace," the class used two adjacent rooms. Wilkinson teamed with another teacher and, at that time, two student teachers. She orchestrated in an unobtrusive manner scores of tasks in a quiet, low-key fashion.

Had Lillian Weber, Vito Perrone, Charles Silberman, William Kilpatrick, Harold Rugg, and Elizabeth Irwin been looking over my shoulder as I watched Wilkinson and her colleague work with the 50 children that April morning, I am sure they would have been pleased with the presence of the "Palace" at Jamestown. Had they walked the halls with me and looked into the other 17 self-contained classrooms, they would have seen only one other classroom similar to the "Palace"[1]

Over the years I served as Superintendent, I visited Wilkinson, who had taught for 32 years (as of 1980), at least ten more times and saw her classroom change into a one-grade self-contained room yet retaining flexible groupings and learning centers that were integrated into the instructional day. Wilkinson's informal classroom was unusual at Jamestown and among 500 other Arlington elementary teachers between 1975 and 1980.

Unusual also was Bobby Schildt's social studies classroom in 1975 at Hoffman-Boston, an alternative junior high school in Arlington. When I saw Schildt's room for the first time during my visits in my initial year as superintendent, there wasn't any class for me to see. She had individual-ized her courses into a series of projects, contracts, and learning stations that she collectively called a social studies laboratory. For each course, students would gather once a week as a class to discuss some topic. For the rest of the week, students worked at various tasks and centers completing contracts they had negotiated with Schildt. She spent class time asking questions of individual students, helping some that were stuck, and reading and commenting on work that would be placed into student cubbies along the wall. Teacher-made, teacher-gathered, and commercial materials overflowed the room.

As with Wilkinson, I saw Schildt a number of times over the years. When I last saw her in 1981, she was still teaching social studies to seventh through ninth graders, although then it was in an alternative school that had been consolidated into a seventh through twelfth grade secondary school. But the laboratory was no more. The high degree of independent and individual work through contracts and learning stations were now carried on periodically, woven together with more whole-class discussions, simulations, role-playing, and small group work.

The subtle changes that occurred in these Arlington classrooms mirror, in a number of important ways, what happened nationally to efforts aimed at reforming teaching practices. In this chapter, I will sketch out the swift shift in attention from informal education to a renewed, intense preoccupation with the teaching of basic skills, minimum com-petencies, and accountability that swelled in the mid-1970s and spilled over into the early 1980s. Then I will try to reconstruct what happened in classrooms both nationally and in one school district, Arlington County, Virginia, after this abrupt shift.

The swiftness in which media and popular interest in informal class-rooms vanished was breathtaking. Within a brief period of time, roughly between 1968 and 1974, open classrooms and alternative schools attracted national attention, became a *de rigeur* innovation, and began the slide off the edge of the public's radar screen. Mirroring that rise and fall in both public and professional interest are the number of references to newspaper articles, trade books, television programs, journal articles, academic research, and research notes in the *Readers' Guide, Educational Index, The New York Times,* and *Washington Post* indices and other similar listings.

While other school reform impulses have surfaced and coalesced into movements, as this one had, their lifespans usually stretched over a few decades. Somehow this impulse of informal education and alternative schools were telescoped into less than a decade (allowing for regional and local differences). It seemed almost as if, by 1975, the public and school professionals, for any number of reasons, flicked the dial and switched television channels to another station. Or to shift images, I recall the cartoons I saw as a child when the narrator said the sun set and I saw the sun clunk down on the horizon. Whatever image I would use, the point about the brief life span of informal education is evident. By 1975, the climate surrounding open classrooms and alternative schools had changed substantially. Obviously, such generalizations about a country with nearly 15,000 school districts, millions of teachers and children in the 1970s cannot hold for all schools. Yet while an incoming tide seldom arrives evenly, there is still a high tide.

Exactly when the shift occurred varies from place to place. One reporter marked the end of the passion for informal schools in the founding of alternative schools committed to traditional approaches. Pasadena, California established its John Marshall Fundamental School in 1973; Palo Alto, a leader in informal education, created the Hoover Contemporary School in 1974 with a program, according to its brochure, that concentrated upon:

> ... academic skills and subject matter and the establishment of good study habits ... in a quiet and orderly environment.... A majority of the school hours will be devoted to the teaching of reading, writing, spelling, language and arithmetic.

More and more school districts established "Basic Alternative Schools" as Prince Georges County, Maryland did in 1975. Arlington's entry came in 1978 with the Page Traditional Alternative School. "Back to the basics," a phrase with far more political baggage packed into it than affection for the familiar trinity of basic skills, became a rallying slogan throughout the mid-1970s.[2]

Whether it was a knee jerk reaction to the perceived changes that had occurred in schools and classrooms (often captured in a code word borrowed from an earlier generation of critics, "permissiveness"), or persistent reports of declining test scores, increasing school vandalism and disrespect for teachers, or the educational version of the political conservative climate that spilled onto schools with state mandates for teacher accountability and minimum competency tests—I cannot say.

Whatever the explanations, there was a renewed passion for orderliness, stability, and academic skills captured in symbols that plucked nostalgic strings within both citizens and parents: rows of desks facing the blackboard and teachers desk, the teacher in front of the room, required homework, detentions, dress codes, spelling bees, letter grades on report cards, tougher promotion standards and school–wide discipline rules.

Implicit in these slogans and symbols was that most teachers had either converted, or threatened to convert their classrooms, into open or quasi-open classrooms where children made choices, standards were undefined, basic skills were neglected, and order was problematic. The issue, I believe, is not whether this is a misrepresentation of informal classrooms—which it is, although a persistent search among two million classrooms would probably turn up instances of whatever anyone would like to demonstrate about teachers. The issue is the gap between available evidence and the profound misconception of the frequency and spread of open classrooms. As the limited data I gathered from New York City, Washington, D.C., and North Dakota for 1967 through 1975 suggest, open classrooms did, indeed, turn up in numerous and unpredictable places, catching on in an ink-splattering fashion, but at no point in the brief passion for the reform did it ever capture more than a small minority of teachers and schools. What the slogans reveal about schools is less about what went on in classrooms but far more about the historic vulnerability of public schools to political issues in the culture as selected and translated for the public by newspapers, magazines, and, more recently, television.

What remains unclear, however, is why some teachers converted from teacher-centered practices to informal ones, why others modified their approaches by selectively incorporating some but not other informal techniques, and why some of these teachers, over time, slipped back into their previous patterns. Also, why have most teachers ignored both rhetoric and new practice, and persisted in their teacher-centered classrooms? Finally, what about teaching practices since the waning of open classrooms?

The rhetoric of "back to the basics" hid more than it revealed about teaching. As I have tried to show, there was some movement away from the teacher-centered regularities—practices which seemed consistent with the claims of those wanting more stress on fundamental skills. What occurred seemed to be the introduction of more variation around teacher-centeredness and the legitimacy, if not viability, of varied forms of student-centered practices. To assess what happened in classrooms since 1975, I shall look at Arlington, Virgina, and then review some recent national studies of teaching practices.

ARLINGTON, VIRGINIA, 1974–1981

In turning to this school district, I am no longer an historian collecting data, evaluating sources, sifting the evidence, and drawing inferences from scattered fragments of information—all filtered through my values and experience as a teacher and administrator. When I write about Arlington, I write as a participant.

In 1974, I was appointed superintendent in Arlington. I served nearly seven years and left in 1981 to begin writing this study and teach at a university. The seven years I spent in Arlington were both exhilarating and exhausting. Viewing a school system from the cockpit of the superintendent's office, however, is a narrow perspective. While I will try to broaden the view in the narrative beyond what I saw, I raise the issue of my position to signal readers that other accounts of Arlington would probably vary both in detail and emphasis.

Because of my position, I visited classrooms repeatedly over a seven year period and informally gathered a great deal of information about teaching practices in the district. I saw over half of Arlington's teachers in their rooms. Few people, professional or lay, have automatic access to as many classrooms as a superintendent does, should he or she choose to use this privilege. I did. My visits to classrooms began six weeks prior to formally assuming the post. The School Board agreed to my request to spend a month and a half visiting schools and sitting in classes in order for me to become acquainted with principals and teachers before I took over the formal duties of the post. The Board, staff, and community knew that my last job previous to becoming Arlington's superintendent was as a social studies teacher in a Washington, D.C., high school. Because the Board and I agreed that improvement of student performance was one of our top agenda items, it was reasonable that I spend time with principals and teachers.

My routine for school visits was set in those initial six weeks. I would go unannounced to a school, stop in the principal's office, chat with him or her for a few minutes and then begin to walk through the building, stopping in classrooms. Most often my stay in a classroom ranged between 15 minutes to a half-hour, with most being closer to the 20 minute mark. I jotted notes in a folder about what the teacher and students were doing, the arrangement of the classroom, and any unusual items I noticed going on in class, and student-teacher exchanges. If it were possible to speak with the teacher without disrupting the class, I did. If I could, I often would ask questions about the tasks students were working on, the materials the teacher was using, and so on. As the years went by, teachers grew accustomed to these visits and would often take the time to mention items on their personal agenda in the school, the district, parents, union, etc.

Often in a cryptic pidgin-shorthand, I took notes so that I could write to the teacher thanking her or him for answering my questions, praising something about the class that I was impressed with, or simply to continue a point that we had been discussing. While I did not write every single teacher after each visit, notes from me were common. The purpose for my visiting classrooms and writing notes was explicitly stated and reaffirmed repeatedly in the articles I wrote in local newspapers, speeches to the staff, and statements at public meetings: I believed that teachers should know that the superintendent was as concerned and interested in instruction as they were. One of the few ways I had to demonstrate that concern was to allocate my time—roughly one and a half days a week—to listening, watching, and answering questions in face-to-face exchanges with teachers principals, and students. In addition, at least twice during the school year, I taught workshops for teachers and administrators interested in improving thinking skills through the use of questions. All of these activities brought me in touch with a substantial number of teachers and, I would like to believe, communicated some of my priorities about instruction and student performance. A few words about the school district and community in these years are necessary to establish the setting for the examination of classrooms.[3]

The Setting

Arlington, Virginia, is located across the Potomac River from Washington, D.C. Once a quiet middle-class white suburb with segregated schools, it has become a city with a flourishing multi-ethnic population in the last decade. In those years Arlington simultaneously got smaller, older, and more culturally diverse. The facts are plain: in the last decade population dropped from almost 180,000 in 1966 to about 160,000 in 1978; there were fewer and smaller families with school-age children; there were sharp jumps in number of young singles and adults over 55 years of age. Coincident with these changes, scores of different nationalities moved into the county, swelling minority population, but with insufficient numbers to counteract the other shifts.[4]

The impact of these changes upon schools has been dramatic. Pupil enrollment shrank from 26,000 in 1968 to 14,000 in 1982. From nearly 40 schools (including 3 high schools) in 1968, to 31 schools in 1982. Also from less than a 15 percent minority in 1970, the number of ethnic pupils doubled to over one-third in 1980. The jump came most sharply in non-English speaking minorities, particularly Hispanic, Korean, and Vietnamese children.[5]

If demographic changes were one pincer squeezing schools, the other was the rising cost of schooling. Spending more to buy less was as true for a school system as it was for families in the mid- to late-1970s. With diminishing revenue intersecting with inflation, the pincers tightened.

Since the appointed five-member School Board is fiscally dependent upon the elected five-member County Board, state and federal revenue shortfalls plus inflation unraveled school budgets in these years, precisely at the time that the cumulative effects of the demographic changes were being felt. The arms of the pincers closed.

What prevented the pinch from hurting Arlington schools too badly was that the County, measured by family income and assessed valuation of property, was wealthy. That wealth somewhat eased the painful transformation from suburb to city, especially during a recession. Arlington's prime location—close to Washington and improved further by the Metro rail system—and the County Board's cautious fiscal policies gave it the lowest tax rate in the metropolitan area (1980). Nonetheless, the County Board had to struggle with the politics of retrenchment. Irate property owners, most of whom no longer had children in school, wanted lower taxes. Their demands competed with requests from citizens who wanted higher school budgets, subsidies for the elderly, improved police, recreation, and social services.

Caught like everyone else in recessions, county officials tightened belts, bit bullets, and pursued other less vivid fiscal metaphors. The County emerged from the mid-1970s recession with most services intact, the lowest tax rate in the metropolitan area, and a school system that had become an annual target for holding costs down and reducing expenditures.

Political change also occurred. There had been a gradual but persistent shift from a Republican County Board to one composed of a coalition of Independents and Democrats. By 1971, this liberal bloc had attained complete control of the County Board. By 1978, however, three Republicans had been elected to the five-member Board, thereby reasserting a majority they had enjoyed a decade earlier. Since the County Board appointed School Board members, those who served on the School Board throughout the 1970s had been appointed by the liberal majority. Due to the lag between the Republicans attaining a majority on the County Board (1978) and appointments to the County Board, it was not until 1980 that the School Board had a three-member Republican majority.[6]

As part of this political shift in the 1970s, change also occurred in the School Board's relationship with its superintendent. When previous Republican School Boards in the 1960s left operational decision making to its executive officer, appointees of the liberal majority intervened more actively in what most superintendents would have considered their turf. Inevitably, friction developed between the superintendent who had been appointed in 1969 by a School Board content to let their hired expert transact school business and the new, far more activist School Board. In 1974, the superintendent resigned. I was appointed that year.

I find it difficult to summarize my tenure as superintendent without succumbing to such temptations as listing achievements, cloaking errors, or telling battlefield stories. To avoid these obvious pitfalls, while risking a tumble into less evident traps, I will try to summarize my agenda and that of the School Board as it changed over the period, and the inescapable issues that seized substantial amounts of my attention.

The Board that appointed me in 1974 was concerned with the consequences of shrinking enrollment, declining test scores, and what was viewed as an experienced instructional staff that was either unaware or resistant to further changes prompted by a diverse student population. In the first few years my staff and I spent much time in establishing a process by which the Board and community could determine in an orderly manner whether or not to close schools and, if schools were to close, which ones. By 1975, the decision making process for school consolidation was in place and the trauma from the closing of the first elementary school reverberated through the affluent portion of the County. By 1980, five elementary schools and two junior highs had been merged with nearby schools. Moreover, a secondary reorganization that moved the ninth grade to the high school and retained four intermediate schools (seventh and eighth grades) had been approved by the School Board. The merger process appeared resilient enough to weather the controversy that erupted periodically over school closings.

The other task that consumed much time was creating an organizational framework for improving student performance. By 1976–1977, a framework for instructional improvement was put in place. The pieces to that framework were as follows:

- School Board established a set of instructional goals for system, e.g. improving reading, math, writing, and thinking skills; improving students understanding of humanities and human relations.
- Superinendent and staff established organizational devices for converting those goals into school and classroom priorities.

  1. Each school staff, with advice from parents, drew up an Annual School Plan that concentrated upon the Board's goals.
  2. Superintendent reviewed each School Plan, met with each principal at mid-year to discuss progress and make changes, and, at the end of the year, received an assessment of the plan.
  3. Superintendent and principals discussed periodically the School Academic Profile which listed test scores and other student outcomes linked to the Board's goals.
  4. Administrator and teacher evaluation forms and procedures were revised to incorporate the objectives of the Annual School Plan into each professional's formal evaluation.
  5. Curriculum objectives, kindergarten through twelfth grade in all subjects, and skill areas were being revised to align them with one another and link them to School Board goals. Instructional materials, including textbooks, were reviewed and modified to make them connected to curriculum objectives. County-wide tests were constructed to assess the aims of the revised curriculum and to determine their fit with the materials in use. Analysis of test items missed on county-wide curriculum-based tests and national standardized achievement tests were completed and shared with principals and teachers annually to determine areas for improvement.

In short, a major effort was made over a three year period to tighten the generally loose linkages between system goals, district curriculum, school goals, texts and materials, tests, and normal evaluation procedures in order to concentrate the instructional staff's attention on fewer, more worthwhile targets. In doing so, the School Board and I hoped that a positive climate toward academic improvement would be generated.

Test scores—the coin of the realm in Arlington—at the elementary level climbed consistently for seven straight years. Plateaus in achievement and some gains, but not many, were established at the junior and senior high schools, but progress was less evident. The staff identified for the School Board and community substantial gaps in academic achievement between minority and white students in 1978 and began to close those gaps. Other performance indicators such as the number of students continuing their education, dropping out of school, county-wide tests, and Scholastic Aptitude Tests also reflected well on the efforts of the teachers and administrators.

This reconstruction of the years since 1974 suggests that events and decisions involving the Board and Superintendent flowed smoothly throughout the organization, falling neatly into their proper niches. Far from it. Unexpected events proved to be disruptive and complex, often producing unexpected consequences. Consider, for example, how the transfer of a veteran principal from the mother high school in the district produced a political controversy that trailed the School Board and Superintendent for seven years leaving, in its wake, a court suit, the election of one of the transferred principal's advocates to the County Board and, when the Republicans secured a majority on that Board, the appointment of that very principal, by then retired, to the School Board.

Another unexpected crisis occurred in 1976, when the Governor of Virginia sued Arlington School Board and County Board for unconstitutionally carrying on collective bargaining since 1967. The Governor lost in the local court but won the appeal in 1977 in the State Supreme Court. After a decade of bargaining and establishing personnel procedures with four different unions (including all administrators), the School Board found it was now illegal to sit down with teacher or administrator representatives to negotiate salaries or working conditions.

Simultaneous with the 1977 Virginia Supreme Court decision, a number of retrenchment measures were forced onto the schools by the County Board, itself coping with a reduced flow of revenues, which forced the School Board to cut back both personnel and programs. Reductions in teaching positions and specialist categories occurred throughout the 1970s. With 85 percent of the budget pinned down in salaries, and inflation soaking up existing funds, teachers saw their salaries lag behind an unrelenting, spiraling cost of living. After the collapse of collective bargaining, teachers received a 2 percent salary increase that angered them as a slap in the face. The resentment from this 2 percent increase erupted in subsequent years with the union calling for a work-to-the-rule action and a majority vote of the membership asking for my resignation in 1979.

Take a volatile political setting where Arlington-style liberals and conservatives periodically switched control of County offices, often using the schools as a community punching bag, add economic changes that yielded less revenues for County services, and mix in a different direction charted by the School Board and Superintendent that caused staff changes and concentration on different agenda items. What resulted made for flashy headlines, seven years of evening meetings marked by long hours, and a feisty climate for organizational change. So much for the setting.

Schools and Classrooms

Turn now to the schools. There were 36 schools in 1975 (25 elementary, including 1 alternative; 6 junior highs, and 3 senior high schools, excluding 2 alternative secondary schools). Of the elementary schools, six were completely open space and nine contained additions of substantial portions of the building that were open. Teachers were experienced (over half were at the top of a 15-step salary schedule) and highly educated (52 percent had a Masters or higher degree). Average class size ranged between 22 and 26 students at all school levels throughout the 1970s. Books, materials, and supplies were adequate; in some cases, abundant. Per pupil expenditure— a large proportion of which mirrored teacher salaries—rose from nearly $2,000 in 1974 to $3,000 in 1981. By that year, five elementary schools and two junior high schools had been closed, the two secondary alternative schools had been consolidated into a single program (grades 7 through 12), and a reorganization had pushed the ninth grade into the high schools, leaving the former junior highs as two-grade intermediate schools.[7]

Professional acceptance of innovation and responsiveness to most school problems was high. A veteran Associate Superintendent of Instruction (1964–1980) had developed networks of teachers and administrators proud of and loyal to Arlington schools as a pacesetter. Under this leadership, the school district had either adopted or, at least, considered numerous innovations throughout the 1960s, including team teaching, individually prescribed instruction, computer-assisted instruction, new curricula (social studies, science, and math), alternative schools, open space, and, of course, informal education. No formal School Board or Superintendent mandate occurred to apply system-wide these new efforts. There was, however, an informal expectation that professionals were to be on top of whatever novel approaches were being tried elsewhere in the nation and investigate their appropriateness for Arlington. Like an archeological dig, traces of previous innovations could be seen at various strata within the entire organization when I became Superintendent in 1974.

So it was with open classrooms. In the June, 1969 issue of "Profile," a publication sent to all staff members, two of the five pages described the new "Learning Center Approach." Acknowledging that the "experiment" proved "exciting and creative" to teachers in Arlington and across the nation, a group of teachers at four elementary schools offered enthusiastic endorsement of the practice. Workshops had been held to train teachers in setting up centers, stocking them, and establishing management systems to track student performance in the centers. Already variations in the use of centers had emerged by 1968–1969.

> Some teachers prefer to have one or two centers for smaller groups while they work with a larger group.... There are those who prefer to have their students involved in learning centers for the entire class day while others will spend a portion of the day dealing with the entire class in a traditional manner and then allot the rest of the time for the students to pursue projects in the centers.[8]

Tempering enthusiasm with caution, teachers recognized that "learning centers demand a great deal of work and creativity on the part of the teacher." Teachers who were interviewed saw the workload as "impossible without the help of teacher aides." Others were just skeptical. Bessie Nutt at Henry said:

> I'm still wondering in my own mind if this is a new trend in education or just another gimmick. Meanwhile, I am keeping an open mind and experimenting a bit.[9]

Three years later at Jamestown, where Carmen Wilkinson had begun opening up her class and space in 1966, there were 50 fifth and sixth graders being team-taught by 3 teachers who jointly were responsible for 8 learning centers in science, social studies, math, and language. The three teachers spent a great deal of time arranging for materials in each center. All three said that they spent part of each weekend preparing materials and activities for the following week.

I cannot ascertain how widespread the use of learning centers was in Arlington—as an index of informal classrooms—in the early 1970s. Wilkinson, who traveled to various schools in the County to give worshops and had a steady stream of visitors to her classroom, estimated that two or three teachers in each building opened up their classrooms to various degrees. The Drew Elementary school, an alternative school, introduced centers, nongraded primaries, and team teaching when it opened in 1971. By 1975, when I visited all of the elementary teachers at least once, I found about 25 teachers who used centers daily, permitted students to move freely, and organized their instruction for small groups and individuals with some time set aside for large-group teaching. That teachers who chose to establish centers in their rooms varied in their embrace of open classroom practices is evident from the quotes. That teachers could choose to do so in a climate of acceptance is also clear.[10]

Between 1975 and 1981, I informally observed, at least two or more times, 280 elementary classrooms, or about 40 to 50 percent of the teachers who served in those years. The results of those visits are displayed on Table 6.1 with the results of my observations of 63 classrooms in 2 North Dakota cities.

Table 6.1   Patterns of Instruction, Elementary, 1975–1981

	Teacher-Centered Instruction		Mixed		Student-Centered Instruction		Number of Classes	
	Arl. %	*N.D.* %	*Arl.* %	*N.D.* %	*Arl.* %	*N.D.* %	*Arl.* %	*N.D.* %
Classroom arrangement	42	43	18	30	39	27	(223)	(63)
Group instruction	49	62	50	25	1	13	(215)	(63)
Classroom talk	45	60	52	23	2	16	(215)	(63)
Student movement	60	37	0	0	40	63	(125)	(63)
Class activities	34	59	64	30	2	11	(213)	(63)
Classrooms with one or more centers					23	32	(209)	(63)
Classrooms observed in at least two school years with one or more centers					8	(NA)	(150)	

What is apparent in the County figures is considerable reliance, but not dominance, upon a teacher-centered configuration. Student-centered patterns registered substantially in two areas: arrangement of space and student movement. A mixed pattern in instructional groupings (large, small, and individual), classroom talk, and activities suggest higher levels in student participation. Just under one in four classrooms contained learning centers. On closer inspection of those classrooms with centers one finds a half-dozen teachers used centers as an integral part of the instructional day. In most cases, the centers were used for enrichment, skill practice, or free choice activities before and after formally scheduled lessons, e.g. at the end of the reading period, before lunch, after recess, etc. I did track a dozen teachers (8 percent) who had centers when I visited classrooms during two different school years. Of all the teachers who had at least one center in the classroom, there was no consistent relationship between the presence of the centers and the kind of space the teacher taught in, i.e. open space or self-contained, except for one school where 7 of the 11 classrooms had learning centers. The school had been built as open space but teachers had thrown up bookcases and temporary partitions to divide the space into self-contained rooms.

Examine the figures for the Grand Forks and Fargo teachers whom I observed briefly in 1981. While the percentages are not comparable in either sample size or duration of observation, the visits occurred in a similar time period and in settings that were much like Arlington in a number of areas: class size, history of responsiveness to innovations, and experienced and highly trained staffs.

What turns up in the comparison is the twofold similarity in strength of teacher-centered instruction, albeit to a higher degree in the two North Dakota cities, and less presence of student-centered instruction, particularly in Arlington. Two student-centered categories, however, show surprising strength: classroom arrangement and student movement, quite similar to what occurred in Washington, D.C., classrooms (1967–1976) in the use of classroom space and New York City (1967–1976) for student mobility.

In visiting Arlington classrooms for nearly seven years I came to expect a number of regularities. Almost half of the teachers (43 percent) put up a daily schedule on the blackboard. If it were time for reading, the teachers would work with one group and assign the same seatwork or varied tasks to the rest of the class. If it were math, social studies, science, or language arts generally the teacher would work from a text with the entire class answering questions from it or either from dittoed sheets or workbooks. These regularities in alloting time and grouping students were common except for those teachers who used learning centers, grouped more often in subjects other than reading, and assigned different tasks to different students.

High School

Shift now to the high school. In the early 1970s, Arlington was no different than many communities in experiencing the growing concerns expressed by students, teachers, and parents over the curriculum being unrelated to problems students faced, rules for maintaining school discipline that made 17-year-olds feel like 2-year-olds, and the lack of opportunity to do independent work both in and out of the school. The search for a type of education where students assumed responsibility for learning drove a small group of teachers and students at Wakefield High School to initiate experiments where different classes were held and students could choose anything they wanted to study for a week. These experiments led to a drive for a separate alternative high school.[11]

A group of teachers and students at Wakefield designed a new school and presented it to the School Board. Concerns for the size of high schools, student decision making, electives, and a variety of instructional practices produced a plan for a small (225 students) alternative high school open to any tenth to twelfth grade student on the basis of a lottery. The School Board approved the venture and Woodlawn opened its doors in a converted, abandoned elementary school in 1971. Two years later an alternative junior high, prompted by similar impulses, was also endorsed by the School Board and placed in the former all-black secondary school,

Hoffman-Boston. In 1979, both schools were consolidated into one alternative secondary school, grades 7 through 12, called H-B Woodlawn, with an enrollment of over 400 students and a waiting list of parents hoping to have their children admitted into the school.[12]

Similar to alternative schools elsewhere in the country that opened in the early 1970s, the governance of the school through a head teacher and a town meeting, its informality, small classes, and tolerance of differences marked the school clearly as unique in Arlington. Students and teachers were on a first name basis; a first floor bulletin board became an instant communication center with its notes, announcements, and pleas pinned to the wall; students designed elective courses with teachers; teachers developed internships in Arlington and Washington, D.C., including tutoring in nearby elementary schools. During the day, there was much student traffic in and out of the building to take internships, jobs, and courses unavailable at Woodlawn at other high schools.[13]

Teaching in such a school was different, according to Amos Houghton, a veteran teacher who volunteered to work in the Woodlawn program.

> Teaching here is infinitely more challenging than in the traditional school. I'm putting in more hours. I've never read so much in my life. But the ultimate reward is the depth in which you get to know the student personally in a school of 200 instead of 1,600. Oh, I've had some adjusting to do. This is not a neat and tidy school. But I've been able to learn from my own son that this is not as important as a relaxed atmosphere....
>
> We don't have rules like hall passes that must be signed by a teacher for a student to leave the room. We've dropped the authoritative aspect in the teacher-student relationship and we find that kids are not tensed up, don't feel persecuted and are more amenable to our ideas.[14]

Table 6.2 Patterns of Instruction, High School and H–B Woodlawn, 1975–1981

	Teacher-Centered Instruction		Mixed		Student-Centered Instruction		Number of Classes	
	H.S. %	H-BW %	H.S. %	H-BW %	H.S. %	H-BW %	H.S. %	H-BW %
Class Arrangement	85	61	10	0	1	31	(91)	(11)
Group Instruction	94	36	6	45	0	18	(87)	(11)
Classroom Talk	72	33	27	33	1	33	(85)	(12)
Student Movement	96	27	1	0	2	73	(85)	(11)
Class Activities	72	25	26	42	0	33	(86)	(12)

Glebe Elementary, 1975 (*Arlington Public Schools, Public Information Office*).

Discussions, student reports, lectures, independent study, textbooks, projects—all were used by various Woodlawn teachers. How different their classroom practices were from mainstream teachers is captured partially in Table 6.2.

Regular high school teaching practices in Arlington resembled quite closely those of New York City and Washington, D.C., between 1967 and 1976. The niche that high school teaching occupies in Arlington matches the ones that I have described previously: rows of tablet-arm chairs facing a teacher who is talking, asking, listening to student answers, and supervising the entire class for most of the period—a time that is occasionally punctuated by a student report, a panel, or a film.

I sat in classes and listened to discussions, recitations, and, on occasion, student reports. I watched teachers send students to the chalkboard, use the overhead projector, give tests, and run movie projectors. What the teacher would probably do in any given high school class, I came to realize, was one of the very few hunches that I would risk betting on and have a decent chance of winning. The range and sequence of activities, I discovered, was predictable: teacher takes attendance; makes an assignment from the text; collects homework done from previous day; picks up a point from previous lesson or homework; questions students on points from the textbook or homework. Periodically, a film, a test, student reports, or a field trip would interrupt the above activities. The sequence of activities might differ from subject to subject, e.g. science labs or language tapes, assignment given at end of period rather than beginning, but the teacher activities listed above capture, I believe, about 90 percent of what teachers and students did in the classrooms that I observed. The universe of classroom tasks was a small one dominated by regularities that resembled planets orbiting the sun in a predictable manner.

As this study has shown, teaching repertoires in Arlington differed little from New York City and Washington, D.C., in the 1970s and looked considerably alike the teaching of colleagues a generation earlier across the country, allowing, of course, for exceptions.

One exception in Arlington was H-B Woodlawn, with half of the staff represented in Table 6.2. Practices were similar but there seemed to be more variety in the mix of techniques, particularly student participation, that turned up in classrooms. Mixed and student-centered patterns in each of the categories appear as frequently used alternatives to the familiar teacher-centered instruction.

Between 1974 and 1981 in Arlington, a middle-sized district undergoing substantial demographic changes under the aegis of a school board and superintendent trying to steer a course of action targeted upon improving student performance, classroom teaching showed traits common to earlier periods when impulses for instructional reform weakened and slipped away. Forms of teacher-centered instruction dominated classrooms. The tediously familiar pattern of some variety in elementary

Swanson Intermediate School, Social Studies Class, 1979 (*Arlington Public Schools, Public Information Office*).

teaching practice within a teacher-centered and mixed configuration narrowing into a pristine version of teacher-centeredness at the high school is apparent in Arlington.

Certain informal practices did penetrate elementary teacher repertoires producing, as described also in other settings, a hybrid form of informal teacher-centered practice. No such cross-fertilization seemed to have occurred at the high school level in Arlington, except for the occasional teacher in each building or at H-B Woodlawn.

National Data on Classroom Practice

Arlington is one school district. A fair question to pose is whether classroom practice in Arlington in the 1970s and early 1980s was unique. Comparisons with 63 elementary classrooms in 2 North Dakota cities in

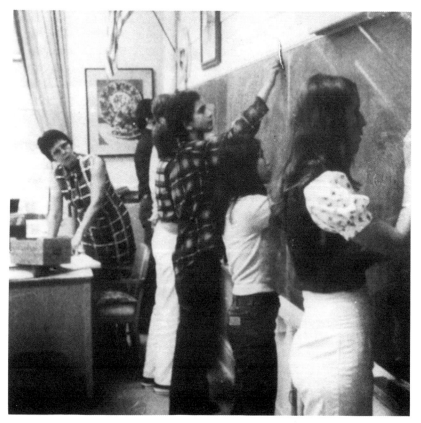

Washington-Lee High School, Math Class, 1974 (*Washington-Lee Yearbook, 1974*).

1981 suggest a general convergence in patterns, with the differences a matter of degree, rather than kind. There are some recent data that offer points of comparison and contrast: two National Science Foundation (NSF) studies completed in 1978 and John Goodlad's large-scale "Study of Schooling."

The NSF *Case Studies in Science Education* (CSSE) sent writers and researchers into 11 districts across the nation in 1976–1977. Concentrating upon science, math, and social studies programs in 11 high schools and their feeder schools, the field researchers constructed from interviews, documents, and observations richly textured case studies of urban, rural, large, small, wealthy, poor, white, and black schools. To corroborate the findings emerging from the case studies, NSF commissioned a survey of over 7,000 teachers, principals, central office administrators, and state supervisors.[15]

No clear portrait of elementary classroom teaching breaks through the thick descriptions of the cases. The full range of teaching practice is described, sometimes in painstaking detail when the observer takes the reader through a class discussion that isn't going anywhere and tedium blankets the reader's eyes or, on occasion, when the prose about a gifted teacher wraps itself seductively around the reader and won't let go until the last paragraph.[16]

The mass of detail, however, overwhelms. Sorting out the details into regularities in instruction is difficult since frequency counts were beyond the scope of the writers' task and were alien to these case studies. Nonetheless, amidst the variety of practices the observers described some general patterns were evident in nine of the cases that included elementary schools. Principal investigator Robert Stake found in the 11 cases the teacher's centrality to all classroom activity. Moreover, the textbook was the primary authority of knowledge and math, science, and social studies; it was "presented as what experts had found to be true."[17]

In high schools, observers, after mentioning the occasional superb math or science teacher who hooked students' attention and steered it elegantly for 50 minutes, commented on the remarkable similarities in teaching that cut across subject matter, class size, teacher experience, or curriculum. A sampling from the cases makes this point.

• Rob Walker on the math department of Central High School (all names of schools are pseudonyms) in a Houston, Texas suburb:

> "I am a very traditional teacher. I use a chalkboard, a textbook, and handouts." If half the faculty did not say this precisely, they came close. I believe it is a fair representation of the faculty's pedagogical style....

• Mary Smith on Fall River High's science program in a small Colorado city:

Introductory Biology—instructional methods are largely lectures, lab investigations, review sheets, and occasional films and guest speakers. The text used is from the Biological Sciences Curriculum Study (green version).

Chemistry—the text *Modern Chemistry* is used but the approach is traditional. The vast majority of class time is spent in lectures and laboratory experiments.

● Louis Smith on science in Alte High School in a St. Louis suburb. He jotted down a number of statements that summarized what he saw "across schools, levels, disciplines, and departments":

1. In most classrooms, a section of the blackboard with assignments for each day of the week.
2. Teachers' grade books literally full, cell by cell, of pages of numbers.
3. Teachers carrying a stack of laboratory notebooks home to be graded (in the evening) or into class to be returned (in the early morning before school).
4. Lab books full of red ink comments.
5. Frequent classroom byplay around the question, "Does it count?".
6. Reviews before tests, taking of quizzes and tests, returning and checking of tests.... [18]

If numbers appear infrequently in the volume of case studies, they are densely packed into every page of another NSF volume reporting the results of a 1977 national survey. Stratified by geography, socio-economic status, and other variables, almost 5,000 questionnaires from teachers were returned for a response rate of 76 percent. Teachers reported their classroom techniques and manner of grouping students for instruction. In the following Tables I have selected those techniques that approximate the ones I have used throughout this study. [19]

A number of commonalities are obvious from the self-reports. First, lecture and discussion were favored methods throughout the grades, except for elementary math. Second, certain teacher practices increased in frequency as students moved through the grades into high school: lecture, discussion, tests and quizzes—except for high school science teachers' use of lab equipment. Third, classroom practices associated with student-centered classrooms, such as student reports and projects, use of manipulatives and lab materials—either decreased as students got older (again, except for science) or did not reach beyond a reported 25 percent in use.

When Table 6.4 on instructional groupings reported by teachers is examined even more familiar patterns reassert themselves. Teaching the entire class as a group increases in frequency in the higher grades, according to teacher responses, so that by high school, regardless of subject, over half of the class time is spent in whole-group instruction; teaching in small groups decreases in practice as the students move through the grades, except in science. This form of instructional grouping, however, did not exceed one-quarter of the time in the three subjects at all levels, except for K–3 math. Working "individually" is ambiguous since

Table 6.3   Frequency* in Use of Selected Math and Science Techniques, 1977

	Math			Science			Social Studies		
Grade:	K–3 %	4–6 %	10–12 %	K–3 %	4–6 %	10–12 %	K–3 %	4–6 %	10–12 %
Lecture	47	58	90	40	66	87	56	59	80
Discussion	86	88	87	76	90	89	88	91	95
Individual Assignment[†]	80	83	61	18	42	46	27	52	42
Teacher Demonstration	71	64	53	35	37	41	NA	NA	NA
Students at Blackboard	81	78	58	12	18	10	10	13	6
Tests or Quizzes	45	64	78	7	30	62	20	38	60
Students use of lab materials and manipulatives	66	34	14	37	36	72	31	30	11
Student Reports or Projects	12	10	5	19	18	23	21	27	22
Sample number	(297)	(277)	(548)	(287)	(271)	(586)	(254)	(281)	(490)

* Frequency is defined as a technique reported by teachers to be used daily or at least once a week.
† "Teacher supervises students working on individual activities."[20]

the question included answers of teachers who assigned the entire class the same task and students worked alone while the teacher supervised the work.[21]

Emerging, then, from a national cross section of teachers' self-reports in 1977 are regularities in practice generally consistent with those in Arlington: teacher-centered patterns in total group instruction, classroom talk, and class activities converged with teacher self-reports of frequency in

Table 6.4   Average Percentage of Time Spent in Various Instructional Arrangements by Subjects and Grade Range

	Math			Science			Social Studies		
	K–3	4–6	10–12	K–3	4–6	10–12	K–3	4–6	10–12
Entire class as group	36	38	54	52	52	52	59	50	68
Small groups	29	25	22	18	18	19	15	15	11
Students working individually	36	38	24	30	30	30	26	35	21
Sample Number	(293)	(271)	(539)	(272)	(262)	(576)	(254)	(281)	(453)

lecture-discussion and whole group instruction. Furthermore, the patterns of increasing teacher-centeredness as students move from elementary to high school converge. By "converge" I only suggest a similar path in both cases although percentages do differ and categories are not identical. How much to discount for the inflation built into teacher reports is another item that needs to be factored into a judgment of how closely the two sets of data overlap.

Study of Schooling

A final set of data come from John Goodlad's team of researchers who have been working since 1972 on "A Study of Schooling." A technical report of over 1,000 elementary and secondary classroom observations in 38 schools across the nation, representing different regions, racial, socio-economic, and ethnic backgrounds of students and school sizes, was published in 1981. Although the study covered the goals of schools, parent and student views of what schools do, student expectations of the curriculum, and other issues, I will concentrate on the report that dealt with what teachers did in classrooms.[22]

Classroom data were elaborate. Trained observers did Five Minute Interactions (FMI), using an instrument to count the number of classroom events that occurred within 5 minutes, 4 times during a high school class and 16 times daily in an elementary classroom. The target events were how teachers spent time on different tasks and exchanges between students and teacher: who is doing what to whom, how, and in what context. This offered a continuous picture of classroom exchanges. Another information pool came from Snapshot data. Brief descriptions were taken in each classroom to locate what activity was going on, who directed the activity and the form of grouping for the activity.[23]

From both sets of data on over 1,000 elementary and secondary classrooms, Ken Sirotnik, who headed this portion of "A Study of Schooling," noted the following:

- Approximately half of the time is devoted to teacher talk.... Relatively speaking, teachers 'out-talk' students by a ratio of about three to one.
- The model classroom configurations which we observed ... looked like this: the teacher explaining/lecturing to the total class (or a single student), asking direct, factual-type questions or monitoring or observing students; the students 'listening' to the teacher or responding to teacher-initiated interaction.
- The majority of students at all schooling levels—nearly two-thirds in elementary and three-fourths in secondary—work as a total class.... Less than 10% are found working in small group configurations.[24]

In examining Sirotnik's tables, a number of specific activities resembled closely those included in this study. For example, observers counted classes where there was a learning center. Of 129 elementary classrooms, 39 percent had at least 1 learning center. No explanation of how the centers were used appeared in the report, however. In one table of activities in elementary and high school classrooms, I chose a number of familiar classroom tasks already discussed at length in this report.[25]

Table 6.5   Percentage of Time Teachers Used Selected Activities[26]

	Elementary	High School
Preparation for assignments or instructions; cleanup	12.1	13.2
Explain, lecture, read aloud	18.9	25.8
Discussion	6.8	5.2
Work on written assignments	29.1	15.2
Taking tests or quizzes	2.6	5.6
TOTAL	69.5	65.0

For about two-thirds of each class, elementary and high school students spent their time in only five activities—ones generally labeled as teacher-centered. These figures are generally consistent with the 1977 NSF survey data which tallied teacher responses for frequently used techniques and the Arlington figures for regular high schools in the category "Class Activities." Percentages from "A Study of Schooling," however, exceed by a considerable margin Arlington's figures for these tasks. In comparing the various sets of data for another category—grouping for instruction—keep in mind that two of the data sets come from direct observation (albeit with vastly different instruments) and teacher reports in dissimilar settings.

Table 6.6   Forms of Instructional Grouping*

	Entire Class		Small Group—Individual[†]	
	Elementary, %	High School, %	Elementary, %	High School, %
Study of Schooling	63	71	9	15
National Science Foundation Survey	48[‡]	58	26	21
Arlington	49	94	1	0
North Dakota cities	62	(NA)	13	(NA)

* All percentages are founded off.
[†] "A Study of Schooling" has a category "Medium/Large" group which accounts for the remainder.
[‡] NSF separated math, science, and social studies. Percentages that I used are means for the three subjects.

Degrees of difference in the figures are apparent. Precision in this area is, simply stated, lacking. What remains significant, I believe, in the face of differing methodologies, settings, and research designs are the commonalities in grouping for instruction, i.e. entire class is frequently used, and small group and individual is a much less common teaching practice. Frequencies vary for any number of reasons ranging from the nature of the data—survey and direct observation—to the instruments used or actual differences in classrooms.

No unambiguous statement can be made about teaching practice but perhaps these monotonous, repetitive configurations that show up persistently will help nail down the notion that there is, indeed, a stubborn stability to certain teaching patterns. Numbers, of course, help in making the point. Narrative, however, may fill in gaps in the meaning that escapes decimals and percentages. So I end this chapter with the experience of Ellen Glanz.

Teacher Playing Student

Typical of that group of experienced teachers who work in suburban affluent, white districts, Glanz spent a year as a student in the high school in which she taught. In becoming a student she took her teacher perspective and tilted it by sitting behind a student's desk in class after class, facing teachers, her colleagues. Her one-year experience illuminates classroom instruction in an unusual manner.[27]

A social studies teacher for six years at Lincoln-Sudbury Regional High School in Sudbury, a suburb twenty miles from Boston, Glanz proposed to her superintendent a project that would enable her to find out what it was like to be a student in high school. The superintendent gave her permission to take courses like any other student, provided the teacher, Glanz's colleague, agreed to her being in class. Glanz enrolled as a senior in' 1978–1979. Her schedule included advanced expository writing, calculus, Russian history, advanced French, drawing, and trampoline.[28]

Successful in being accepted as a student after the novelty wore off, she attended classes, did homework, took tests, and, as she remarked with a touch of pride, was even "kicked out of the library for talking." She kept a journal of her experiences and thoughts. Periodically, she met with teachers to share her observations and, by the end of the project, wrote two reports for the high school staff, parents, and students. Her observations from the perspective of a teacher-turned-student, pull together a number of points that both the text and tables made earlier.[29]

"I was curious to discover how different other teachers' classes were from those I attended as a child and a teenager." What she found out was that they "were not very different."

> Most teachers teach in much the same way they were taught—in an essentially didactic, teacher-centered mode.... The teacher knows the material and presents it to students, whose role is to 'absorb' it.

The system, she said, nurtures "incredible passivity." In class after class, "one sits and listens."

> In one class during my second week as a student, I noticed half way through the hour that much of the class was either doodling, fidgeting, or sleeping. Before long, I found my own mind wandering too.

Yet this teacher was touted as one of the finest in the school. "I realized," she said, "that what was boring was not what the teacher was saying but the very act of sitting and listening for the fourth hour in a row."[30]

When it comes to teaching methods, Glanz observed that most techniques teachers used "promote the feeling that students have little control over or responsibility for their own education." She pointed out the agenda for the class is the teacher's. He or she plans the tasks and determines who does what to whom, when. There is, she found, little opportunity for students to "make a real difference in the way a class goes, aside from their doing their homework or participating." She described how her English teacher surprised the class one period by letting two students lead a discussion. After some practice, "students were far more attentive and the teacher learned when and how to intervene to lead the discussion ... without taking control."[31]

After completing the year, writing the reports, and returning to her five classes a day, Glanz asked about the stubborn regularities in teaching approaches that she saw. "We must realize that in all likelihood, despite the problems I've described, classes will remain basically as they are right now." Why? Because subject matter—French, math, anatomy, history— "dictates an essentially didactic class model since the subject matter is not known intuitively by students and must be transmitted from teacher to student. And the ultimate authority and control will and should remain with the teacher."[32]

While Glanz suggests ways of improving teacher methods, involving students in classroom activities, and reducing the tensions that she saw clearly between the two separate worlds of teachers and students, it is apparent that she believes that the way it is in a high school can be improved but probably will stay much as it is because of what is taught, who has the knowledge, and where the authority rests. Glanz's description of her life as a student is similar to a number of other books and research efforts that put an adult into a high school for a limited amount of time. It is also consistent with the figures presented earlier. Her explanation, however, is an attempt to figure out why things are as they appeared to her. That task is now before me. Of the two questions I asked in the Introduction, I have answered the first one: how teachers taught. The second question on why teachers taught the way they did is discussed in the next chapter.[33]

NOTES

1. In 1966, Wilkinson asked whether her principal, Kitty Bouton, could secure a larger room for her effort to introduce informal teaching practices. Bouton received approval to have a wall knocked out thereby creating a large double room with ample space. Seeing it for the first time, according to Wilkinson, she exclaimed: "It's like a palace!" She told me that the word took on a negative meaning in the early 1970s. Interview with Carmen Wilkinson, March 22, 1982.
2. *The New York Times*, September 15, 1974.
3. It was, of course, these informal and frequent classroom observations over the seven years that produced the puzzling questions which prompted me to do this study. The research proposal that the National Institute of Education (NIE) approved in 1980 omitted Arlington as a site to study. It was after I left the post and began collecting data in Denver, Washington, New York City, and rural schools in the interwar decades and for the early 1970s that I saw the merit of examining a school district in the mid-to-late 1970s that had already experienced the surge of enthusiasm for informal education and open space. Because I had not included Arlington in the original proposal, I requested permission from NIE to add the district and they agreed. Thus, notes taken for one purpose were sifted to see how applicable they would be for another purpose. Most were; many were not.

   To protect the confidentiality of the teachers I visited, no individual will be identified except for those who have consented after I left Arlington or have published articles themselves. The two teachers I described in the opening pages of this chapter, for example, agreed to be included by name. The data I present, then, will be aggregated by elementary and high school.
4. Larry Cuban, "Shrinking Enrollment and Consolidation: Political and Organizational Impacts in Arlington, Virginia, 1973–1978," *Education and Urban Society*, 11 (May, 1979), pp. 367–95.
5. ibid., p. 368; Arlington closed its last all-black elementary school in 1971. Drew Elementary became a county-wide alternative school. Students interested in attending the school that was advertised as using informal approaches were bussed to Drew. A number of slots were held for black students in the Drew neighborhood.
6. Without getting caught in the nuances of what "liberal" means in the context of Northern Virginia politics in the early 1970s, I used the word since it was the label the press attached to the coalition and was often used by members of the group itself.
7. Arlington Public Schools, *School News*, January, 1980, n.p.
8. Arlington County Public Schools, *Profile*, June, 1969, p. 3.
9. ibid., pp. 3–4.
10. This estimate is taken from my notes written during my first year as Superintendent when I visited elementary classrooms. Interview with Carmen Wilkinson, March 22, 1982.

11. *Northern Virginia Sun*, September 7, 1971; *Washington Post*, May 31, 1971.
12. Superintendent Memorandum to School Board, "Status Report on Alternative Schools," June 15, 1979, p. 22.
13. *Arlington Journal*, February 14, 1974; I visited Woodlawn numerous times and observed classrooms, listened to students, and, in general, was familiar with the details of the school and its ethos.
14. ibid.
15. Robert E. Stake and Jack A. Easley, *Case Studies in Science Education*, Vol. 1, "The Case Reports."
16. ibid., 3–61, 62, 63, 64, 65.
17. ibid., "The Project," n.p.; pp. 3–90, 91.
18. ibid., p. 3–90.
19. National Science Foundation, *Report of the 1977 National Survey of Science, Mathematics, and Social Studies Education*, (Washington, D.C.: National Science Foundation, 1978).
20. ibid., pp. B–56, 57, 59, 60–1, 63–5, 67, 110.
21. ibid., p. 110.
22. Kenneth A. Sirotnik, "What You See Is What You Get: A Summary of Observations in Over 1000 Elementary and Secondary Classrooms," Technical Report No. 29, (Los Angeles: Graduate School of Education, 1981).
23. ibid., pp. 2–5.
24. ibid., pp. 8, 10, 14.
25. ibid., Table 1, n.p.
26. ibid., Table 3, n.p.
27. Ellen Glanz, "What Are *You* Doing Here?" (Washington, D.C.: Council for Basic Education, 1979).
28. ibid., pp. 1–4.
29. ibid., p. 5.
30. ibid., pp. 12–13.
31. ibid., pp. 14–15.
32. ibid., pp. 25.
33. See, for example, Philip Cusick, *Inside High School* (New York: Holt, Rinehart and Winston, 1973).

Part III

Stability and Change in Classrooms, 1890–1980

6

Explaining How They Taught: An Exploratory Analysis

> I must show the school as it really is.
> I must not attack the school, nor talk overmuch about what ought to be, but only about what is.
>
> WILLARD WALLER, *The Sociology of Teaching*

Remember the metaphor of the hurricane. Images of storm-tossed waves on the ocean surface, turbulent waters a fathom down, and calm on the ocean floor lent themselves well to agitated squabbles over curricular theories, textbooks, and classroom instruction. In the years after reform impulses pumped different ideas and practices into public schools, the metaphor helps to reveal the impossibility of generalizing about teaching behavior simply from the dominance of reform ideas and language in professional journals, popular magazines, and discourse among educators. Even crude classroom maps are better guides to revealing practice than reformer intentions or rhetoric. Moreover, these maps reveal the limits of the metaphor since it isn't calm on the ocean floor.

If anything, the last five chapters have charted some (but by no means all) features of the classroom terrain. I have collected data in five categories, embracing an important portion of visible teaching behaviors that educators label "instruction." Note, however, that these categories in no way equal the richness or complexity of classroom life. They do not capture the artistic elegance of those teachers whose subtle techniques can individualize instruction with the nod of a head, the wink of an eye, and a friendly arm around a shoulder. Or the abundant wealth in exchanges between students and teachers that produce a classroom culture complete with traditions to be honored, norms to be respected, and roles to be played. Thus, the study is limited in order to concentrate upon those practices teachers engage in regularly.

Drawn from a large number of varied sources in diverse settings over nearly a century, the data show striking convergence in outlining a stable core of teacher-centered instructional activities in the elementary school and, in high school classrooms, a remarkably pure and durable version of the same set of activities.

To the question—how did teachers teach?—answers can now be drawn from a substantial body of evidence, direct and contextual, from 1900 clearly showing what the central teaching tendency was and what variations of that dominant strain existed. Precision in methodology and sampling of historical sources were limited. However, the collection of almost 7,000 different classroom accounts, and results from studies in numerous settings, revealed the persistent occurrence of teacher-centered practices since the turn of the century—at the sizable risk of dulling a reader's sensibilities by presenting similar patterns and numbers. This historical inquiry into classroom instruction and the imprecise responses were in the spirit of one researcher who said, "far better an approximate answer to the right question, which is often vague than an exact answer to the question which can always be made precise."[1]

Previous chapters also disclosed that changes in teaching practices did, indeed, occur. Reforms left their signature on some classroom chalkboards. Some teachers, mostly elementary, created their versions of child-centered classrooms where students could move about freely to work in activity centers, where clustered desks made it easy for students to work together, and where teacher-student planning occurred daily. Subjects were correlated and ample time was spent by students working in small groups and independently on projects.

Other teachers—a much larger number—chose certain student-centered practices to initiate for part of a day or once a week which they felt would benefit children and not unsettle existing classroom routines. Some began grouping students for certain periods a day; others established a science or reading center in a corner of the room. Some pulled desks into a circle or groups of four so that children could talk to one another as they worked; others chose a unit, say, on Indians, and tried to integrate many subjects into the three weeks spent on the project. These new practices, often implemented on a consciously selective, piecemeal basis, were incorporated slowly into the regular modes of instruction that typified the average day. Hence, practice altered.

The modification of teacher practices that produced hybrid forms of teacher-centeredness occurred in substantial numbers of elementary schools in the interwar years and since the late 1960s. Teachers chose particular student-centered approaches and blended them into their daily routines. By the 1980s, classrooms were far less formal places for children than a century earlier. Varied grouping procedures, learning centers, student mobility, and certain kinds of noise were acceptable. But far fewer teachers had incorporated teacher-student planning of activities, determination of content, and allocation of class time into their lesson plan. Even less variation was apparent among high school teachers.

Why did these different patterns emerge? To ask "why" shoves a historian into pursuing causation. Unambiguous cause-effect relationships seldom march up to researchers and tap them on their shoulders. Moreover, because of some excesses in previous writings, historians have been leery of dealing openly with causes, substituting for the word such nouns as "factors," "influences," and "elements." Yet historians, in my judgment, cannot escape trying to explain what they have documented.

Let me state plainly what I mean by "why", since the word is slippery. To ask why the dominant form of instruction continued to be teacher-centered since the late nineteenth century and why hybrids of teacher-centered progressivism and informal education developed in elementary but less in high school classrooms, could produce a search to:

- Seek out motives, i.e. of reformers, teachers, administrators
- Lay blame, i.e. intransigent teachers, penurious school boards
- Justify the status quo, i.e. that's the way the system has been and it works
- Understand why something developed

This latter meaning of the word "why"—understanding the sources for continuity in teacher-centeredness and modest changes—is, I believe, essential knowledge that policymakers, scholars, and school officials need. This search for explanations is an inquiry into the determinants of classroom instruction, a search that, if successful, could produce reliable knowledge upon which informed improvement efforts could be built.

This exploratory effort to map and explain classroom instruction contains much imprecision in methodology. Nonetheless, there are criteria that would help sort out some explanations from others. Obviously, given the data and its inevitable gaps, there is no one single, comprehensive, or final explanation. Explanations that would meet certain criteria would be, at best, suggestive and provide only further hypotheses for exploration. My criteria for selecting explanations are drawn directly from the patterns that emerged from the data:

1. Does the argument explain the pattern of teacher-centered instruction in both elementary and high school classrooms?
2. Does the argument answer why some instructional changes occurred at the elementary and not at the high school level?
3. Does the argument further explain why teachers selected particular progressive and informal practices, and not others?

These criteria exclude, for now, the possibility that there are separate explanations for separate questions which are also mutually exclusive. I exclude these possibilities now in the hope of initially finding simple, answers rather than complex ones. Yet these possibilities exist.

I return now to the five candidate explanations I sketched out briefly in the Introduction. Let me review them and add more detail where relevant. Each has a plausible ring in explaining either the persistent regularity or change in teaching practices. The danger of building weak arguments that could be later torn apart in order to present *the* correct one is inherent in this approach. I am aware of this and in building these possible explanations I have tried to avoid that trap by distilling from the literature on stability and change in schooling those arguments that are consistent with evidence presented in the last five chapters and fit the more narrow issues of pedagogy raised in this study. Nonetheless, it remains a danger and I want to alert the reader to it.

EXPLANATIONS

There are five explanations. Three (Schooling as Social Control and Sorting, Classroom and School Structures, and the Culture of Teaching) try to account for the constancy of teacher-centered instruction. Two (Teacher Beliefs and Implementation of Change) try to explain both continuity and change in practice. In presenting each explanation, I argue as if I were an advocate of the position. Following the five explanations I analyze the strengths and flaws of each.

Schooling as Social Control and Sorting

The school is the only public institution in the life of a growing child that stands between the family and the job market. The overriding purposes of the school, not always apparent but nonetheless evident, are to inculcate in children the prevailing social norms, values, and behaviors that will prepare them for participation in the larger culture. The structure of school life, what knowledge is highly valued, and what pedagogical practices occur, mirror the norms of the larger class and economic system. This explanation focuses largely upon schools being the primary mechanisms for social control, the sorting of diverse students into niches, and distributing the dominant cultural knowledge to the next generation.

Those teaching practices that seek obedience, uniformity, productivity, and other traits required for minimum participation in bureaucratic and industrial organizations, are viewed as both necessary and worthwhile. In the primary grades, for example, work and play emerge as a distinct dichotomy with work considered more important by the teacher and play viewed as something to be done after tasks are completed. Work includes whatever the teachers directs children to do. Free-time activities are called play. Moreover, time to work is stressed. Tasks must begin and end when teachers say they do. Also work periods often involve every child working alone on the same task, at the same time. Thus, classrooms with helper charts listing children's names with tasks to be done and daily schedules of activities that teachers place on blackboards reflect these points on work and time.

As the students grow older, homework, tests, grades, focus upon classroom competitiveness and productivity. Within this argument, certain teaching practices are functional: whole group instruction where waving hands vie for the teacher's attention; a question-answer format that rewards those better at factual recall; classroom furniture arranged to produce a uniform appearance; textbooks, a primary source of knowledge, yield reams of homework to which credit is given or withheld and becomes the basis for tests and quizzes. Dominant teaching practices, then, endure because they produce student behaviors consistent with the requirements of the larger society especially, in the high school.

The origins of the high school as a college preparatory institution serving a fraction of the population, capture both the social sorting and control functions precisely—according to this argument. College entrance requirements, Carnegie units, examinations, varied curricula mirroring future vocational choices channeled students into classes where knowledge and instruction are matched to vocation, e.g. business English, advanced placement English; physics and general science; calculus and consumer math. These external demands of university and marketplace shape the high school's structure and teaching, yet plumbs deeply into the junior high and upper elementary grades. The persistent press upon elementary teachers to have their children up to grade level to be prepared for junior high is duplicated by junior high teachers who press to have their students ready for the high school.

Progressive and informal pedagogy, on the other hand, nourish individual choices, independent behavior, expressiveness, group learning skills, knowledge from many sources, joint student–teacher decision making, and student participation in both the verbal and physical life of the classroom. Such behaviors are beyond the behaviors believed to be matched to the requirements of the university and the marketplace, although they do describe certain behaviors characteristic of future professionals, managers, and executives. Such a fit helps to explain why progressive changes and open classrooms were often associated more with private schools and groups of upper-middle class, highly educated parents living in affluent areas than with public schools in white and blue–collar districts.

This argument about schools as mechanisms for social sorting and control is another explanation for the stability in pedagogical practices since the turn of the century.[2]

School and Classroom Structures

Organizational structures drove teachers into adopting certain instruction-al strategies that varied little over time. By structure, I refer to the way school space is physically arranged; how content and students are orga-nized into grade levels; how time is allotted to tasks; and how rules govern the behavior and performance of both adults and students. These structu-ral configurations, the argument runs, derive from the primary impulses of public schooling: to get a batch of students compelled to attend school absorb certain knowledge while maintaining orderliness. The Carnegie Unit, age-grading, self-contained classrooms, class size, and teaching load aim at improving the school's productivity.

The classroom organization, located within the larger school structure like a small Russian wooden doll nested within another larger one, is a crowded setting in which the teacher has to manage 25 to 40 or more students of approximately the same age who involuntarily spend—depend-ing upon their age—anywhere from 1 to 5 hours daily in a space no larger than a luxurious master bedroom. Amidst continual exchanges with individual students and groups—up to 1,000 a day in an elementary classroom, according to Jackson—the teacher is expected to maintain control, teach a prescribed content, capture student interest in the subject matter, vary levels of instruction according to student differences, and show tangible evidence that students have performed satisfactorily.

Within these overlapping school and classroom structures, teachers rationed their energy and time in order to cope with conflicting and multiple demands, constructed certain teaching practices that have emerged as resilient, simple, and efficient solutions in dealing with a large number of students in a small space for extended periods of time.

So, for example, rows of movable desks and seating charts permit the teacher, like Gulliver in Lilliput, easy surveillance and help to maintain order. The teacher's desk, usually located in a visually prominent part of the room near a chalkboard, underscores quietly who determines the direction for what the class will do each day. Class routines for students raising their hands to answer questions, to speak only when recognized by the teacher, and to speak when no one else is talking—the principle of turn–taking—establishes an orderly framework for instruction when it is delivered to groups. Students asking permission to go to the pencil sharpener or to leave the room reaffirm the teacher's control over student mobility and the imperative of orderliness.

Teaching the entire class at one time is simply an efficient and convenient use of the teacher's time—a most valuable and scarce re-source—to cover the mandated content and to maintain control. Lectur-ing, question–answer format, recitation, seatwork, homework drawn from texts are direct, uncomplicated ways of transmitting knowledge and directions to groups. Given the constrictions placed upon the teacher by the daily school schedule, and the requirements that a course of study be completed by June—the above instructional practices permit the teacher in a timely and efficient manner, to determine whether students have learned the material.

Student-centered approaches in organizing space, instructing in small groups, correlating subject matter, encouraging expressiveness and student decision making generate noise, movement, a muted view of teacher authority, and make a shambles of routines geared to handling batches of students. These approaches appear out of touch with existing school and classroom structures and would seemingly require a complete overhaul of basic modes of classroom operation, placing the entire burden of change upon the shoulders of the teacher. It comes as little surprise, according to this explanation, that few teachers are willing to upset their intimate world for the uncertain benefits of a student-centered classroom.

Called the "Hidden Pedagogy" by some British writers, in contrast to the explicit teaching methods called for by textbooks and professors, this interpretation of regularities in instruction stresses how teachers coped in a practical manner with the demands of organizational structures, over which they had little control. By constructing solutions in the shape of practical classroom routines and teaching methods—the "Hidden Pedagogy"—teachers survived the crosscutting daily pressures of the classroom.[3]

The Culture of Teaching

A third explanation concentrates upon the occupational ethos of teaching that breeds conservativism and resistance to change in instructional practice. This conservativism, i.e. preference for stability and caution toward change, is rooted in the people recruited into the profession, how they are informally socialized, and the school culture of which teaching itself is a primary ingredient.

Persons attacted to the classroom seek contact with children, appreciate the flexible work schedule, and, while acknowledging the limited financial rewards, still embrace the service mission built into teaching. Entrants, according to this explanation, are usually young people already favorably disposed to schools, having been students for many years. Moreover, of the young who enter teaching women outnumber men, who often move out of the classroom in search of recognition, more influence, and higher salaries. Attracted by work schedules that permit flexible arrangements with family obligations and vacations, the argument runs, women and men, for different reasons, invest little energy in altering occupational conditions. Recruitment, then, brings in people who tend to reaffirm, rather than challenge, the role of schools, thereby tipping the balance toward stability, rather than change.

Even prior to formal entry to teaching via a brief training program, informal socialization has shaped newcomers' attitudes toward continuity. Consider that as public school students for 12 years (over 13,000 hours), entering teachers were in close contact with their teachers. Teaching is one of the few occupations where one learns firsthand about the job while sitting a few yards away, year after year. Teachers intuitively absorbed lessons of how to teach as they watched. Within this explanation, the familiar assertion is heard that teachers teach as they were taught.

Similarly, the act of teaching presses toward preserving what is. The first-year teacher, after a brief apprenticeship, is thrust into the classroom with the same responsibilities as a 20-year veteran. The private anguish of a sink-or-swim ordeal which usually consumes the first few years of the neophyte is alleviated by occasional advice and sharing of folklore from experienced colleagues. From the very first day, facing the complicated process of establishing routines that will permit a group of students to behave in an orderly way while the subject matter is taught, the teacher is driven to use those practices that he or she remembered were used or take the counsel of veterans who advised their use. Experienced colleagues may help informally and, in doing so, entrants absorb through a subtle osmosis the norms and expectations of the school and what it takes to survive as a teacher. The folklore, occupational gimmicks, norms, and daily teaching reinforce what *is* rather than nourish skepticism, especially if one wishes to persist in the profession.

Thus, classroom practices tend to be stable over time. After all, homework assignments, discussion, seatwork, tests, and an occasional film to interrupt the routine were all methods familiar to newcomers in their own schooling and, more often than not, seemed to keep the class moving along. To use them in their own classrooms would be preserving what some exemplary teachers and esteemed college instructors had used. Rather than making fundamental changes—such as teaching in small groups, integrating varied content into units, planning lessons with students, and letting class members choose what to do—tinkering with methods, polishing up techniques, introducing variations of existing ones would be consistent with the basic conservatism, according to this explanation, that is bred by the occupation.[4]

Beliefs: Individual and Shared

The ideas teachers hold about the purposes of the school, how children develop, the role of subject matter in instruction, how classroom space should be organized, and the exercise of authority determine teaching practices. This explanation stresses that 19th century ideas of child-centered instruction, implemented by practitioners such as Sheldon, Parker, Dewey, and others, reached a popular audience in the twentieth century, after academics and writers wrote journal and newspaper articles.

Growing numbers of teachers, particularly at the elementary level, put these ideas to work in classrooms. The Eight Year Study and other experiments are instances of the spread of these ideas at the secondary level.[5]

The teacher who believes that children working together in small groups can teach one another much of what he or she wishes to convey, will organize classroom furniture differently than a teacher who views learning as a filling-up process. Also the teacher who conceives of block-building as an exercise to develop large muscles in five year olds will plan for that task differently than one who views it simply as another play activity. Finally, the teacher who looks for connections between textbook content and daily events because he or she believes that knowledge related to a context will be learned by students, will depart from the text far more often than others to explore these connections. Coverage of subject matter will be sacrificed in a trade-off that offers students a larger grasp of deeper understandings than dates, numbers, or similar facts could convey.

Among teachers, however, other ideas are far more deeply embedded. Knowledge must be transmitted to young people; the role of the school is to develop the mind and instill social values; students learn best in well-managed, noiseless classrooms where limits are made plain, academic rigor is prized, and where rules are equitably enforced by the teacher; and the teacher's authority, rooted in institutional legitimacy and knowledge, must be paid respectful attention. These, and similar beliefs, are held by most teachers, especially in high schools. They account for the perserverance in such teaching practices as reliance upon textbooks, little student movement, and a concern for tranquil classrooms marked by the "hum of knowledge." The familiar dichotomy of teaching-children-a-subject or teaching–a-subject-to-children captures a substantial piece of these belief systems.[7]

Beliefs, then, shape what teachers choose to do in their classrooms and explain the core of instructional practices that have endured over time.[8]

Feckless Implementation

A core of teaching approaches endured because reform efforts to alter those approaches were ineffectually executed. Had thoughtful, systematic, and comprehensive efforts been undertaken to implement instructional changes, the argument runs, far more progressive and informal educational practices would be apparent in the 1980s. Where implementation succeeded, teaching practices altered.

Except for Denver and New York in the 1930s, few school districts developed conscious strategies that would put into practice new ideas about teaching. Where classroom reforms were adopted, invariably, they stemmed from a decision made at the top administrative level. Implementation was given little thought beyond a batch of directives being sent out and briefings for principals and teachers, according to this argument.

Indeed, seldom were teachers directly or formally involved in planning or determining the conditions for implementation except, again, in Denver in the interwar years (which still remains unique among school districts). In most instances, formal endorsement occurred but there were few organized efforts to put progressive or open classroom approaches into practice, e.g. Child Development Program in 1938 (Washington, D.C.); expansion of the Activity Program in 1941 (New York City); also, in the same year, Denver's decision to mandate General Education courses, results of the Eight Year Study, in all high schools; open classrooms in Fargo and Grand Forks (North Dakota) in the 1970s.

A laissez-faire, free market approach marked the posture of middle-sized and large school systems after the superintendent and school board embraced instructional reforms. A "dogma-eat-dogma," Darwinian world where reforms struggled among themselves for survival, often characterized school districts. Individual advocates or bands of partisans for a special change would fight doggedly for a niche, i.e. resources to last a couple of years. If successful, the district grapevine and sporadic contacts with like-minded professionals and parents would spread word of the change. Perhaps, if conditions were just right, formal notice of the successful reform by a top administrator, superintendent, or board of education would lead to its expansion. Serendipity, more than plan, would explain expansion. Absent, more often than not, were administrative mechanisms to disperse information, organizational linkages between school practices and district-wide goals, and teacher participation in the process.

Student-centered approaches, then, infrequently penetrated classrooms because of the unwillingness or incapacity of school officials to convert a policy decision or formal approval of an instructional change into a process that would gain teacher support for classroom adoption. The explanation contains within it the adage implementors are fond of using: It was a terrific idea; it is a shame that it wasn't ever tried. The explanation also suggests that the very adoption of the innovation without subsequent organizational effort may have even strengthened the stability of existing practices by spreading the illusion of classroom change.[9]

Applying the Criteria

All of these arguments hurdle the first criterion of explaining the durability of teacher-centered instruction in elementary and high school classrooms. In meeting the other two criteria, however, dropouts occur. The lack of effective implementation, for example, explains why so few changes in teaching practice did penetrate classrooms (except in New York City and

Denver) during the 1930s when concerted organizational efforts were undertaken. But the argument fails to account for why student-centered practices occurred among grade school teachers and hardly spread among high school staff. Nor does the interpretation account for teacher selectivity in implementing some approaches but not others.

Similarly, the argument of a teacher culture explains nicely the durability of a core of teaching practices. It accounts for high school classrooms especially retaining the look, smell, and activities of classrooms of previous generations. But its elasticity is limited. Evidence that teachers, singly and in groups, did establish student-centered classrooms in various places in both periods when progressive and open classroom methods were in vogue reveals that large numbers of teachers, while shaped by that occupational culture, did break away from its confining traits. Nor does the argument help in understanding why hybrids of approaches developed among teachers.

The same problems afflict the social control and sorting argument. Its power is rooted in connecting the larger culture and social structure to the mundane activities that teachers carry out daily in their classrooms. Partially, it even helps to explain the organizational structures that were established in schools, i.e. grade levels, time schedules, curricular tracks, 1 teacher for 30 students, etc. Stability in pedagogical practices have social meaning—they are not simply artifacts independently created, detached from a context. Yet the distinctions in the amount of change between levels of schooling and teacher-centered versions of progressivism and open classroom practices that emerge from the data are missing from this argument. Finally, there is the larger, more substantial issue accompanying any social control and sorting explanation for phenomena: latent functions. That is, what teachers do in their classrooms is only a surface reality, for it masks the underlying functions that are the true purposes of the institution, i.e. social control and sorting of students into economic niches.

This may be true, although it borders on the impossible to prove that what are asserted as latent functions are, indeed, the *real* purposes. The best that could occur, I believe, is a correlation between evidence and the assertion that, for example, the teacher's domination of classroom talk is a means of reproducing the larger social order's power relationships and hierarchial control mechanisms.[10]

Individual beliefs, as an explanation, is more robust because it carries with it implicitly the notion of potential teacher change. Beliefs are learned. They can be dropped, learned anew, integrated with others into a unique synthesis. Changes in ideas occur slowly. Hence, changes in teacher practice follow shifts in belief patterns among teachers. This argument hurdles two fo the criteria: it accounts for durability because of entrenched beliefs concerning what was appropriate teaching dating back to the late nineteenth century; it accounts for some teachers changing their beliefs and embracing new ones.

The argument also explains why teachers may have decided among pedagogical practices since beliefs may be accepted partially at first and then wholly as classroom experience meshes with belief. Classrooms are unforgiving crucibles for testing out ideas. A few meet the rigors of daily instruction fully; some have partial merit, while others are discarded onto the ideological debris that surrounds public schooling. But the explanation fails to clarify why more student-centered pedagogy turned up in elementary rather than high schools.

What teacher beliefs lack in an explanation, the argument of school and classroom structures supplies a missing piece. The suggestion that organizational structures shape practice assumes that elementary and high schools are similar in structure but not identical. Where the two organizations differ markedly is in complexity of content students face in classrooms, allocation of time to instruction and external arrangements imposed upon high schools from other institutions.

Children in elementary grades learn fundamental verbal, writing, reading, and math skills. Content is secondary and often used as a flexible vehicle for getting at those skills. But in the upper grades of elementary school, and certainly in the secondary school, not only are more sophisticated skills required of students but these skills are hooked directly into complex subject matter that in and of itself must be learned. Literary criticism, historical analysis, solving advanced math problems, quantatitive analysis in chemistry—all require knowledge of complicated facts and their applications. High school teachers will remain didactic in methods because subject matter drives methodology in the classroom.[11]

Also in elementary schools, student and teacher contact time differ markedly at both levels. The self-contained classroom remains the dominant form of delivering instruction. Generally, teachers spend 5 or more hours with the same 30 or more students. They see far more of a child's strengths, limitations, capacities, and achievements than a high school teacher who sees 5 groups of 30 students less than an hour a day. Over a year, the elementary teacher sees a class of 30 children nearly a 1,000 hours; a high school teacher sees any one class no more than 200 hours during the year or about one-fifth of the time that elementary colleagues spend with pupils. Contact time becomes an important variable in considering issues of grouping, providing individual attention, varying classroom tasks and activities, and rearranging furniture. In elementary schools, the *potential* to make changes in these and other areas is present just because the teacher has more contact time with the same children; such potential is absent for 25 students within a 50-minute period. Whether such changes occur in the lower grades, is, of course, an entirely separate issue, but the structural difference in time allocation allows for possible changes in elementary classrooms.[12]

Finally, external pressures from accrediting associations, college entrance requirements, and vocational qualifications have far more a direct, unrelenting influence upon high schools than lower grade classrooms. In the high school classroom, strong pressures derive from Carnegie units, College Boards, Scholastic Aptitude Tests, Advanced Placement, certifying agencies, and other external constraints that push teachers to complete the textbook by June, that drive students to prepare for exams, seek jobs, and take the proper courses for graduation. While similar urgencies exist in elementary grades, particularly the press to get children ready for the next grade, the tensions seldom pinch as they do in the higher grades. More time is available in elementary schools. Flexible arrangements are possible. Grades can be combined. Groups within a class can include a range of ages and performance. Retaining a student for another year, while uncommon, occurs more frequently in elementary than in high schools. These three structural differences—emphasis on subject matter, contact time, and external pressures—may well account for why changes occurred with some frequency in elementary schools and much less so in high schools.

If this argument meets the criteria and also explains teacher-centered instruction as a series of teacher-engineered solutions designed to cope with the physics of school and classroom structures within which they labored, then there is still the final hurdle of explaining why teachers selected certain student-centered practices and not others. Here this argument falls short. It does not offer a plausible reason for why those teachers who embraced new practices chose ones that produced hybrids of teacher-centered open classrooms and progressivism, e.g. classroom rearrangements, more student movement, learning centers, projects, and varied groupings wedded to teacher-centered approaches.

None of the explanations meet all three criteria. From the diverse arguments, bits and pieces touch upon various facets, capturing a highlight here and a significant theme there. Anyone could carve from these five perspectives a number of reasonably coherent explanations that would meet all three criteria. Let me shape a synthesis of these arguments—again acknowledging that it is one of many choices—that I believe explains why teacher-centered instruction perservered; why elementary classrooms changed more than those in high schools; and why mixed versions of progressivism and informal education have developed.

Situationally Constrained Choice: A Preliminary Explanation

My explanation is midway between speculation and conclusion. It is more informed than a guess, but it falls short of being a confident assertion. Why I chose this configuration of arguments rather than another set is because it met the three criteria, and rang true to my quarter-century experience as a teacher and administrator. My experience—a fourth criterion—acted as a sieve. All of the findings that have been extracted from the data fit this hypothesis in a satisfying manner, given my experiences.

The school and classroom structures, I believe, established the boundaries within which individual teacher beliefs and an occupational ethos worked their influences in shaping a practical pedagogy. Intertwined as these two influences are, disentangling them and assigning a relative weight to the influence of each I found virtually impossible to do. The constraints, pressures, and channeling that the school and classroom contexts generate is the invisible, encompassing environment that few recognize potentially shapes what teachers do daily in classrooms. How difficult it is to analyze the commonplaces—that which is seen daily and taken for granted as organic, unchanging, brick-hard features of the environment. Seymour Sarason, in an attempt to see the school differently, used the device of a visitor from outer space asking basic questions about school structure. Imagination is required. For example, to envision a voluntary tutorial with a student meeting daily in the teacher's living room contrasted with an eighth grade U.S. History class of 30 students in a school of 1,500 students is to see starkly the different environments, stripped of non-essentials. How tutor/student and teacher/class define instruction and learning suggests the overriding importance of organizational structures. For public schools, chairs in rows, recitations, whole group instruction, worksheets, and textbook assignments need to be viewed as a series of successful solutions invented by teachers to solve daily problems of managing a score or more of students while they also acquired information and values. Coping with these structures, teachers constructed workable pedagogical solutions that have proved useful in personally maintaining control while carrying out instruction.[13]

Within this organizational framework, the culture of teaching, itself shaped by structural arrangements, further funnels both newcomers and veterans into teaching regularities that folk wisdom reinforces as essential for classroom survival. Teachers copying mentors and former teachers was not wholly a knee jerk, unthinking reaction but was also a realistic appraisal of what teaching approaches were necessary to survive the year.

What leavens the deterministic drift of this argument is the potential for change associated with teacher beliefs. Certainly, the larger social milieu shaped belief systems. Moreover, organizational imperatives influenced what people thought. Yet different ideas about children's development, how they learn, and the purposes for schooling beyond cultivating minds, permeated the larger culture and penetrated educators' thinking since the turn of the century. Child-rearing manuals were influenced by developments in psychology. Radio programs, films, and magazines touted the New Education. Both helped shape different attitudes toward children and schools. Too often one forgets that while parents and citizens absorbed these ideas, teachers—as both parent and professional—did also. Ideas once embraced are not easily let go. You cannot unring a bell.

What continually intrigued me as I worked through the data was the recurring phenomenon of veteran elementary teachers, many of whom had taught for more than a decade, who created for the first time centers, different seating arrangements, projects, varied groupings, etc. Leona Helmick in rural Michigan (1937), Mrs. Spencer (1924) and Gloria Channon (1969) in New York City, Carmen Wilkinson (1981) in Arlington, and others who were often trained in conventional approaches and socialized by years in the classroom, still adopted, partially or wholly, another perspective of teaching. Generally, a small number of teachers in a district (and mostly in elementary schools) were the ones who persisted in maintaining the alterations they made to their classes long after the initial enthusiasm for the activity method, projects, learning centers, and open classrooms faded and colleagues returned to their familiar practices. Although these teachers were few, for any number of reasons, they already had developed over time, beliefs different from their fellow teachers about how children learn and what classrooms should be. Within the organizational structure of the elementary school, where heavy external pressures were less evident, larger blocks of time were available, and skills were stressed more than content, pedagogical practices could flow more easily from these ideas. Researchers might explore this phenomenon since it suggests renewed attention upon experienced teachers who already control their classrooms yet wish to try out different approaches. Were there substance to this idea, it would question a current notion that experienced teachers hold unchanging, entrenched beliefs and attention should be paid to new (or young) teachers as classroom innovators. Furthermore, it might give substance to the point I suggested earlier, that teachers who combined both teacher- and student-centered approaches were pathfinders. Such teachers created hybrids of instruction that coped with classroom complexities.

This argument of situationally-constrained choice, one of a number that could have been constructed, offers an explanation that accounts for both constancy and change in teaching practice, although the tilt is decidedly toward continuity. More important, I believe, it suggests that teachers had some, but not a great deal of, autonomy to make classroom choices derived from their belief systems. The margin of choice, exploited to its fullest by a small number of teachers, however, was quite slim.

The issue of teacher autonomy weaves covertly in and out of any speculation about classroom change. Of the five explanations, two suggested that teachers were gatekeepers of reform practice and freely chose what they would do in their rooms. The implementation argument assumed that if certain organizational mechanisms were in place, teachers would have been either coerced by formal authority, or persuaded by incentives of the virtues in certain instructional changes. The other argument focused upon teacher beliefs which could change were teachers exposed to different ideas about children and learning. Within the other explanations, the degree of teacher freedom to alter what is done in classrooms is diminished greatly by either adaptations to the larger social structure outside of the school or the professional culture itself.

Teacher Autonomy

Thus, blaming the teacher for resisting instructional changes—"teacher-bashing," as the British label this line of argument—is a common response to the tenacity of teacher-centeredness. Such a response assumes that most teachers were free to adopt changes, if they merely chose to. When they did not, it was because they were stubborn or fearful of classroom consequences. Teacher-centered instruction became an artifact of intransigence or fear.[14] Attributing to teachers the personal power to halt and divert change is a common tendency in locating explanations for events in personal behavior rather than assessing the potent influence of the setting or the blend of both factors. Yet consider, for example, what basic decisions directly affecting instruction were sealed off for decades from teachers:

1. How many and which students should be in the class?
2. Which students should leave the class because they are not profiting from instruction?
3. What extra instructional help will students get?
4. How long should the school day or class period be?
5. Should teachers have planning time in the daily schedule and, if so, when?
6. What texts will be used for each subject?
7. What grades or subjects will each teacher teach?
8. What should be the format and content of the report card?
9. What standardized tests will be given?
10. What content will the teacher teach?

The results of these decisions, nested in a structure outside the classroom, established the context for what teachers did in their classrooms.

The point here is to differentiate between contextual decisions affecting instruction over which teachers have had little influence from those classroom decisions that teachers could, indeed, make:

- How the classroom space and furniture is arranged (once portable furniture was installed in rooms)
- How students should be grouped for instruction
- Who should talk and under what circumstances
- To what degree and under what circumstances should students participate in classroom activities
- What tasks are most appropriate to get students to learn what is expected
- What instructional tools (texts, television, film, photographs, radio, etc.) are most productive in reaching classroom goals?

Teachers decided each of these issues; their decisions constituted the margin of change available to them. Yet these decisions could not escape the influence of the twin impulses pumped into the classroom from the outside: teachers must maintain order in their classrooms and get students to learn the required curriculum.

The issue of how much autonomy teachers had over school and classroom decisions is fundamental to any analysis of instruction since what policymakers and school administrators assume teachers can and cannot do is often built into decisions touching classrooms. Is the teacher a captive of processes that inexorably shape what happens in classrooms? Is the teacher a leader who determines what needs to be done within the classroom and who does it? Or is the teacher in the classroom an ineffable mix of captive and leader who is dependent upon both circumstances and time? My speculation stressed that structural and cultural influences were sufficiently potent to maintain teacher-centered practices, especially in high schools. In classrooms, teachers had partial autonomy. A narrow margin of opportunity for change existed (more in elementary than in high schools). The freedom to alter the classroom and exploit that margin increased in those teachers who, for any number of reasons, embraced different beliefs about children, learning, and what schools should do. They believed that those ideas could be introduced to their classrooms and forged ahead in a trial-and-error fashion.

Far more stability than change, my argument goes, characterized classroom instruction. Change did occur, mostly at the elementary level, and far less in high schools, but it was limited to certain areas. What I have yet to explain is why hybrids of teacher-centered progressivism and informal education appeared.

Recall that more informality in seating and student movement developed in elementary classrooms over the years. Varied groupings showed up; teachers divided classes into two or three groups for reading, math, or other activities. Individual attention from the teacher increased somewhat. Activity centers and projects were embraced by substantial numbers of teachers in one generation and learning centers by a later one. Why these areas were selected, initiated, and installed by growing numbers of teachers (far from a majority, however) and not student-teacher planning of content, alloting of time during the day, and choice of activities, is a puzzle to which I now turn.

Why Did These Hybrids Develop?

This question can be split apart: why did teachers who chose to introduce new techniques limit what they selected? Why did teachers choose the particular student-centered approaches that mark these hybrids?

To answer these questions, I need to divide teachers since 1900 into three general groups. First, the largest group and numerical majority, including over 90 percent of high school teachers contained teachers who chose to continue instruction in a manner to which they were accustomed—or, as I have argued, were shaped by organizational structures and occupational culture. A second, and considerable group of teachers—probably up to 25 percent of the teacher population—accepted many of the ideas but tried out only a few, limiting themselves to particular techniques. Finally, there was a fraction of teachers, probably in the 5–10% range and concentrated in elementary schools, who believed in progressivism and informal education. They introduced as faithful a replica of those ideas as they could that was tailored to their classrooms and the available resources. These last two groups, I estimate, added up to at least one-third of all teachers, again, drawn mostly from elementary schools. From these teachers mixed versions of progressivism and open classrooms developed. And for these teachers, the two questions I ask are applicable.

Why did teachers limit their choices to certain student-centered practices? Two reasons, I believe, dulled the appetites of teachers for classroom change: the personal cost in time and energy and the lack of help to put complex ideas into practice. What most teachers do ordinarily requires a major investment of time and emotional, if not physical, energy. Consider planning what content to cover and how to carry it off; doing it amidst unexpected events; interacting with children continually while teaching; making hundreds of small decisions daily while in front of the class; marking papers; handling disputes between children—and a dozen other activities. Effective execution of these tasks spell the difference between maintaining a harmonious order or helplessly watching a parade pass through the room. To incorporate student-centered practices and begin revising the customary role of teacher expands the personal investment of time, energy, and effort while posing a threat to classroom routines.

Consider supplying the class with varied materials in order to match up students' interests and performance level with classroom tasks. To do so requires teachers to find new materials in the school or district and, if not available, then elsewhere. Otherwise, teachers make the materials themselves. Recall rural Vermont teacher Mary Stapleton and to what lengths she went in 1932 to individualize instructional materials similar to what she heard about in Winnetka. Or imagine how much work goes into starting learning centers for the first time, much less the continuing work of changing them weekly. Or consider the emotional energy and managerial skills that go into operating a class where children move about doing many varied tasks simultaneously while the teacher listens to a child or speaks to a small group.

Monitoring what children are doing, what skills they need to work on, and resolving unexpected problems as they arise demands the teacher's additional investment in radar equipment, if not an intensive management course. Students deciding on classroom rules, content to be studied, or similar areas require of the teacher certain skills and more patience in anticipating, responding, revising, and accepting diverse noises and student activity than they had been used to.

The initial five chapters contained many examples of different stages in classroom student-centeredness. Such changes in conventions and classroom traditions imposed a direct, unrelenting obligation upon the teacher to invest far more time and effort beyond what teacher-centered colleagues invested. If there is any continuous theme in what teachers have said about opening up their classrooms or introducing progressive practices, it is that far more is expected of the teacher. Afternoons and evenings are often spent in preparing materials and marking papers. Coming to school early in the morning before the children arrive in order to rearrange centers and set up activities for the day was common among such teachers. Arlington's Carmen Wilkinson, with over 30 years experience, told me:

> We have a lot of work. The curriculum is overloaded and we have so many assessments to do. So much paperwork. Yet I teach Spanish in the first grade. That's not in the curriculum. Every other Friday, we cook. That's not in the curriculum. But I feel that they need these extras. Teachers need to expand their own thinking and their own creative ideas.[15]

Anyone reading even a small portion of teacher accounts describing what they have done in their classrooms would come away impressed with the amount of extra work that had to be done to alter practice.

Help was necessary. Help was needed in the shape of another pair of hands, another person to work with individuals and small groups, grade papers, prepare seatwork, etc. Help was needed in developing materials and building centers; how-to sessions in managing students engaged in six different classroom tasks; how to distinguish between instructional and disruptive noise, cope with distractions, and help pupils work through decisions. Help was needed in providing time for teachers to talk, plan, and work through some of the thornier classroom issues of control, management, implementing curriculum, risking one's self-esteem in trying something new, etc. Many student-centered classrooms in the 1970s had student-teachers, aides, or parent volunteers to help in open classrooms. The Innovation Team (Washington, D.C.), the New School's support team (North Dakota), Workshop Center for Open Education (New York City) are instances of the awareness that teachers lacked the resources to do it all by themselves and needed technical assistance.

Most teachers who endorsed progressive and informal educational ideas lacked access to that kind of aid or already felt overloaded with existing classroom demands. In a sink-or-swim fashion, most teachers who ventured into progressive and informal practices had to learn these skills by themselves, from like-minded colleagues either in school or elsewhere, from books, summer courses, etc. Dorothy Boroughs, the P.S. 198 fourth grade teacher in 1970–1971 took a course in open classrooms, visited a school where two teachers had opened their classrooms without any outside help, and had even placed a math center in one corner of the room. Yet, as the article pointed out, doing all she had to do to keep abreast of her students, school requirements, and her expectations of what was necessary to get her class to read on grade level left her little time and few emotional resources to pursue actively changes in her classroom.

All of this is to say that what is required involves far more rethinking of daily classroom events, what materials must be secured, how to spend time, and what children are to do for those teachers who wish to adopt student-centered practices. The time and effort burden falls directly and solely upon the teacher's shoulders. No professor, reformer, principal, or superintendent had to stay after 4 o'clock in the afternoon to put up learning centers. What clear and consistent yield could teachers count upon for their students and themselves from the additional exertion? What organizational recognition and incentives were there to increase the amount of work taken home and periodic rearrangement of the classroom? What problems with students, other colleagues, and school administrators might occur as a result of classroom changes? Are the inner rewards worth the tradeoff in potential problems and additional work? No unambiguous answers existed to these questions. This is why, I believe, teachers in the second group restricted their embrace of student-centered approaches to just a few.

Between 1900–1980, why did a substantial number of teachers re-arrange classroom space and furniture, permit more student movement, develop projects and learning centers, and use varied groupings as the preferred student-centered approaches? Partisans of child-centered schools two generations ago and open classrooms a decade ago might wince at these artifacts of reform. Yet informality in student-teacher relationships, space and furniture arrangements that resemble a home-like situation, and student freedom to move around in the elementary classroom are more apparent now then they were a half-century earlier.

But, according to Philip Jackson, this informality may be deceptive. He studied a group of 50 elementary teachers identified as "superior" in suburban Chicago in the early 1960s. He found them informal but made some careful distinctions.

> "Informal" as these teachers use the term, really means *less* formal rather than *not* formal (original emphasis), for even in the most up-to-date class-rooms, much that goes on is still done in accordance with forms, rules, and conventions. Today's teachers may exercise their authority more casually than their predecessors, and they may unbend increasingly with experience, but there are real limits to how far they can move in this direction. As a group, our interviewees clearly recognized and respected those limits. For them, the desire for informality was never sufficiently strong to interfere with institution-al definitions of responsibility, authority, and tradition.[16]

Jackson's comments echo John Dewey's observations of substantial changes in "life conditions" of the classroom but such "atmospheric" modifications have not "really penetrated and permeated the foundations of the educational institution." Moreover, Dewey continued, "the fundamental authoritarianism of the old education persists in various modified forms."[17]

The key that might unlock the puzzle of teacher selectivity in choosing certain student-centered practices, I believe, is what both Jackson and Dewey mention—teacher authority. Formal power is delegated to the teacher to transmit knowledge and skills to students in an orderly manner. Maintaining classroom control, an essential exercise of that authority, is a fundamental condition for instruction to occur. Classroom control, of course, can be expressed in a number of forms ranging from coercively direct to charmingly subtle. Still, to the teacher, managing a group of students in an harmonious manner is paramount.

An asymetrical power relationship in the classroom permits the teacher to establish conventions that express the muscle that he or she implicitly has: calling the roll, making assignments, changing students' seats, asking questions, interrupting students to make a point, giving directions, telling students to perform tasks, drinking coffee in front of the class, giving grades, reprimanding students, praising individual effort, etc. These actions reinforce daily the teacher's perogatives, making it plain who is in charge of the classroom.

While there are hundreds of such behaviors that teachers and students engage in weekly that certify the teacher's power, there are, nonetheless, key decisions that are discretionary which touch the very core of classroom instruction and the teacher's authority. Who, for instance, allots time for each of the dozens of tasks assigned daily? Who determines what content will be studied? Who determines what instructional methods will be used? These and other decisions can be arrayed in a series of squares with those closer to the center representing the core of instructional authority.

Many teachers exercise their authority by deciding what will occur in each square, from seating charts for students to which students will knock dust from the erasers. To such teachers, student participation in any decision in the outer areas is viewed cautiously. At the beginning of this century, all decisions were made solely by the teacher. As progressive ideas about children's development and learning entered the thinking of educators, increased student talk, movement, and participation in the life of the classroom became professionally acceptable forms of conducting lessons.

Substantial numbers of teachers, concerned with maintaining order and limiting classroom noise, yet attracted to the new ideas about children and their development struck compromises between what was viewed as minimum teacher perogatives (i.e. the inner core) and the new beliefs.

Most experienced teachers, for example, establish student loyalty and compliance to their authority in the initial weeks of a school year. They can then count on students consistently responding to their requests. In such a setting, rearranging desks, students moving around more than they had, establishing learning centers, or dividing pupils into groups is far less threatening to a teacher's control than students determining what should be studied, when, and under what conditions. Not only are such increments of student involvement in the classroom less menacing, once the teacher's mandate is accepted by students, but these levels of participation offer the best of both worlds: control is maintained through the existing routines and traditions established by the teacher that undergird the moral

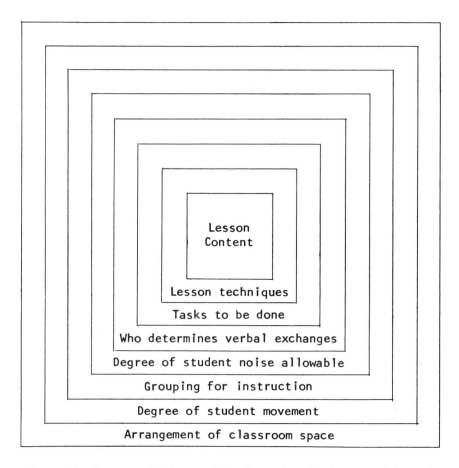

Figure 6.1 Classroom decisions made by the teacher. I make no special case for the order in which I have arranged the decisions. The point is that the closer to the center one gets, the more the decisions touch the core of the teacher's authority.

order of the classroom—all within a less formal, relaxed atmosphere. The fist is tucked gently inside the pillow.[18]

Thus, John Dewey's observations about the limits of the penetration of child-centered practices in classrooms are consistent with the evidence I have gathered. So, also, is the notion that hybrid forms of progressivism and open classrooms that emerged in this century may well have strengthened the teacher's authority in the elementary school making it congruent with shifts in society's attitudes toward child-rearing, individual expression, and participation in decisionmaking. These hybrids of instruction became awkward compromises that teachers fashioned to handle the conflicting social values that inevitably come to roost in America's classrooms.

These answers to the two questions on the development of teacher-centered forms of progressivism and informal education offer one explanation that is halfway between speculation and a confident hunch. How persuasive my analysis is at this point is less important than considering the implications of the findings on how teachers taught over the last century for schools in the 1980s.

IMPLICATIONS OF FINDINGS

On school reform and teacher improvement, issues of interest to policymakers, school officials, teachers, and scholars, these data on stability and change may have something to say.

Reform

This is not the place for an essay on school reform. I want to concentrate on those reforms aimed at changing instruction and the constraints inherent in change efforts targeted upon the classroom. Whether ideas came from child-centered advocates, technologically inspired reformers who see microcomputers in every classroom, enthusiasts dedicated to outflanking teachers by getting teacher-proof materials in student hands, or researchers intent upon spreading results of effective teaching studies— the unchanging, consistent target was moving the classroom teacher from one set of practices to another. In all of these sporadic efforts to change teacher classroom behavior was the dependable fact that future attempts would be made regardless of what previous efforts had or had not demonstrated. I make no judgment here about the quality or value of any instructional reform over the last century; I do not assume that a proposed change was superior to the practice it intended to replace; nor do I assume that stable teaching practices were ineffective in getting students to learn and thereby should have been changed. I do assume, however, that there are definite limits to any reforms aimed at altering classroom behavior. To ignore these limits is, I believe, injudicious given the current knowledge that exists both in experience and research.

This study, if anything, demonstrates how impervious high school classrooms were to such efforts for nearly a century. What few changes occurred in curricular content, classroom talk, and the formal recitation were overshadowed by the persistent continuity of teaching practices extending back decades into the shadows of a previous century. A plausible argument can be made that the reforms were either ritualistic, inappropriate, sloppily implemented, or untimely and the remarkable, century-long stability of high school instructional practice is, if anything, a sign of resilient vitality.

While the argument may be plausible, it would be, I believe, unpersuasive. The same argument, as I have shown, cannot be made for elementary teaching practice. Moreover, the Denver experience in five high schools with the Eight Year Study offered a glimpse of how a reform was adopted and installed in each of the schools. Yet also clear was the uneven spread of the experimental Progressive Education classes into the rest of the staffs and the minor traces of course content that remained in the curricula after 1943. And this in a district where top administrators supported these changes for almost two decades.

I raise this issue of marginal change because over the last decade in which blue-ribbon commissions, panels of professionals, and prestigious corporate coalitions have studied the high school, little attention has been paid to classroom instruction in any of their descriptions, analyses, and recommendations. Most changes that were recommended stressed organizational and structural changes aimed at tying high schools and their students to the larger community. Little notice was given to the kinds of instruction or its quality. What makes these studies quaint is that students have spent and continue to spend over three-quarters of their school time sitting in classrooms. More high school studies are imminent. Except for the Stanford University study and one jointly sponsored by the National Association of Secondary School Principals which do include curriculum and instruction, it appears that teaching will play no larger a role in their analyses than an earlier generation of studies.[19]

Nor does it appear that the current wave of corporate enthusiasm for overhauling the high school will touch the internal organs of the classroom. The loud call by the business community for high schools to produce better-equipped graduates possessing fundamental skills, positive attitudes toward the workplace, and flexibility in learning new tasks has produced a clutch of reports, collaborative ventures, and lobbying at both the local and state levels. State legislative agendas shaped by education-business coalitions call for stiffer graduation standards (e.g. more math, science, etc.), higher entrance requirements for public universities, a longer school day, tougher textbooks, competency tests for new teachers, rigorous evaluations of senior teachers, and more state testing that is matched to present curricula. A developing wisdom for retooling high schools often includes these and related items. While such agendas echo earlier efforts to restructure high schools grave omissions of essential issues provoke skepticism. There are, for example, no references to what happens in elementary schools, what factors determine high school instruction, and the practical pedagogy that teachers have invented to cope with the complexity of teaching in high school.

What seems to be missing from these studies and state legislative initiatives is an awareness of the profound difference between altering the external and structural conditions that shape what happens in schools (e.g. high school requirements, better tests, etc.) and trying to improve classroom teaching.[20] Connections between the external context (e.g. college requirements) and high school structure (e.g. the six-period school day), both of which shape what occurs in classrooms, have been largely ignored in these efforts to improve high schools. The assumption seems to be that teachers teaching 5 classes a day and students sitting in those rooms over 75 percent of the school day are either unchangeable features of the terrain or presumed worthwhile and thereby unsuitable targets for improvement. By manipulating the number and kinds of courses student take, entrance and exit requirements, cognitive skills of teachers, textbooks, and the like—somehow, in some mysterious way, teacher practice will change for the better and produce higher test scores. Certainly, this is a plausible hypothesis but burying hunches in policy is risky, particularly when those affected by the policies are unaware that guesses may drive decisions. Based upon this study of classroom instruction, the margin for change in teaching regularities is slim. Within the current high school organization the dream that stiffer requirements, more class time, and external tinkering with conditions outside of the school will turn high schools around will remain but a dream.

What directions in reform might work? Given that the margins for change may be slim, what would I predict might work in the light of the results of this study? Two directions clearly emerge. First, elementary schools offer a lower risk, higher return on altering teaching practices than in high schools; second, reforms that aim to improve teacher-centered approaches in either elementary or secondary schools have far more likelihood of success than those targeted on introducing student-centered practices. Let me expand on each of these.

The structural differences between elementary and high school offer a potentially rich arena for reform. Yet so little notice is paid to this level by the political actors who often spell the difference between dreamy intentions and fully funded programs. Whether it is because the investment is long-term and far more costly than short-term stakes in high schools, or whether the outcomes are so entangled with other variables, or other reasons, I am uncertain. The results of this study, at least on the point of how much change is possible, is unambiguous: the promise for alteration in the practical pedagogy that teachers have constructed is far rosier in the lower grades than in high school classrooms.

The second direction for reforms that offers promise is toward those improvement efforts that build on the existing teacher-centered pedagogy. Such efforts need, I believe, to be especially sensitive to the classroom teacher and attempt to understand the world that the teacher faces daily. To pursue that direction, reforms aimed at altering teacher routines need to secure the teacher's commitment. The teacher needs to be persuaded that a change will be better for children, not undercut his or her authority, and can be adapted to the current setting. Where modest changes have occurred, they have occurred because teachers have abosrbed rival beliefs that compete with existing ones. They embraced different ways of viewing the classroom. Also, I have argued that changing teachers' minds needs to be closely bound to tangible help in putting those ideas into practice. Because most instructional reforms impose increased demands upon the teacher's limited time and energy, help from outside the classroom is essential. While there are some Michaelangelos in the classrooms, like other professionals, teachers fall—for the most—in the middle range and therefore need aid at the classroom level in implementing any alteration in basic classroom conventions. The advisory network, liaisons, Innovation Teams, Workshop Center for Open Education, and other resources to permit teachers to plan and talk together seem to be minimum tools in modifying classroom practices. Current research on teacher collaboration supports this finding; also the growing body of literature on school-based improvement efforts that teachers participate in buttress this point.[21]

Data on the enduring patterns of instruction suggest revised notions of what constitutes success in modifying classroom practice. Remember New York administrator Joseph Loftus's generous estimate in 1941 that 25 percent of the system's teachers had initiated "in some degree" activity methods. The source for the quote faintly hinted that the statement was asserted proudly. If so, how could pride be expressed with three-quarters of the staff continuing in the dominant teacher-centered instructional patterns—approaches that he found wrongheaded?

In view of the powerful constraints on teacher behavior and the difficulty in capturing their attention, 25 percent may well be viewed as a victory. It certainly would be a victory in other highly competitive arenas. If Nielson television ratings, for example, register that high a viewing audience for a program, that show is judged first-rate. Or, if a textbook publisher gains that share of the school market, it is a bonanza. Direct mail executives would jump in joy over a 10 percent return. The point is that standards for judging the effectiveness of an instructional reform penetrating classrooms hinges upon an awareness of how limited teachers are in determining what goes on in their rooms. Beyond the constraints to instructional reform mentioned, the usual standards of defining the success of a reform may need to be revised in the light of evidence demonstrating that large numbers of teachers selectively implemented different classroom approaches.

Improving Teacher Performance

Basically, there are four strategies to upgrade the quality of classroom instruction: revise selection policies in schools of education and districts hiring teachers; improve preparation programs for apprentices; remove incompetents; retrain existing corps of teachers. Rather than go over the pluses and minuses for each approach, let me focus instead on the implications of the findings in this study for particular strategies. I derive four implications, provided that my assumptions are accepted. Assuming that this core of durable practices is a set of teacher-constructed solutions to cope with the school and classroom they find themselves in and a product of occupational socialization that newcomers experience, I suggest the following directions to pursue for those who plan to enter the classroom, newcomers, and veterans.

1. *Schools of Education.* Preparing entrants to the profession is one institutional form of gradual change that has had a mild, if not unfocused, effect upon instruction. Data on the enduring stability of teacher-centeredness places college professors of teacher education committed to improving classroom instruction in a familiar dilemma: prepare teachers for what exists in public schools or prepare them to alter what is. Over the decades, patchwork compromises have been fashioned, leaving those who prepare and certify teachers profoundly dissatisfied. Current efforts in a number of states to upgrade credential requirements for teachers, establish entry-level tests, and similar measures also mirror public dissatisfaction with the classroom. These solutions to improve teaching quality will produce teachers who can pass test items assessing minimum literacy skills and who will have spent more seat-time in college classrooms. Yet anyone serious about seeking instructional reform knows that it is a courageous leap to view literacy tests or course credits as anything more than proxies for teaching effectiveness. Few states or colleges, however, have yet pursued aggressively the obvious suggestion concerning selection and training. These approaches would need to be altered to produce classroom teachers who are more aware of the organizational and professional constraints they must face; more adaptable, resilient, and analytic problem solvers; and more technically proficient in those techniques that they must master in order to survive. The idea is for a college to produce a teacher trained in the craft, equipped with the generic intellectual skills necessary to move beyond survival, and alter what occurs in the classroom, if the teacher is so inclined to transcend the typical instructional pattern. Dan

Lortie has offered a number of concrete suggestions that develop some of these points.[22]

2. *District In-Service Efforts.* Staff development could focus more sharply on two areas. One is improving teacher knowledge and skills for those tasks that they carry out with predictable regularity, regardless of whether a classroom is teacher- or student-centered: questioning, lecturing, explaining, or extracting meaning from textbooks. In short, there is a craft portion to teaching that needs to be learned as an apprentice and improved continually even while practicing techniques on a daily basis in the classroom.

The other area is teachers helping teachers in their own schools. Reducing the isolation and nourishing collegiality are necessary, but far from sufficient, conditions to enable teachers to pursue some directions in instruction that were unfamiliar or risky yet were viewed as helpful to children. Anyone reading a fraction of teacher accounts since 1900 cannot escape the strong impression of how longely teaching is, how insulated the classroom is from other adult contacts. A shelf full of studies have confirmed this classroom isolation. Staff development opportunities and strategies designed to bring teachers together in their schools to plan, initiate, research, evaluate, and write can chip away at the physical and psychological barriers that separate teachers from one another but, far more important, they can mix practitioner folk wisdom, ingenuity, and organizational moxie in efforts to solve common problems. Trying to build schools that provide settings for teachers to both serve and learn with colleagues remains, I believe, a worthwhile task.[23]

3. *Implementing Changes in Classrooms.* The findings of this study also raise some questions while adding data to the substantial issue of putting ideas into practice. A growing number of case studies of botched school innovations, research on street-level bureaucrats (social workers, policemen, teachers) who use their discretion in coping with heavy demands that cannot all be met, and an increasing sensitivity to a "bottom-up" rather than "top-down" perspective of implementation has moved policymakers to focus attention on service deliverers, i.e. teachers and principals.[24]

Educational policymakers have generally given a rhetorical bow to the importance of the classroom teacher and school principal in implementing instructional or curricular change and then assigned to each organizational level what tasks were to be done. Offers of aid were often mixed with threats of sanctions; these were the frequently used engines that drove the implementation machine. Routines and directives were the nuts and bolts that held it together.

This study showed that this process occurred in Washington, D.C., with the Child Development Program (1938), the expansion of New York

City's Activity Program (1941), and Denver's mandate for General Education (1941). A generation later, alternative schools, high school reforms, and informal classrooms were designed at 110 Livingston Street in New York, the Presidential Building in Washington, D.C., and the state legislature in Bismarck, North Dakota. This top-down approach was common.

Different approaches emerged in occasional efforts to mobilize teachers and principals to plan to implement new policies that they were charged to carry out. Under Newlon and Threlkeld (1922–1937), Denver administrators and teachers jointly worked through a series of complicated steps that produced system-wide curriculum revision in elementary and secondary subjects. When the course of study was completed, directives replaced collaboration; principals were told to make sure that teachers used the syllabi as intended. It is unclear what happened at each school to install the final step of the implementation process. Washington's first alternative high school, Freedom Annex, was planned wholly by teachers and students, although it lasted less than two years. Arlington's Woodlawn, the 1971 alternative high school, was designed by teachers, students, and parents. Open Corridors in New York City worked only with those principals and teachers who wanted to introduce informal approaches into their schools and classrooms. These instances of a bottom-up implementation strategy were uncommon.

Rather than argue the merits of one or the other approach, or even a mix of the two, it is well to keep in mind the persuasive body of research that underscores the importance of teacher and principal direct involvement, commitment, and clear understanding of the change as essential ingredients in transforming a policy into practice. Furthermore, if research-based knowledge is less than convincing, then the experienced-based knowledge of practitioners has produced this recommendation repeatedly. Perhaps, a more radical step needs to be taken. Policymakers intent upon classroom innovations might be required to submit a teacher-impact statement. In other words, an instructional plan designed largely by non-teachers must be accompanied by an analysis of how the proposal would affect the teacher's role, classroom organization, materials, and routines. While this is a bureaucratic device, such a suggestion becomes a forceful reminder that top-down policy decisions need to consider practitioner concerns and classroom consequences.

This study on how teachers taught provides some data that can be used to argue that teachers' commitment and involvement seldom responds to mandates or coercive threats beyond brittle compliance. Where classroom changes occurred, again making the distinction between the appearance of change and its effects, teachers seem to have been active collaborators in the process. The point is that those policymakers who approach implementation from the viewpoint of teachers and not from the typical downward perspective can find some support in this study.

4. *Teacher Effectiveness*. Over the last half-century, researchers and school policymakers have sought to pin down precisely what teaching effectiveness is, which teachers have it, and how they got it. The history of that search has been documented numerous times. What is of special interest to this study are recent findings drawn from a number of correlational studies of certain teaching practices at the elementary level that have yielded strong, positive relationships to student test scores on standardized achievement tests in reading and math.[25]

Which practices have shown up favorably?

- Teacher focuses clearly on academic goals[26]
- Teacher concentrates on tasks alloting the instructional period to instructional tasks rather than socializing[27]
- Teacher presents information clearly; organizing instruction by explaining, outlining, and reviewing; and covers subject matter extensively[28]
- Teacher monitors student progress toward instructional objectives, selecting materials and arranging methods of increase student success[29]
- Teacher paces instruction to fit students[30]
- Teacher feedback is quick and targeted on content of instructional tasks[31]
- Teacher's management abilities prevent disturbances by encouraging cooperation[32]

Barak Rosenshine, reviewing a number of studies, specified six instructional "functions" that have shown repeatedly to have produced improved academic achievement, as measured by test scores:

1. Checking previous day's work
2. Presenting new content/skills
3. Initial student practice (and checking for understanding)
4. Feedback and correctives (reteaching, if necessary)
5. Student independent practice
6. Weekly and monthly reviews[33]

There are substantive, and telling, criticisms of correlational research that isolates certain teacher behaviors, links them to high student test performance at one point in time, and then uses these relationships as a basis for instructional improvement efforts or teacher education curriculum.[34]

Putting aside such criticisms, the point is that this line of research has surged ahead in specifying particular teaching practices as effective. Notice that the sampling I have displayed resembles (somewhat) the stable core of teaching practices in this study that have persisted since the beginning of the century. The similarity, of course, is not wholly accidental. The practices that have been recently investigated, carefully counted, and compared in effectiveness through pre- and post-tests are themselves teaching activities that have been used for decades in classrooms across the country with great confidence in their efficacy. Let me add quickly that these practices identified as effective are not only associated with teacher-centered classrooms; open classrooms, in their various incarnations, contain most of these practices as was seen in the New York City Activity Program, North Dakota schools, and Washington schools.[35] I said "resemble" to avoid any foolish leap to inferences linking what I detailed as durable teaching practices and these specific teaching behaviors emerging from recent studies labeled as effective. Beyond the substantive methodological issues associated with correlational research, there are a host of contextual variables, often absent from such investigations, that involve teachers, students, school, class size, grade, and time of observation which influence outcome measures.

The resemblance, however, seems to be sufficiently tantalizing to explore further those teaching practices that show up strongly in correlational findings to determine what can be learned from their past use in classrooms.[36]

On what note I should end this study of constancy and change has bothered me since I began writing the Introduction. My impulses tended toward optimism. After all, one doesn't go into teaching and administration, shuttle back and forth between both kinds of jobs for a quarter-century, without having some strong beliefs about children, improvement of existing institutions, and public service—among the many motives that impel men and women into public school work. Yet, I never felt my optimism soared unreasonably or was not anchored in modest expectations. Unlike the Grand Academy of Lagado where Gulliver saw workers trying to extract sunshine from cucumbers, turning ice into gunpowder, and weaving cloth from spiderwebs, I had a restrained, cautious, but nonetheless, buoyant view of improving schools.[37]

But the data can be easily interpreted as presenting an unrelenting, pessimistic picture for any fundamental modification in teaching behavior and school reforms that promise anything beyond marginal, incremental tatters of change that may be insubstantial or, worse, irrelevant. Perhaps.

Another interpetation can be drawn from the data that avoids the optimism-pessimism dichotomy and converts elements of both into a mix that can be put: what schools and teachers can and cannot do. Recall the metaphor of farming to describe schooling. The essential point was learning to work through an ancient, unchanging process of growth by building efforts around what seeds, plants, insects, and climate were likely to do. By understanding the durability and limits to this process, farmers can improve the yield of crops. But these organic forces, over which a farmer is helpless to exercise control, have to be worked with, not ignored.

Based upon this study, there are, I believe, analogs of organic processes like seeds, plants, and climate in schools and classrooms—shaped by organizational constraints and other factors—that need to be worked through in order to improve what happens within the walls of the building. Certainly, teaching load, age grading, Carnegie Units, self-contours of a practical pedagogy just like an organic force. They become and drought. Yet, until the man-made structures are modified fundamentally, they blow like a wind, flood like a storm, and shape the contours of a practical peoagogy just like an organic force. They become what Willard Waller called the "human nature of the classroom," fundamental traits that need to be reckoned with if changes are to occur.[38]

I draw my optimism from these metaphors because they suggest clearly that until those powerful school structures are altered there is some margin for change, an elasticity that imagination and large chunks of energy can stetch. There are, to be sure, effective farmers; they produce abundant crops. There are effective teachers; their students' praise recognizes them. There are effective schools scattered across the country where principals and teachers have constructed settings, in the most unlikely places, where learning, growth, and deep satisfaction exist.

Concentrating upon what teachers can do well in classrooms, on what schools can achieve effectively within certain boundaries is a sensible response to the potent processes at work in schools. Labels such as "teacher-centered," "traditional," "child-centered", and "open classrooms" may help researchers and promoters but they do what all labels inevitably do: categorize and simplify. Such names help not a bit in identifying, under what conditions, what will work with children in boosting both academic performance and personal growth. I have found no magic to either classrooms labeled one way or the other. Effective practices exist in different settings in spite of the severe constraints teachers face. These practices, once identified, should be cultivated as carefully as a gardener who anticipates the approaching harvest.

Thus, in steadfastly refusing to go beyond the question of how teachers taught to touch the issue of instructional quality, I confess that it is the very issue of quality upon which I end this book. The variety of what teachers do in classrooms is finite. It is limited by a number of circumstances over which teachers have little influence. Despite these limits, questions of teaching effectiveness become even more demanding since the repertoire of practices is narrower than previously thought or promoted. I suggested a basis for determining the quality of what teachers can do well in classrooms. No longer should the central issue about instruction be: how should teachers teach? Based upon my experience and study of classrooms over the last century, I believe the central question is simply: how can what teachers already do be improved?

NOTES

1. J. Tukey, "The Future of Data Analysis," *Annals of Mathematical Statistics*, 33 (1962), pp. 13–14.
2. Alternative models of explaining puzzling questions is common. I do wish, however, to acknowledge the many discussions I have had with David Tyack. He uses this mode felicitously in "Ways of Seeing: An Essay on the History of Compulsory Schooling," *Harvard Educational Review*, 46 (August, 1976), pp. 355–89; the sources from which I draw the Schooling as Social Control argument are: Basil Bernstein, "On the Classification and Framing of Educational Knowledge," in Michael Young (ed.) *Knowledge and Control* (London: Coller-Macmillan, 1971), pp. 47–69; Peter Woods, *The Divided School*, (London: Routledge and Kegan Paul, 1979), chapters 1, 7, 20; Michael Apple and Nancy King, "What Do Schools Teach?" *Curriculum Inquiry*, 6 (1977), pp. 341–69; Samuel Bowles and Herbert Gintis, *Schooling in Capitalist America* (New York: Basic Books, 1976).
3. Philip Jackson, *Life in Classrooms* (New York: Holt, Rinehart, and Winston, 1968), chapter 1; Seymour Sarason, *The Culture of the School and the Problem of Change* (Allyn and Bacon, 1971), chapters 1, 7, 10, 11; Louis Smith and William Geoffrey, *The Complexities of an Urban Classroom* (New York: Holt, Rinehart and Winston, 1968), chapters 3–4; Robert Dreeben, "The School as a Workplace," in W. Traver (ed.) *The Second Handbook of Teaching* (New York: Rand McNally, 1973); J. W. Getzels, "Images of the Classroom and Visions of the Learner," *School Review* (August, 1974), pp. 527–40; Carol Weinstein, "The Physical Environment of the School: A Review of the Research," *Review of Educational Research*, 49 (Fall, 1979), pp. 577–610; John Meyer and Brian Rowan, "The Structure of Educational Organizations," in M. Meyer, (ed.) *Environments and Organizations* (San Francisco: Jossey-Bass, 1978): Hugh Mehan, *Learning Lessons* (Cambridge, Mass.: Harvard University Press, 1979), chapter 3. The term "Hidden Pedagogy" comes from Martin Denscombe, "The 'Hidden Pedagogy' and Its Implications for Teacher Training," *British Journal of Sociology of Education*, 3 (1982), pp. 249–65.
4. Willard Waller, *The Sociology of Teaching* (New York: John Wiley, 1965), chapters 22–23; Dan Lortie, *Schoolteacher* (Chicago: University of Chicago Press, 1975), chapters 2–3; Estelle Fuchs, *Teacher Talk* (New York: Anchor Books, 1969); Wayne Hoy, "Pupil Control Ideology and Organizational Socialization," *School Review*, 77, (1969), pp. 257–65; John Goodlad, "Study of Schooling: Some Findings and Hypotheses," *Kappan*, 64 (March, 1983), pp. 465–70.
5. I avoid the word "ideology" for reasons cited by Carl Kaestle, "Ideology and American Educational History" (paper delivered at meeting of History of Education Society, October 3, 1981, pp. 1–10). While I know that beliefs held by teachers and administrators are shaped by larger social forces and often intersect with both personal and social issues, I also recognize that these beliefs can be grouped into related propositions which, if comprehensively described, could be labeled "ideology." To map out those intersections and groupings systematically would be beyond the scope of this study. Thus, I do not use the word "ideology." In this explanation, I concentrated more on the apparent linkages between individual behavior and ideas and less on the impact of belief

systems upon group behavior.

6. Chittenden, et al., p. 17.
7. Leonard Covello, *The Heart is the Teacher* (Totowa, N. J.: Littlefield, Adams, and Company, 1970), p. 197.
8. Gary Fenstermacher, "A Philosophical Consideration of Recent Research on Teacher Effects," *Review of Research in Education*, 6, pp. 177–82; Mary H. Metz, "Clashes in the Classroom: The Importance of Norms for Authority," *Education and Urban Society*, 11 (November, 1978), pp. 13–47; Lortie, chapter 5; Chittenden, et al., chapters 4–7. The work of Lee Shulman at Michigan State University and now at Stanford University has focused upon the cognitive tasks that teachers must engage in to process information for decision making. "How teachers behave and what they do," he has written, "is directed in no small way by what they think." Lee Shulman and J. E. Lanier, "The Institute for Research on Teaching," *Journal of Teacher Education*, 28 (1977), p. 44. See Shulman and A. S. Elstein, "Studies of Problem Solving, Judgment, and Decision Making," in F. N. Kerlinger (ed.) *Review of Research in Education*, 3, (1975), (Itasca, Ill.: Peacock Publishers, 1975).
9. Gross et al., *Implementing Organizational Innovations*, chapters 4–5, 7, 8; Smith and Keith, chapters 1, 5, 7, 9–11; David Goodwin, *Delivering Educational Service: Urban Schools and Schooling Policy* (New York: Teachers College, Columbia University, 1977), chapter 6; Aaron Wildavsky and Jeffrey Pressman, *Implementation*, (Berkeley, Calif.: University of California Press, 1973); Milbrey McLaughlin, "An Exploratory Study of School District Adaptation" (Los Angeles: Rand Corporation, 1979).
10. For example, see Peter Woods, *Divided School*, chapters 5–7.
11. Mary H. Metz, *Classroom and Corridors* (Berkeley, Calif.: University of California Press, 1978), pp. 250–1.
12. Lortie, p. 147.
13. Sarason, p. 63.
14. Woods, p. 12; See Lee Ross, "The Intuitive Psychologist and his Shortcomings: Distortions in the Attribution Process," *Advances in Experimental Social Psychology*, 10 (1977), pp. 173–220.
15. Interview with Wilkinson, March 22, 1982.
16. Jackson, *Life in Classrooms*, p. 29.
17. Dworkin, pp. 129–30.
18. This point is made often in David Swift, *Ideology and Change in the Public Schools* (Columbus, Ohio: Charles Merrill Publishing Company, 1971).
19. A. Harry Passow, "Secondary Education Reform: Retrospect and Prospect," (New York: Teachers College, Columbia University, 1976).
20. See Larry Cuban, "Corporate Involvement in Public Schools: A Practitioner/Academic Perspective" (Washington, D.C.: National Institute of Education, 1983); David Tyack and Tom James, "Learning from Past Efforts to Reform the High School," *Kappan*, 64 (February, 1983), pp. 400–406.
21. This point has been made by many other school participants and researchers. See, for example: Larry Cuban, "The Powerlessness of Irrelevancy," *Educational Leadership*, 25 (February, 1968), pp. 393–6; Milbrey McLaughlin and Paul Berman, the Change Agent Studies, *The Process of Change*, Volume 3 (Los Angeles: Rand Corporation, 1975); Milbrey McLaughlin, "Implementation as Mutual Adaptation in Classroom Organization," *Teachers College*

Record, (1976). On teacher collaboration, see Judith Little, "Norms of Collegiality and Experimentation: Workplace Conditions of School Success," *American Educational Research Journal*, 19 (Fall, 1982), pp. 325–40; Tom Bird and Judith Little, "Finding and Founding Peer Coaching" (Speech to American Education Research Association, 1983): school-based reform efforts are summarized in Jane L. David, "School-Based Strategies: Implications for Government Policy" (Palo Alto, Calif.: Bay Area Research Group, 1982).

22. Lortie, pp. 228–34.
23. See Jackson, Life in Classroom, chapter 1 and pp. 159–77; Sarason, pp. 105–8.
24. Richard Elmore, "Organizational Models of Social Program Implementation," *Public Policy*, 26 (Spring, 1978); Michael Lipsky and Richard Weatherley, "Street Level Bureacrats and Institutional Innovation: Implementing Special Education Reform," *Harvard Educational Review*, 47 (1977); Eleanor Farrar, et al., "Alternative Conceptions of Implementations" (Cambridge, Mass.: Huron Institute, 1978).
25. For reviews of the literature on teacher effectiveness, see: N. L. Gage, *The Scientific Basis of the Art of Teaching* (New York: Teachers College, Columbia University, 1977), chapters 1 and 3; Michael Dunkin and Bruce Biddle, *The Study of Teaching* (New York: Holt, Rinehart and Winston, 1974), chapters 5–10; *Journal of Teacher Education*, 27 (Spring, 1976) is devoted to research on teacher effectiveness.
26. Barak Rosenshine, "Content, Time, and Direct Instruction," in P. L. Petersen and Herbert Walberg (eds.) *Research on Teaching* (Berkeley, Calif.: McCutchan Publishing Co., 1979).
27. ibid.; also T. L. Good, "Teacher Effectiveness in the Elementary School," *Journal of Teacher Education*, 30 (1979).
28. Rosenshine; William J. Tikunoff and Beatrice Ward, "Ecological Perspectives for Successful School Practice: Knowledge of Effective Instruction," n.d., n.p.
29. ibid.
30. ibid.
31. ibid.
32. T. L. Good and D. A. Grouws, "The Missouri Mathematics Effectiveness Project," *Journal of Educational Psychology*, 71 (1979).
33. Barak Rosenshine, "Teaching Functions in Instructional Programs," paper delivered at NIE Conference at Airlie House, Virginia, February, 1982, p. 5.
34. Walter Doyle, "Research on Classroom Contexts," *Journal of Teacher Education*, 32 (November–December, 1981), p. 3; Gary Fenstermacher, "A Philosophical Consideration of Recent Research on Teacher Effects," *Review of Research in Education*, 6, pp. 157–83.
35. Communication from Kim Marshall, Boston Public Schools; the idea that the persistence of particular teaching practices occurred simply because they worked, i.e., solved efficiently classroom problems, was mentioned also by Tommy Tomlinson, "The Troubled Years: An Interpretive Analysis of Public Schoolings Since 1950," *Kappan*, 62 (January, 1981), pp. 373–6.
36. Tommy Tomlinson, "Effective Schools: Mirror or Mirage," *Today's Education*, (April–May, 1981), pp. 48–50.
37. Joseph Sisk, "Untested Assumptions," *Harpers* (May, 1981), p. 70.
38. Waller, preface.

Appendix

The five categories that I use to capture dominant instructional patterns are: classroom arrangements, group instruction, classroom talk, student movement, and classroom activities. I recognize that these categories in no way capture the totality of teaching. They are, at best, windows of the classroom. They are visible to observers. They describe the terrain of the classroom while accounting for the major chunks of time that teachers and students spend together. And, most important, these categories are within the power of the teacher to determine for his or her classroom: how the space should be arranged, who should talk, what homework to assign, where students should go within the room, etc.

The issue is whether or not certain patterns in these categories cluster together to create regularities in classrooms. I believe that they do. In the discussion below, I offer reasons for this belief. References are to those books and articles listed in the bibliography.

1. *Organization of space in the classroom.* If movable desks or student chairs are arranged in rows facing either the blackboard or teacher's desk then there is a high probability that the instruction is teacher-centered. The rationale for the assertion is:

   a. Such an arrangement is intentional (except for the classrooms where desks were bolted to the floor). Furniture arrangement is seldom mandated by a school board, superintendent, or principal. The teacher decides (or accepts prevailing norms) use of classroom space. Furniture placement, consciously or not, expresses the teacher's views of how best to teach, maintain order, and how students learn.

   b. When all students face the teacher or blackboard where directions, assignments, tests, or class recitation occurs whole-group instruction is encouraged. Teacher-student exchanges gain higher priority and legitimacy than ones between students.

   c. Surveillance is easier for a teacher with space arranged in this manner. Threats to classroom order can be seen quickly and dealt with expeditiously.

   d. Such a configuration of classroom space limits students' movement within a classroom to that which the teacher permits.

   (It needs to be mentioned, however, that for the early decades of this century when desks were fixed to the floor, there were teachers who ingeniously and with much energy overcame that obstacle and introduced student-centered practices into the classroom. Such furniture may have discouraged many teachers but it did not prevent some from altering their teaching practices. With movable desks and chairs, other arrangements became possible.)

If desks are arranged into a hollow square, horseshoe, or tables are scattered around the room permitting students to face one another and talk, student-centered instruction becomes a much stronger possibility. But far more information about what happens in the classroom would be needed since teacher-centered instruction can, and often does, occur in these seating arrangements. (Getzel, 1974; Weinstein, Carol, 1979; Sommer, 1969).

2. *Instructional grouping and classroom activities.* If class space is organized into student-centered arrangements, i.e. tables and desks where students can face one another, carrels, rug-covered area for a reading corner, etc., one needs to look for evidence of student movement, student participation in verbal discourse, diverse grouping patterns, and the extent of project activities (or learning centers). Projects (a common term used in the 1920s and 1930s to describe a child-centered activity) and learning centers (a phrase used often in movement to install informal education after 1967) assumed that students can learn effectively as individuals or in small groups while making decisions independent of the teacher.

Thus, the external signs of a student-centered classroom would include furniture arrangements that encourage face-to-face exchanges and small group meetings; work stations in the classrooms (project areas or learning centers) where individual and small groups of students operate in a self-directed manner, and evidence of students moving about without securing the teacher's permission. The teacher's desk is no longer front and center; often, the room lacks a discernible front and rear. (Barth, 1972; Silberman, 1971; Bussis, et al., 1976; Perrone, 1972, 1977.)

Let me add that the simple presence of a project corner or learning centers, like tables scattered around the room, does not make a classroom student-centered. Much of the literature on such settings in the 1920s and 1970s focused upon a process of learning and the teacher's grasp of the underlying principles in child development and learning. Seating arrangements, projects, and centers are a few visible signs but in no way guarantee that the process will occur or that the teacher understands the principles involved. To suggest that only the physical arrangements and available artifacts recaptured in written accounts and photographs represent what a William Kilpatrick or Harold Rugg of the 1920s espoused and a Lillian Weber and Vito Perrone of the 1970s advocated would trivialize complex processes.

3. *Classroom Talk.* The evidence that teachers talk far more than students in classrooms dates back to Romiett Stevens' work at the turn of the century. That pattern of teacher talk consuming most of the instructional discourse in the form of telling, explaining, and questioning is a proxy for a teacher-centered classroom. Student talk in such a classroom is generally confined to responding to content questions from the teacher, asking procedural questions (e.g. will it be on the test?), and covert conversations with classmates. The teacher determines what questions have to be asked, who should be asked, and the quality of the student response. It is a classroom discourse that contains implicit rules that students come to learn over time. (Mehan, 1979; Stevens, 1912; Hoetker and Ahlbrand, 1969.)

These five categories, then, contain the pieces that teachers arrange into instructional patterns. Organizing the classroom space, grouping for instruction, classroom talk, student movement, and classroom activities as they materialize in schools point to a variety of teaching patterns. These categories, I believe, can extract from the data dominant instructional patterns in classrooms.

Bibliography

Abelow, Samuel P. *Dr. William H. Maxwell, the First Superintendent of Schools of the City of New York*. Brooklyn: Scheba, 1934.

Alberty, Beth. *Continuity and Connection: Curriculum in Five Open Classrooms*. New York: City College Workshop Center for Open Education, 1979.

Aldrich, Howard E. *Organizations and Environments*. Englewood Cliffs, N.J. Prentice-Hall, 1979.

Apple, Michael, and Nancy King. "What Do Schools Teach?" *Curriculum Inquiry*, 6 (1977).

Arlington County Public Schools, *Profile* (June 1969).

———, *School News* (January 1980).

———. Newspaper Clip Files in Public Information, 1972–1981.

Bagley, William C. "The Textbook and Methods of Teaching." In National Society for the Study of Education, *The Textbook in American Education*. Bloomington, Ill.: Public School Publishing Co., 1931.

Barr, A. S. *Characteristic Differences in the Teaching Performance of Good And Poor Teachers of the Social Studies*. Bloomington, Ill.: Public School Publishing Co., 1929.

Barth, Roland. *Open Education and the American School*, New York: Agathon, 1972.

———. "Should We Forget about Open Education?" *Saturday Review* (November 6, 1973).

Behavioral Service Consultants. "Final Evaluation Report: Training Center for Open-Space Schools, ESEA Title III Project." Greenbelt, Mary.: Behavioral Service Consultants, 1974.

Bennett, Henry E. "Fifty Years of School Seating." *American School Board Journal*, 100 (March, 1940).

Berg, Andrew C. "A Daily Program for the One-Room Schools of North Dakota." Unpub. Masters Thesis, University of North Dakota, 1929.

Berliner, David. "Studying Instruction in the Elementary Classroom." In Robert Dreeben and Alan Thomas (eds.). *The Analysis of Educational Productivity*. Cambridge, Mass.: Ballinger, 1980.

Bernstein, Basil. "On the Classification and Framing of Educational Knowledge." In Michael Young (ed.). *Knowledge and Control*. London: Collier-Macmillan, 1971.

Berrol, Selma C. "William Henry Maxwell and a New Educational New York." *History of Education Quarterly*, 8 (1968).

Blauch, Lloyd, and J. Orin Powers. *Public Education in the District of Columbia.* Washington, D.C.: Government Printing Office, 1938.

Bowles, Samuel, and Herbert Gintis. *Schooling in Capitalist America.* New York: Basic Books, 1976.

Briggs, Thomas. "The Practices of Best High School Teachers." *School Review*, 43, (December, 1935).

Bursch, Charles W. "The Techniques and Results of an Analysis of the Teaching Process in High School English and Social Science Classes." Unpublished doctoral diss., Stanford University, 1930.

Bussis, Anne M., Edward Chittenden, and Marianne Amarel. *Beyond the Surface Curriculum: An Interview Study of Teachers' Understandings.* Boulder, Colo.: Westview, 1976.

Campbell, Harold. "Class Sizes in New York City." *The School Executive*, 55, (December, 1935).

Campbell, Jack. *The Children's Crusader: Colonel Francis W. Parker.* New York: Teachers College Press, 1967.

Campbell, Robert, *The Chasm.* Boston: Houghton-Mifflin, 1974.

Center for Urban Education. *Open Door: New York City.* New York: Center for Urban Education, 1970.

Changes in Classroom Teaching Made During 1937–1939 in One-Room Rural Schools in the Area of the Michigan Community Health Project. Battle Creek, Mich.: W. L. Kellogg Foundation, 1940.

Channon, Gloria. *Homework.* New York: Outerbridge and Dienstrey, 1970.

Chittenden, Edward, et al. *First Year Evaluative Study of the Workshop Center for Open Education.* New York: Workshop Center for Open Education, 1973.

Cohen, Sol. *Progressives and Urban School Reform.* New York: Teachers College, Columbia University, 1964.

Cort, H. R., et al. *An Evaluation of the Innovation Team.* Washington, D.C.: Washington School of Psychiatry, 1969.

Covello, Leonard. *The Heart Is the Teacher.* Totowa, N.J.: Littlefield, Adams, 1970.

Cremin, Lawrence. *Transformation of the School.* New York: Vintage, 1961.

_____. "The Free School Movement: A Perspective." *Notes on Education*, (October, 1973).

Cuban, Larry. "Reform by Fiat: the Clark Plan in Washington, 1970–1972." *Urban Education*, 9 (April, 1974).

_____. "Hobson v. Hansen: A Study in Organizational Response." *Educational Administration Quarterly*, 11 (Spring, 1975).

_____. "Determinants of Curriculum Change and Stability." In Jon Schafferzick and Gary Sykes (eds.) *Value Conflicts and Curriculum Issues.* Berkeley, Calif.: McCutchan, 1979.

_____. "Shrinking Enrollment and Consolidation: Political and Organizational Impacts in Arlington, Virginia, 1973–1978." *Education and Urban Society*, 11, (May, 1979).

Cubberley, Ellwood P. *The Portland Survey.* Yonkers-on-the-Hudson, N.Y.: World Book, 1916.

Cushman, C. L. "Conference Appraises Denver Secondary Program." *Curriculum Journal*, 9 (November, 1938).

Cusick, Philip A. *Inside High School.* New York: Holt, Rinehart and Winston, 1973.

Dayton, Ohio Public Schools, *Annual Report of the Board of Education, 1895– 1896.* Dayton, Ohio: Board of Education, 1896.

Deal, Terrence, and Robert Nolan. *Alternative Schools: Ideologies, Realities, Guidelines.* Chicago: Nelson-Hall, 1978.

Dearborn, Ned H. *The Oswego Movement in American Education.* New York: Teachers College, Columbia University, 1925.

DeLima, Agnes. *Our Enemy the Child.* New York: New Republic, 1925.

Denver Public Schools, School District Number 1 in the City and County of Denver, *Annual Report.* Denver, Colo.: Denver Public Schools, 1919–1941.

———. *Denver Program of Curriculum Revision.* Monograph 12, 1927.

———. *General Information and Courses of Study: Senior High School.* Denver, Colo.: Denver Public Schools, 1929.

———. "Handbook for the Application of Progressive Education Principles to Secondary Education." Denver, Colo.: Denver Public Schools, 1936.

———. "History of East High School." Denver, Colo.: East High School, 1948.

———. *Angelus.* Denver, Colo.: East High School, 1920–1945.

———. *Viking.* Denver, Colo.: North High School, 1920–1945.

———. *Thunderbolt.* Denver, Colo.: Manual Training High School, 1920–1945.

———. *Classroom Interests.* Denver, Colo.: Denver Teachers, 1921–1938.

———. *School Review.* Denver, Colo.: Denver Public Schools, 1920–1940.

———. Newspaper Clip Files in Public Information Office, 1920–1940.

Denver Public Library. Newspaper Clip Files on Public Schools. 1916–1940.

Devaney, Kathleen. "Developing Open Education in America: A Review of Theory and Practice in the Public Schools." Washington, D.C.: Department of Health, Education, and Welfare, 1973.

———. "The New School of Behavioral Studies in Education." Grand Forks, N.D.: Center for Teaching and Learning, 1974.

Dewey, John, and Evelyn Dewey. *Schools of To–Morrow.* New York: E. P. Dutton, 1915.

Dewey, Evelyn. *New Schools for Old.* New York: E.P. Dutton, 1919.

District of Columbia, Board of Education. *Annual Report to the Commissioners of District of Columbia* Washington, D.C.: Government Printing Office, 1908– 1941.

———. "School Achievements in Twenty Years." Washington, D.C.: Board of Education, 1941.

———. George Rhodes, Jr. "Action Programs in Progress in the Secondary Schools." Washington, D.C.: Board of Education, 1970.

———. Central High School. *The Bulletin.* Washington, D.C.: Central, 1925– 1938.

———. Central High School. *Handbook.* Washington, D.C.: Central, 1919, 1926.

———. Central High School. *Brecky.* Washington, D.C.: Central, 1919–1950.

———. Dunbar High School. *Crimson and Black Handbook.* Washington, D.C.: Dunbar, 1925.

———. Dunbar High School. *The Dunbar News Reel.* Washington, D.C.: Dunbar, 1942.

———. Dunbar High School. *Liber Anni.* Washington, D.C.: Dunbar, 1920–1940; 1965–1975.

———. Eastern High School. *The Easterner*. Washington, D.C.: Eastern, 1925–1940.

———. Cardozo High School. *Purple Wave*. Washington, D.C.: Cardozo, 1965–1975.

———. Roosevelt High School. *The Roughrider*. Washington, D.C.: Roosevelt, 1965–1975.

———. Woodrow Wilson High School. *Woodrow Wilson*. Washington, D.C.: Wilson, 1939–1945.

District of Columbia Public Library. Newspaper Clip Files in Washingtonia Room. 1919–1981.

Divoky, Diane. "New York's Mini-Schools." *Saturday Review*, 18, (December, 18, 1971).

Dodge, Vincent. "The Fargo-Madison School Program: A Cooperative School–University Effort." Grand Forks, N.D.: Center for Teaching and Learning, 1974.

Donovan, John. *School Architecture*, New York: Macmillan and Co., 1921.

Doyle, Walter. "Research on Classroom Contexts." *Journal of Teacher Education*, 32, (November–December, 1981).

Dreeben, Robert. "The School As a Workplace." In W. Traver (ed.) *The Second Handbook of Teaching*. New York: Rand McNally, 1973.

Dropkin, Ruth (ed.). *Changing Schools*, New York: City College Workshop Center for Open Education, 1978.

Duke, Daniel L. *The Retransformation of the School*. Chicago: Nelson-Hall, 1978.

Dunkin, Michael, and Bruce J. Biddle. *The Study of Teaching*. New York: Holt, Rinehart, and Winston, 1974.

Dunn, Fannie, and Marcia Everett. *Four Years in a Country School*. New York: Teachers College, Bureau of Publications, 1926.

Dworkin, Martin (ed.). *Dewey on Education*. New York: Teachers College University Press, 1959.

Eddy, Elizabeth. *Walk the White Line*. New York: Doubleday, 1967.

Elmore, Richard. "Organizational Models of Social Program Implementation." *Public Policy*, 26 (Spring, 1978).

Elofson, Theresa. "Open Education in the Elementary School: Six Teachers Who Were Expected To Change." Urbana, Ill.: Center for Instructional Research and Curriculum Evaluation. 1973.

Fargo-Moorhead Forum. 1967–1975.

Featherstone, Joseph. "The British and Us." *The New Republic* (September, 11, 1971).

———. "Tempering a Fad." *The New Republic* (September 25, 1971).

Fenstermacher, Gary. "A Philosphical Consideration of Recent Research on Teacher Effects." *Review of Research in Education*, 6 (1978).

Finkelstein, Barbara. "Governing the Young: Teacher Behavior in American Primary Schools, 1820–1880." Unpublished Ed. D diss., Teachers College, Columbia University, 1970.

———. "The Moral Dimensions of Pedagogy." *American Studies* (Fall, 1974).

Flaxman, Anne, and Kerry Hanstead (eds.). *1977–1978 National Directory of Public Alternative Schools*. Amherst, Mass.: National Alternative Schools Program at School of Education, University of Massachusetts at Amherst, 1978.

Flexner, Abraham, and Frank Bachman. *The Gary Schools.* New York: General Education Board, 1918.

Folger, John, and Charles Nam. *Education of the American Population.* Washington, D.C.: Government Printing Office, 1967.

Fox, Lorene K. *The Rural Community and Its School.* New York: King's Crown Press, 1948.

Fuchs, Estelle. *Teachers Talk.* New York: Anchor Books, 1969.

Fuerst, Sidney M (ed.). "Methods in New York Schools." *New York Teachers' Monographs,* 2 (June, 1900).

Gage, N. L. *The Scientific Basis of the Art of Teaching.* New York: Teachers College, 1977.

Getzels, J. W. "Images of the Classroom and Visions of the Learner." *School Review* (August, 1974).

Giles, H. H., et al. *Exploring the Curriculum.* New York: Harpers, 1942.

Gladstone, Carol. "What Constitutes a Remedial Reading Lesson." *High Points* (March, 1975).

Glanz, Ellen. "What Are You Doing Here?" Washington, D.C.: Council for Basic Education, 1979.

Goodlad, John, et. al. *Looking Behind the Classroom Door.* Worthington, Ohio: Charles Jones, 1974.

Goodwin, David. *Delivering Educational Service: Urban Schools and Schooling.* New York: Teachers College, 1977.

Graham, Patricia. *Progressive Education: From Arcady to Academe.* New York: Teachers College, 1967.

Grand Forks Herald. 1967–1975.

Green, Constance M. *The Secret City.* Princeton, N.J.: Princeton University Press, 1967.

Greene, Mary F., and Orletta Ryan. *The School Children.* New York: Pantheon, 1965.

Gross, Neal, et al. *Implementing Organizational Innovations.* New York: Basic Books, 1971.

Handorf, George G. "An Historical Study of the Superintendency of Dr. Frank Ballou in the Public School System of the District of Columbia." Unpublished Ed.D. diss., American University, 1962.

Hansen, Carl. *Danger in Washington.* West Nyack, N.Y.: Parker 1968.

Hart, Charles. *Memories of a Forty-Niner.* Philadelphia: Dunlap, 1946.

Harvard Educational Review. "Alternative Schools," 42 (August, 1972).

Haskins, Jim. *Diary of a Harlem Schoolteacher,* New York: Grove Press, 1969.

Heffron, Ida. *Francis W. Parker.* Los Angeles: Ivan Deach, 1934.

Helgeson, Stanley, et al. *The Status of Pre-College Science, Mathematics, and Social Science Education: 1955–1975.* Vol. 1. Columbus, Ohio: Center for Science and Mathematics Education, 1977.

Hoetker, James, and William Ahlbrand. "The Persistence of the Recitation." *American Educational Research Journal,* 6 (March, 1969).

Hoffman, Nancy. *Woman's 'True' Profession.* New York: McGraw–Hill, 1981.

Hoiberg, Larry. "We're Putting It All Together at Washington Elementary School." Grand Forks, N.D.: Washington School, 1971.

Horwitz, Robert A. "Psychological Effects of the Open Classroom." *Review of Educational Research,* 49 (Winter, 1979).

Hoy, Wayne. "Pupil Control Ideology and Organizational Socialization." *School Review*, 77, (1969).

Huebner, Theodore. "Suggested Standards in the Supervision of Foreign Languages." *High Points*, 21, (November, 1939).

Hughes, J. M., and E. O. Melby. "A Cross-Section of Teaching in Terms of Classroom Activities." *Educational Method*, 10, (October, 1930).

Hundley, Mary G. *The Dunbar Story*. New York: Vantage, 1965.

Jackson, Philip. *Life in Classrooms*. New York: Holt, Rinehart, and Winston 1968.

_____. *The Teacher and the Machine*. Pittsburgh: University of Pittsburgh Press, 1968.

Jersild, Arthur, et al. "An Evaluation of Aspects of the Activity Program in the New York City Public Elementary Schools." *Journal of Experimental Education*, 8 (December, 1939).

_____. "Studies of Elementary School Classes in Action." *Journal of Experimental Education*, 9, (June, 1941).

Kaestle, Carl. "Ideology and American Educational History." Paper Given at History of Education Society. (October 3, 1981).

Karunkakaran, Chitra. "Life and Work in Several Communities: A Case Study of Open Education." Chicago: Center for New Schools, 1978.

Katz, Michael. *Class, Bureaucracy, and Schools*. New York: Praeger, 1971.

Kaya, Esin. "An Evaluation and Description of the Advisory and Learning Exchange, 1973–1974." Washington, D.C.: Advisory and Learning Exchange, 1974.

King, Amy. "Evolution of the Study Group." *Journal of the Education Association of the District of Columbia*. (June, 1936).

Kohl, Herbert. *36 Children*. New York: New American Library, 1967.

Koos, Leonard V., and Oliver L. Troxel. "A Comparison of Teaching Procedures in Short and Long Class Periods." *School Review*, 35, (May, 1927).

Krause, L. W. "What Principles of Modern and Progressive Education Are Practiced in Intermediate-Grade Classrooms." *Journal of Educational Research*, 35, (December, 1941).

Krug, Edward. *The Shaping of the American High School*. Vol. 1. New York: Harper and Row, 1964.

Kutz, Ronald. "An Analysis of the Use of Math Manipulative Materials in North Dakota." Grand Forks, N.D.: Bureau of Educational Research and Services, 1977.

Landry, Richard. "Comparative and Longitudinal Analyses of Teaching Intern Classrooms on Selected Dimensions of Openness: Third Year." Grand Forks, N.D.: Center for Teaching and Learning, 1975.

Lauter, Paul, and Florence Howe. "The Short, Happy Life of Adams-Morgan Community School." *Harvard Educational Review*, 38, (Spring, 1968).

Joseph Lelyveld. "Class 4–4: Educational Theories Meet Reality." *The New York Times*. October 9, 1970.

_____. "The Most Powerful Man in the School System." *The New York Times Magazine*. March 21, 1971.

Lewis, Mayme. "Report of Visit to Horace Mann School, New York." *The Journal of the Columbian Educational Association*. (May, 1925).

Levy, Gerald. *Ghetto School*. New York: Pegasus, 1970.

Lipsky, Michael, and Richard Weatherley. "Street-Level Bureaucrats and Institutional Innovation: Implementing Special Education Reform." *Harvard Educational Review*, 47 (1977).

Loftus, John. "The Nature of the Activity Program." (September 9, 1936).

———. "New York's Large-Scale Experimentation with an Activity Program." *Progressive Education*, 17 (February, 1940).

Lopate, Philip. *Being With Children*. New York: Bantam, 1975.

Lortie, Dan. *Schoolteacher*. Chicago: University of Chicago Press, 1975.

Louisiana Educational Survey. Section B. *The Negro Public Schools*. Baton Rouge, La.: Louisiana Educational Survey, 1924.

Lynd, Robert, and Helen. *Middletown*. New York: Harcourt, Brace, 1929.

McGuffey, Verne. *Differences in the Activities of Teachers in Rural One-Room Teacher Schools and of Grade Teachers in Cities*. New York: Teachers College, 1929.

McLaughlin, Milbrey. "Implementation As Mutual Adaptation in Classroom Organizations." *Teachers College Record*. (1976).

———. "An Exploratory Study of School District Adaptation." Los Angeles: Rand, 1979.

McPherson, Gertrude. *Small Town Teacher*. Cambridge, Mass.: Harvard University Press, 1972.

March, James. "Footnotes to Organizational Change." *Administrative Science Quarterly*, 26 (December, 1981).

Marler, Charles D. "Colonel Francis W. Parker: Prophet of the 'New Education'." Unpublished Ed.D. diss., Stanford University, 1965.

Marshall, Hermine, "Open Classrooms: Has the Term Outlived Its Usefulness?" *Review of Educational Research*, 51 (Summer, 1981).

Marshall, Kim. *Law and Order in Grade 6–E*. Boston: Little, Brown, 1972.

Mayhew, Katherine C., and Anna C. Edwards. *The Dewey School: The Laboratory School of the University of Chicago*. New York: D. Appleton-Century Co., 1936.

Mehan, Hugh. *Learning Lessons*. Cambridge, Mass.: Harvard University Press, 1979.

Metz, Mary H. "Clashes in the Classroom: The Importance of Norms for Authority." *Education and Urban Society*, 11 (November, 1978).

———. *Classrooms and Corridors*. Berkeley, Calif.: University of California Press, 1978.

Meyer, John, and Brian Rowan. "The Structure of Educational Organizations." In M. Meyer (ed.) *Environments and Organizations*. San Francisco: Jossey-Bass, 1978.

Minor, Pearl. "A Unit in Creative Writing." *National Educational Outlook Among Negroes* (May, 1939).

Moore, David T. "Alternative Schools: A Review." New York: Institute for Urban and Minority Education, Teachers College, 1978.

Morrison, J. C. "The Curriculum Experiment with the Activity Program and Its Implications for the Further Study of Education." *New York Society for Experimental Study of Education Yearbook*. New York: Thesis Publishing, 1943.

Myers, Donald, and Lilian (eds.). *Open Education Re-examined*. Lexington, Mass.: Lexington Books, 1973.

National Society for the Study of Education. *Curriculum Making: Past and Present*.

Twenty-Sixth Yearbook. Part 1. Bloomington, Ill.: National Society for the Study of Education, 1926.

_____. *The Textbook in American Education*. Thirtieth Yearbook. Part 2. Bloomington, Ill.: National Society for the Study of Education, 1931.

_____. *The Activity Movement*. Thirty-Third Yearbook. Part 2. Bloomington, Ill.: National Society for the Study of Education, 1934.

Nearing, Scott. *The New Education*. New York: Row, Peterson, 1915.

Newlon, Jesse. "The Need of a Scientific Curriculum Policy for Junior and Senior High Schools." *Educational Administration and Supervision*, 3 (May, 1917).

Newlon, Jesse, and A. L. Threlkeld. "The Denver Curriculum Revision Program." In *Curriculum Making: Past and Present*. Twenty-Sixth Yearbook. Bloomington, Ill.: National Society for the Study of Education, 1926.

New York (City) Board of Education. *Annual Report of the Superintendent of Schools*. New York: Board of Education, 1910–1942.

_____. *The Teachers' Handbook: A Guide For Use in the Schools of the City of New York*. New York: Board of Superintendents, 1921.

_____. *Progress of the Public Schools, 1924–1929*. New York: Board of Education, 1929.

_____. *Report of Survey of Public School System, City of New York, 1924*. New York: Board of Education, 1929.

_____. *Working Together: A Ten Year Report*. New York: District 23 and 24 Principals, 1937.

_____. *Exploring a First Grade Curriculum*. New York: Bureau of Reference, Research, and Statistics, 1947.

_____. *The First Fifty Years: A Brief Review of Progress, 1898–1948*. New York: Board of Education, 1949.

_____. *School Profiles, 1970–1971*. New York: Division of System Planning, 1971.

_____. *Facts and Figures, 1977–1978*. New York: Board of Education, 1978.

_____. DeWitt Clinton High School. *Clintonian*. New York: DeWitt Clinton High School, 1920–1975.

_____. *High Points*. New York: Board of Education, 1918–1975.

New York Principals' Association. *The Principal*. November 14, 1921.

New York State Department of Education. *The Activity Program: The Report of a Survey*. Albany, N.Y.: Department of Education, 1941.

New York (State) University. *Examination of the Public School System of the City of Buffalo*. Albany, N.Y.: State University of New York, 1916.

The New York Times. 1920–1940 and 1965–1975.

North Dakota Statewide Study of Education. *Educational Development for North Dakota, 1967–1975, An Overview*. Grand Forks, N.D.: Center for Teaching and Learning, 1973.

O'Shea, William. "What Are the Progressive Steps of the New York City Schools." *Educational Review*, 74 (1927).

Otto, Henry, et al. *Community Workshops for Teachers in the Michigan Community Health Project*. Ann Arbor, Mich.: University of Michigan Press, 1942.

Passow, Harry A. "Secondary Education Reform: Retrospect and Prospect." New York: Teachers College, Columbia University, 1976.

_____. *Toward Creating a Model Urban School System*. New York: Teachers College, 1967.

Patridge, Lelia E. *The Quincy Methods*. New York: E. L. Kellogg, 1889.

Perrone, Vito. "Open Education: Promise and Problems." PDK Fastback. Bloomington, Ind.: Phi Delta Kappan Educational Foundation, 1972.

———. "A View of School Reform." In Ruth Dropkin and Arthur Tobier (eds.) *Roots of Open Education in America*. New York: The Workshop Center for Open Education, 1976.

———. *Two Elementary Classrooms: Views from the Teacher, Children, and parents*. Dubuque, Iowa: Kendall/Hunt, 1977.

Peshkin, Alan. *Growing Up American*. Chicago: University of Chicago Press, 1978.

Ravitch, Diane. *The Great School Wars: New York City, 1805–1973*. New York: Basic Books, 1974.

Ravitch, Diane, and Ronald Goodenow (eds.). *Educating an Urban People*. New York: Teachers College, 1981.

Raywid, Mary Anne. "The First Decade of Public School Alternatives." *Kappan*. (April, 1981).

Report on Survey of the Public School System of the District of Columbia by the Bureau of Efficiency, 1928. Washington, D.C.: Government Printing Office, 1928.

Resnick, Henry. "Promise of Change in North Dakota." *Saturday Review*, 54, (April 17, 1971).

Rice, Joseph. *The Public School System of the United States*. New York: Arno Press, 1969.

Rist, Ray C. *The Urban School: A Factory for Failure*. Cambridge, Mass.: MIT Press, 1973.

Rogers, David. *An Inventory of Educational Improvement Efforts in the New York City Schools*. New York: Teachers College, 1977.

Rosenshine, Barak. "Content, Time, and Direct Instruction." In P. L. Petersen and H. Walberg (eds.). *Research on Teaching*. Berkeley: McCutchan, 1979.

———. "Teaching Functions in Instructional Programs." Paper delivered at NIE Conference at Airlie House, Virginia. February, 1982.

Rosenthal, Benjamin. "A Case Study of a Lesson in American History." *High Points*, 22, (November, 1940).

Rugg, Harold. *The Child-Centered School*. Yonkers-on-the-Hudson, New York; World Book Co., 1928.

Sarason, Seymour. *The Culture of the School and the Problem of Change*. New York: Allyn and Bacon, 1971.

Schildt, Roberta. Interview. March 22, 1982.

Shanker, Albert. "Interview." *Principal*, 53, (March/April, 1974).

Shaver, James, et al. "An Interpretive Report on the Status of Pre-College Social Studies Based on Three NSF-Funded Studies." In National Science Foundation. *What Are the Needs in Pre-College Science, Mathematics, and Social Science Education?* Washington, D.C.: National Science Foundation, 1979.

Silberman, Charles. *Crisis in the Classroom*. New York: Random House, 1970.

———(ed.) *The Open Classroom Reader*. New York: Vintage, 1973.

Sirotnik, Kenneth. "What You See Is What You Get: A Summary of Observations In Over 1000 Elementary and Secondary Classrooms." Technical Report No. 29. Los Angeles: UCLA Graduate School of Education, 1981.

Sizer, Theodore. *Secondary Schools at the Turn of the Century*. New Haven, Conn.: Yale University Press, 1964.

_____. *Places for Learning, Places for Joy*. Cambridge, Mass.: Harvard University Press, 1973.

Smallwood, James (ed.) *And Gladly Teach: Reminiscences of Teachers from Frontier Dugout to Modern Module*. Norman, Okla.: University of Oklahoma Press, 1976.

Smith, Louis, and William Geoffrey. *The Complexities of an Urban Classroom*. New York: Holt, Rinehart, and Winston, 1968.

Smith, Louis, and Pat Keith. *Anatomy of an Educational Innovation*. New York: John Wiley, 1971.

Snyder, C. B. J. "A Stupendous Schoolhouse Problem." *American School Board Journal*, 65 (October, 1922).

Sommer, Robert. *Personal Space*, Englewood Cliffs, N.J.: Prentice-Hall, 1969.

Sowell, Thomas. "Black Excellence: A History of Dunbar High." *Public Interest*. (Spring, 1974).

Spears, Harold. *The Emerging High School Curriculum*. New York: American Book, 1948.

Spodek, Bernard, and Herbert Walberg (eds.). *Studies in Open Education*, New York: Agathon, 1975.

Spring, Joel. *Education and the Rise of the Corporate State*. Boston: Beacon Press, 1972.

Stake, Robert, and Jack Easley. *Case Studies in Science Education*. Vol. 1. Urbana, Ill.: Center for Instructional Research and Curriculum Evaluation, 1978.

Stephens, J. M. *The Process of Schooling*. New York: Holt, Rinehart, and Winston, 1967.

Sterling, Philip. *The Real Teachers*. New York: Random House, 1972.

Stevens, Romiett. *The Question As a Measure of Efficiency in Instruction*. New York: Teachers College, 1912).

Strayer, George. *Report of a Survey of the Public Schools of the District of Columbia*. Washington, D.C.: Board of Education, 1949.

Stuart, Jesse. *The Thread That Runs So True*. New York: Charles Scribners, 1949.

Suydam, Marilyn, et al. *The Status of Pre-College Science, Mathematics, and Social Science Education, 1955–1975: Mathematics Education*. Vol. 2. Columbus, Ohio: Center for Science and Mathematics Education, 1977.

Swift, David. *Ideology and Change in the Public Schools*. Columbus, Ohio: Charles Merrill, 1971.

Taplin, Winn, and Irving Pearson. "Contributions to Individual Instruction." In *Newer Types of Instruction in Small Rural Schools*. 1938 Yearbook. Washington, D.C.: Department of Rural Education, National Education Association, 1938.

Tenenbaum, Samuel. "Supervision-Theory and Practice." *The School Executive* 59, (March, 1940).

Texas Educational Survey, *Courses of Study and Instruction*. Vol. 5. Austin, Tex.: Texas Educational Survey Commission, 1924.

Thayer, V. T. *The Passing of the Recitation*. Boston: D.C. Heath, 1928.

Thirty Schools Tell Their Story. Vol. 5. New York: Harpers and Brothers, 1942.

Threlkeld, A. L. "Dr. Dewey's Philosophy and the Curriculum." *Curriculum Journal*, 8, (April, 1937).

Tikunoff, William, and Beatrice Ward. "Ecological Perspectives for Successful

School Practice: Knowledge of Effective Instruction." San Francisco: Far West Laboratory. No date.

Tomlinson, Tommy. "Effective Schools: Mirror or Mirage." *Today's Education*. (April/May, 1981).

Tyack, David. *The One Best System*. Cambridge, Mass.: Harvard University Press, 1974.

———. "The History of Secondary Schools in Delivering Social Services." Stanford, Calif.: Unpublished Paper, 1978.

Uggen, Julia. "A Composite Study of Difficulties of Rural Teachers." *Educational Administration and Supervision*, 24, (March, 1938).

U.S. Department of Interior, Bureau of Education. *Report of the Commissioner of Education*. 1891–1892, Vols. 1 and 2. 1900–1901, Vol. 1. 1911, Vol. 2.

———. "Status of the Rural Teacher in Pennsylvania." Bulletin 1921, no. 34. Washington, D.C.: Government Printing Office, 1922.

———. *Biennial Survey of Education, 1920–1922*. 1924 Bulletin. Vol. 1. Washington, D.C.: Government Printing Office, 1924.

———. *National Survey of Secondary Education*. 1932 Bulletin, No. 17. "Summary Report." Washington, D.C.: Government Printing Office, 1932.

———. *Statistics of City School Systems, 1933–1934*. 1935 Bulletin, No. 2, Washington, D.C.: Government Printing Office, 1936.

Waller, Willard. *The Sociology of Teaching*. New York: Wiley, 1965.

Washington Post. 1969–1982.

Washington Evening Star. 1965–1980.

Wasserman, Miriam. *The School Fix, NYC, USA*. New York: Outerbridge and Dienstfrey, 1970.

Weber, George. "Good School Programs in Practice." *CBE Bulletin*, 15, (June, 1971).

Weick, Karl. "Educational Organizations as Loosely Coupled Systems." *Administrative Science Quarterly*, 21, (March, 1976).

Weinstein, Carol. "The Physical Environment of the School: A Review of the Research." *Review of Educational Research, 49, (Fall, 1979)*.

Weinstein, Robert A., and Larry Booth. *Collection, Use, and Care of Historical Photographs*. Nashville, Tenn.: American Association for State and Local History, 1977.

Weiss, Iris. *Report of the 1977 National Survey of Science, Mathematics, and Social Studies Education*. Washington, D.C.: National Science Foundation, 1978.

What Are the Needs in Precollege Science, Mathematics, and Social Science Education? Views from the Field. Washington, D.C.: National Science Foundation, 1980.

Who's Who in America, 11, (1920–1921). Chicago: Marquis, 1921.

———, 19, (1936–1937). Chicago, Marquis, 1937.

Wildavsky, Aaron, and Jeffrey Pressman. *Implementation*. Berkeley, Calif.: University of California Press, 1973.

Wiley, Karen, and Jeanne Race. *The Status of Pre-College Science, Mathematics, and Social Science Education: 1955–1975*, Vol. 3, "Social Science Education." Boulder, Colo.: Social Science Education Consortium, 1977.

Wilkinson, Carmen. Interview. March 22, 1982.

Woods, Peter. *The Divided School*. London: Routledge and Kegan Paul, 1979.

Wrightsone, J. Wayne. *Appraisal of Experimental High School Practices*. New York: Teachers College, 1936.

Zilversmit, Arthur. "The Failure of Progressive Education, 1920–1940." In Lawrence Stone (ed.). *Schooling and Society*. Baltimore: John Hopkins Press, 1976.

Index